Operation Millennium

'Bomber' Harris's Raid on Cologne
May 1942

DIE SCHWERSTEN ANGRIFFE DER LUFTWAFFE VON DER R.A.F. WEIT ÜBERBOTEN

Mehr als

1000

Bomber

auf einmal eingesetzt

In der Nacht vom 30. Mai griff die Royal Air Force Köln mit weit über 1000 Flugzeugen an. Der Angriff wurde auf anderthalb Stunden zusammengedrängt. Der deutsche Sicherheits- und Abwehrdienst war der Wucht des Angriffs nicht gewachsen.

Premierminister Churchill sagte in seiner Botschaft an den Oberbefehlshaber des britischen Bomberkommandos am 31. Mai:

"Dieser Beweis der wachsenden Stärke der britischen Luftmacht ist auch das Sturmzeichen für die Dinge, die von nun an eine deutsche Stadt nach der andern zu erwarten hat."

Zwei Nächte darauf griff die Royal Air Force das Ruhrgebiet mit über 1000 Maschinen an.

Die Offensive der Royal Air Force in ihrer neuen Form hat begonnen

'The offensive of the Royal Air Force in its new form has begun.' Leaflet dropped by the RAF on Cologne the morning after the raid.

OPERATION MILLENNIUM

'BOMBER' HARRIS'S RAID
ON COLOGNE
MAY 1942

by

Eric Taylor

Foreword by General Adolf Galland

SPELLMOUNT
Staplehurst

British Library Cataloguing in Publication Data:
A catalogue record for this book is available
from the British Library

Copyright © Eric Taylor 1987, 2004

ISBN 1-86227-230-1

First published in the UK in 1987 by
Robert Hale Ltd
Clerkenwell Green
London

This edition published in the UK in 2004 by
Spellmount Limited
The Old Rectory
Staplehurst
Kent TN12 0AZ

Tel: 01580 893730
Fax: 01580 893731
E-mail: enquiries@spellmount.com
Website: www.spellmount.com

1 3 5 7 9 8 6 4 2

The right of Eric Taylor to be identified
as the author of this work has been asserted by him
in accordance with the Copyright, Designs
and Patents Act 1988

Typeset by MATS, Southend-on-Sea, Essex
Printed in Great Britain by
TJ International Ltd, Padstow, Cornwall

Contents

Acknowledgements

In writing this book I have been fortunate in having the help and criticism of many people to whom I would express my most sincere gratitude. To Hitler's Minister of Armament Production, the late Albert Speer, I am immensely grateful for much stimulation and helpful information on the greater implications of the first thousand bomber raid; to Herr Rogalla (of the Cologne Oberstadtdirektor's office) and to Herr Dr Eckhardt (Cologne Archivrat), for statistical material and to former Mayor of Cologne, Herr Jan Brügelmann for advice and encouragement.

It is with warm gratitude that I acknowledge my debt to the editor of the *Kolnische Rundschau* and to the feature writer 'Fur Sie Am Telefon' for helping me to contact so many eye-witnesses in Cologne and also to Herr Albert Herchenbach, whose later articles on my research led me to meet and correspond with many more people in Cologne. It would not be practicable in this short acknowledgement to name each of the citizens of Cologne who have given me their accounts of the raid but I should like to mention those whose stories are featured in greater detail in the text. Herr Willy Niessen was a mine of information, having been an avid collector of all airwarfare material since a schoolboy in Cologne at the time of the thousand bomber raid, and I gratefully acknowledge a considerable obligation which I have incurred for the generous and efficient aid he has given me. My most sincere thanks are due also to those who have been kind enough to entertain me in their homes during my research, such as Dr med Berta Weigand-Fellinger and her husband, Herr Theo Stratmann, Herr Toni Stellmaszyk, Frau Hildegarde Steinborn, Frau Klara Zarges and her husband, Herr Peter Blum, Herr Hans Heines, Frau Eddy Else-Becker and Frau Erika Wagner.

From the Air Force side of the picture, I should like to thank newspaper editors and journalists who have helped me to contact so many former bomber crews, ground staff and civilians involved, in particular, the *Daily Telegraph* (Mrs J. Lloyd) *Bradford Telegraph and Argus* (Bill Berry), *Northern Echo* (John Rennie and Caroline Finkle), *Middlesborough Gazette* (Mike Clarke) *Cambridge Evening News, Lincoln Target, Driffield Times, Buckinghamshire Free Press* (Karen Brown), *Yorkshire Evening Press* (John Watts), *Yorkshire Post* (Derek Hudson) *Sheffield Star* and *Matlock Advertiser* (Sam Fay).

Space will not allow me to name all members of bomber crews, ground staff and civilians who have given me accounts of how it was with them in those days but I should like them to know how grateful I am for all their help. Those whose names appear in the text were particularly kind in giving me their time – Fred Simpson, John Macfarlane, David Walker, Alan Smith, David and Brian Craven, Max Pexman, Eric Prince, Ken Williams, Irene Shaw (Mrs Bennett), Jim Davidson, Rusty Hudson, Cyril Manser, Vic Mitchell, Ernest Wilson, Eric Clarke, Tom Allenby, Catherine Price, Jean Caudwell, Ron Lawson, Christine Galbraith, (formerly Mrs Jack Wilson) Ernest Cummings, John Price, Philip Haverly, Mrs Yeomans, Barbara Catchpole, Bob Vollum, Arthur Wilkinson, W.G. Higgs, Norman Tetley and Robert Sage.

In my research I have been greatly helped by staff of the Public Record Office, particularly by Dr Meryl Foster; at the RAF Museum by Group Captain Bill Randle and Mr Hunter; at the Air Historical Branch by Group Captain E.G. Haslam; at the Ministry of Defence Medical Services by Group Captain J.A. Baird, and at the Office of the Judge Advocate General by Miss Norman-Butler. An interesting account of an incident in the raid as seen through the eyes of a German Fighter pilot was given to me by former Luftwaffe pilot, Guenther Hartmann.

Clearly I have been most fortunate in having the help of so many people and it is only fair to them all to say now that the opinions expressed throughout the book are my own. I hold no-one else responsible for them.

Throughout the time that I have spent researching and writing the book I have been the fortunate recipient of expert criticism and counsel from my friend and war historian, Charles Whiting, and I owe a special debt of gratitude to Mrs Sheila Surgener for her indefatigable research into the Air Files at the Public Record Office and for the meticulous checking of the proofs. My most sincere thanks are due to Mrs Anne Milner for her invaluable work in typing the finished manuscript from a script often not easy to decipher.

E.T.

Foreword

The word 'terrible' is derived from 'terror'. And 'terrible' is surely the feeling you get when reading this vivid account of 'Operation Millennium' – the RAF's first thousand bomber raid.

When you have seen – as I have – the devastation inflicted upon a city as big as Cologne in a single night and witnessed the infernos that came to every major German city after that raid on 30-31 May 1942, then you cannot but be shocked by the sheer madness of it all, the absurdity of war.

We – the Germans – have to admit that the Luftwaffe had already launched massive bombing attacks in September 1939 against the Polish capital of Warsaw. The German High Command intended to demonstrate to the Western Allies the superior strength of the Luftwaffe. A year later, during the Battle of Britain, the High Command of the Luftwaffe made a fatal mistake in switching their attack from the British Air Defences to London. Then came the massive raid on Coventry.

The aim of the new strategy of bombing cities was to break the morale of the British people. But though London, Coventry and other major cities suffered, RAF Fighter Command was given time to recover and was saved. And so was Britain.

Hitler's attack on Russia forced RAF Bomber Command – the one force that could strike against Germany – to react immediately. At that time, the German Air Defence in the west was very weak. There were only eight fighter squadrons available for day defence and the night fighter force was only just being built up. The Luftwaffe's squadrons were stretched to the limit covering an area extending from Norway, over the whole of the Russian Front, down to the Caucasus, all over North Africa as well as over France and the Low Countries.

Later, when the 8th USAAF, with its bases in Britain, and the 15th USAAF based in North Africa, came into the air war, the terrible 'round the clock' bombing campaign began.

The Americans concentrated their efforts on massive day attacks against strategic targets while the RAF preferred area bombing by night – with the intention of breaking the morale of the German people.

Thus, Air Marshal Harris repeated the same mistakes made by the Luftwaffe in their bombing of Britain's industrial cities and 'Baedeker' targets.

By the end of 1944 and early 1945 the new navigation aids and bomb sights should have enabled bombers to attack strategic targets, even by night. But the area bombing went on, relentlessly. However, the morale of the German people was not broken.

I believe that the destruction of nearly all the major cities of Germany contributed less to the outcome of the war than the precise bombing carried out by the USAAF on targets of strategic importance.

There is no doubt, however, that civilian morale – and that of the military too – could be broken by the use of nuclear weapons. However, should our world be plunged into a nuclear conflict – may God forbid – there will be neither victory nor defeat.

Eric Taylor's book is the result of extremely careful research work. It is not an accusation but an admonition.

Adolf Galland
Lieutenant General and General of Fighters (retd.)

Prologue

'And some there be, which have no
memorial, who are perished, as though
they had never been ...'
                                    Ecclesiasticus XLIV.9

On the morning of Friday 5 March 1945 a forty-eight-year-old
Irish-American general stood at an empty first-floor window of a
bomb-shattered building and carefully focused his field-glasses.
Before him lay a sea of rubble which had once been German's
fourth largest city, Cologne. He was awestruck. This once great
thriving industrial city, throbbing with energy and power, was now
but a heap of twisted iron and broken bricks, blown-up bridges,
wrecked railways and rolling stock, gutted churches, shattered
towers and shells of factories.

This General, J. Lawton Collins, nicknamed 'Lightning Joe', was
to put the weight of his tired troops into the final attack of this
phase of the campaign. Against him was a stubborn German Army,
already depleted by over two million men lost on the Russian Front
but stoically refusing to budge a metre without a fight, despite
being greatly outnumbered and outgunned.[1] Behind those rugged
remnants of the German LXXI Corps lay the Rhine, the last barrier
to the heart of Germany – not crossed by an invader since
Napoleon.

At precisely 0700 hours 'Lightning Joe' gave the order: 'The
Corps will advance and capture the city of Cologne.'

Tank engines roared into life. Over the 'squawkboxes' came a
constant stream of 'gobbledegook'. Tracks screeched and squealed
over the fallen masonry. Infantry sections moved forward, steadily
but slowly, like men who had been told once too often that the
enemy had withdrawn leaving behind only token resistance. But
this time, for once, the intelligence reports had been right.

By early afternoon it was all over, and the first of the fighting patrols, followed by eager war correspondents, were about to have an experience they would never forget. They had seen war-battered cities and towns before – Caen, Clève, Aachen – but they were not prepared for what they saw in this city, Cologne …

'There was something awesome about the ruins of Cologne, something the mind was unwilling to grasp, and the cathedral spires still soaring miraculously to the sky only made the débâcle below more difficult to accept,' wrote war correspondent Alan Moorehead.[2] 'A city is a plan on a map, and here, over a great area, there was no plan. A city means movement and noise and people; not silence and emptiness and stillness, a kind of cemetery stillness. A city is life, and when you find instead the negation of life the effect redoubled.'

As the first of those GIs crunched their way over broken glass and concrete, they were increasingly dismayed at what they saw and smelt. From below the rubble came the stench of putrescent bodies.

One section which ventured into a concrete air-raid shelter (one of the few buildings left standing in that quarter of the city) was met by a wall of suffocating, foetid heat – the smell of human flesh. The place was packed with old men, scrawny women and crying children, some chewing on crusts, some playing cards, some staring vacantly at the wall, row after row of them. Some men stood up and hesitantly half-saluted, the women hugged their children more tightly and crouched back.

Outside even there was no getting away from smells. The water and sewage systems were fractured; toilets did not work.

Gradually, from out of the charred walls, from cellars and caverns hewed out of the rubble, the Cologne citizens came out into the bright March sunshine, small groups of white-faced survivors who had lived in candle-lit cellars for weeks. All of them had a tense, distant look – the look of people gazing into another world. From one of these groups of dazed citizens the haggard, begrimed figure of what had once been a soldier detached himself and staggered towards the GI corporal. In halting English he said: 'Thank God you're here. Now we're safe!'[3]

Soon, more and more groups of staring people cautiously emerged from damaged buildings. There were few tears. Their faces were set woodenly as they watched and waited.

Behind the leading patrol came the advance parties of the US

104th Division, fanning out as best they could towards the centre and perimeter of the city, looking for snipers. It was not easy going.

A Sherman tank which had driven over mangled animals and half-buried corpses went by with flesh sticking to its tracks, easing its way around craters and jolting over the debris.[4] After the first mass air raids the Germans had cleared the main thoroughfares but in those last few months, when one air raid had been quickly followed by another – the RAF by night and the US Air Force by day, the wreckage had been left, so that under the mass of tumbled masonry the streets were sometimes hidden and had grown level with what was left of the buildings. Most of these were gutted, roofless shells.

Yet beneath all this rubble people were still living. One soldier came staggering out of a cellar carrying a crate of wine. As he stumbled along, he was heard to say: 'There are 40,000 Germans living underground here, and they all have hoards of food and clean table-cloths and flowers on the table!'[5]

Even more macabre situations were to be met on that day. A section advancing awkwardly over piles of concrete and twisted railings found themselves in a clearing of flat concrete and bomb-splintered trees. It was there that a GI got the shock of his young life, for cowering in the shadows of an evil-smelling corner was a hippopotamus. They were in a zoo. One of the most famous in Germany. Recalling this experience later, the former soldier wrote: 'The hippo and two monkeys were the only animals left alive. That hippo became my favourite. We stayed in Cologne a week and I used to go round all the time to feed that hippo "D" bars. As soon as I came over, he'd open his big mouth and I'd throw it in. He was nice ... It was a sad sight though. A shame. There were dead lions and zebras and elephants lying around.'[6]

On that first day in the ravaged city of Cologne one awesome sight quickly followed another. 'There was scarcely anything to remind you of life,' said another soldier. 'What struck me most was not just the destruction and devastation, not the wreckage, but the scenes of half demolition, of things that had remained intact in the midst of utter destruction. I remember how the whole façade of a four-storey tenement had collapsed, and we might have passed it without remarking had it not been for one small object. It was on the first floor, hanging down pathetically but in pristine condition, a white cot. On its side, still immaculate, were painted teddy bears clearly in their red bow ties. A telling reminder of a recent raid. On the ground floor was a barber's shop and the heavy barber's chairs had been blown upside down. Dangling out of the seat of one of them was a pair of black trousered legs.'

The US Army's *Stars and Stripes* newspaper reported the most bizarre story.[7] At the main railway station and goods yard, in a siding, were said to be car-loads of rotting corpses. The Military Government that had moved in to take control said: 'Freight. That can wait. It's not our problem. Tell the evacuation hospital.' The commanding officer at the hospital replied: 'It's not our business. They're dead.' And the problem was passed to the War Graves Registration Unit. But nothing could be moved anyway. The railway track was cratered and the rusty lines twisted skywards. So the soldiers working in the yard put up with the foul smell for a day or two longer. They knew which were the cars with the corpses. 'You could smell them. And over the top of the open freight cars you could see the plain board coffins. There were seven cars of them, loaded to the gills,' said a soldier, 'The soft wood of the coffins was clean and fresh-looking. Some of them were standing on end.'

It seemed very odd that the Germans should stack their dead in this way, and one soldier, more venturesome than the rest, climbed up the freight car for a closer look. He prised open the coffin lid. It was empty. A sharp knock on the others brought forth the same hollow sound. All empty.

But the cars behind the coffins were certainly not empty. From the corners and beneath the doors a yellowish fluid oozed. The smell wafted gently over the coffins and into the noses of those GI transport troops, who eventually just had to open the heavy doors clamped tightly shut. When these did creak open, an overpowering stench came billowing out from those cars – packed with rotting cabbages![8]

The corpses in the city square nearby were real enough though. They were hanging grotesquely with elongated necks from makeshift gallows used by the SS earlier that month. Now it was the turn of the SS to be hanging. Two of them were paying the penalty for their brutality. 'When their gang got into power, they cheated, they swindled, they blackmailed and killed by their own crooked methods by sending their enemies into concentration camps. And more than those two finally got their deserts,' said an angry, withered old lady[9] forty years later, her voice rising with remembered passion. For her, revenge was sweet! How many others, too, rejoiced that this scene of devastation, on 5 March 1945, symbolized final retribution. Indisputably, German National Socialism was doomed.

And remarkably, on that day, from the wreckage the German citizens were rising to meet the Western Allies, 'not as conquerors but as liberators'.

The way it happened was truly a strange spectacle, as John Toland was later to record: 'Some were extremely outspoken in the denouncement of Hitler, and one man wearing baggy trousers and a dirty celluloid collar, called out to war correspondent Iris Carpenter, *"We've been waiting for you to come for a long time!"* '[10]

In the wrecked square in front of the opera house, citizens now pointed derisively at a sign in both German and English. It read:

GIVE ME FIVE YEARS AND YOU WILL NOT RECOGNIZE GERMANY AGAIN.

Adolf Hitler

It was after seeing scenes such as these that Alan Moorehead sat down on the steps of Cologne Cathedral that day, puzzled by the nagging thought: 'How could it all have happened? This utter destruction. How did it come to pass?'

It had all begun one night four years earlier, on 10 May 1941, when Arthur Harris, then commanding No. 5 Bomber Group, stood on the Air Ministry roof at King Charles Street, Whitehall, surveying the success that German bombers were then having in burning out the heart of London. There, on that chilly roof, Harris, alongside the Chief of the Air Staff, Portal, carefully observed the effects of blast bombs, heavy fragmentation bombs and incendiaries. He noted meticulously the effects of the mixture of the three and considered how much more successful the German Air Force could have been if they had achieved a greater concentration of aircraft over the target area and if they had paid greater attention to the detail of the mixture of bombs, thereby creating an even greater conflagration.

Little did Luftwaffe Chief Goering then realize how he was guiding the hand of retribution which was to strike back at Germany so disastrously in the future. For Harris, not known as an emotional man, gazed down upon the sea of flames that was London and was so moved by the suffering of Londoners that he turned to Air Marshal Portal and grunted, 'They have sown the seed. They will reap the whirlwind.'

Three years later, in November 1944, Harris was able to tell Churchill that: 'In the past eighteen months Bomber Command has virtually destroyed forty-five out of the sixty leading German cities ... we have so far managed to keep up and even exceed our average of $2\frac{1}{2}$ cities devastated a month.'

It was done at a terrible cost in lives. Fixty-six thousand British and Commonwealth aircrew died and something like 600,000 Germans as Harris and Churchill stubbornly pursued the policy of hammering away at German industrial cities, trying to win the war by bombing. Much was lost. How much was gained? How far this devastation contributed to final victory we shall never know for sure – the debate continues – but what has never been in doubt is the courage of the bomber crews who went out night after night knowing the odds of survival were against them. Nor can there be any doubt about the courage and steadfastness of those German citizens who endured the RAF's 'area bombing' campaign.

What General Collins saw that Friday morning of 5 March 1945 was the final horrifying result of this 'area' or 'carpet' bombing on German cities which had begun with the first thousand-bomber attack on Cologne in May 1942.

Almost a lifetime has passed since that first terrifying thousand-bomber raid on Cologne. In the intervening years the scars on the city have gradually disappeared and the young of today may ask: 'What was it like? What was it really like to be flying through the flak and the fighters to drop those bombs? What was it really like to be crouching in the bomb-shattered buildings of Cologne at that time?'

These are not easy questions to answer, for we who lived through it remember events, great and small, with the random selection of fallible human memory. And naturally we remember only what we ourselves have seen and heard – a fragment of what really happened that night. It is these fragments, hundreds of them, that I have put together to form a mosaic of experience in an attempt to create a realistic picture of both sides of the raid – the bombers and the bombed.

The vivid pictures of the effects of the area bombing given in this Prologue refer to the total effect, the cumulative effect of the raids which the first thousand-bomber raid began. The statistics about casualties of that raid are given as an appendix (D), taken from the Police President's files in Cologne through the Town Archives.

During the many years I lived in Germany – as a serving officer at Combined Headquarters, Mönchen Gladbach, and in a civilian capacity – many people, RAF, Luftwaffe and civilians, volunteered their help and gave me accounts of their own experiences, frankly and without sparing their own feelings. I am most grateful. Two or three were shy of publicity and I have respected their wish for anonymity but they will nevertheless recognize their stories and, at times, their own accounts which I have sometimes quoted verbatim. Similarly, where it would be needlessly cruel to re-awaken painful memories for the families of those who did not die cleanly and quickly, names have been altered. Without the help of all those people in Germany and in Britain, this book would never have been written. It is not *my* book but *theirs*. They let me look through their eyes and emotions at the weird and horrible night of 30 May 1942.

Obviously, then *The First Thousand Bomber Raid* is not a military textbook explaining tactics and strategy. It is, rather, an impression of moving experiences, graphically recollected, a book which is concerned primarily not with the political level but with the human.

Nor does the book attempt to pass judgement on the morality of area bombing. I have tried to place the raid in such a context of reality that it drives home a vital lesson. War is much too costly and barbarous a method of settling quarrels among the nations of the earth.

Eric Taylor   May 1987, York and Cologne

The Terror Bombing of Germany

'It seems to me that the moment has
come when the question of the bombing
of German cities simply for the sake of
increasing the terror, though under
other pretexts, should be reviewed.'

Winston Churchill
Memorandum to Allied
Chiefs of Staff, March 1945

In the fifteen years since I wrote *Operation Millennium* – the code
name of the first thousand-bomber raid on Cologne, which
according to certain authorities began the terror bombing of
Germany – more information has become available. Files and
documents about the Second World War, once subject to official
secrecy legislation withholding them from public scrutiny, have
been declassified and become available for historical research. But
even with all this additional material, it is still the called
'indiscriminate terror bombing' which continues to arouse the most
heated controversy of the whole war.

The deliberate and remorseless saturation bombing of the
residential areas of sixty major German cities reduced them to
masses of rubble and killed at least 600,000 civilians, more than ten
times as many as were killed in Britain by the Luftwaffe.

The campaign was so devastating that even today, exactly sixty
years after that first massive raid on Cologne, national newspapers
in Britain carry headlines such as that in the *Daily Telegraph* of 25
November 2002, posing the question 'Was this bombing really
necessary?' It is a question military historians frequently raise and
with it goes the question of who was responsible. Was it Sir Winston
Churchill or Bomber Command Chief, Sir Arthur Harris? Have
both of them, asked German military historian, Jorg Friedrich
recently (in his book *Der Brand: Germany Under Bombardment*

1940–45), left themselves open to the charge of being considered war criminals?

Perhaps it is time for the Allies to face up to their bombing history in the way that Germany has faced up to the Holocaust. How far was the Allied pursuance of a bombing policy aimed deliberately at the massacre of civilians? In his new book, Friedrich writes: 'You have to look into the face of the past. Then you can ask if it was a heroic one or a tragic one or perhaps a criminal one.'

Let us take a close look at that face of the past. As far as the aircrew of those bombers were concerned, it was without doubt a heroic face. They spearheaded the fight against Nazi Germany's forces from the second day of the war until a few hours before its end. Knowingly, they risked their lives night after night when the average number of sorties one could hope to survive was fourteen, and when the life expectancy of aircrew joining Bomber Command was eighteen weeks. In those six years of war, their losses were enormous. More than 10,000 bombers were lost, and of the 125,000 airmen serving in various squadrons, 59,000 died. A further 18,000 were wounded or became prisoners of war. The courage of those men has never been in doubt and their contribution to Allied victory is beyond question. They did not *pick* the targets, they *attacked* them.

But, one might ask, was it really necessary to target such densely populated residential areas of cities? Why was such a policy pursued for so long? When did it all start?

We know it started with that first thousand-bomber raid on Cologne on 30/31 May 1942. Immediately afterwards, Churchill said to Harris: 'It will be the herald of what Germany will receive city by city from now on.' Why?

It came out of desperation. In that fateful Spring of 1942 the Allies and their leaders were in no doubt that Germany was poised to dominate the world. France, the Low Countries, Norway, Denmark, Austria, Czechoslovakia, Greece and Yugoslavia had been overrun by the seemingly invincible German Army. Yugoslavia had been beaten in the most brutal fashion of all. In a deliberate attempt to create confusion by terror, Belgrade was bombed from five o'clock in the morning until late at night. Following the pattern of Rotterdam and Warsaw, German bombers hammered the defenceless citizens of Belgrade, swollen by thousands who had come to the city to celebrate Palm Sunday. On that one day 17,000 were killed – the greatest number of civilians killed in a single day since the war began. At the same time other German squadrons bombed all Yugoslav airfields, destroying 600 aircraft on the ground.

All of Europe, save neutral Sweden and Switzerland, was in Hitler's hands or those of his friends and allies – dictators or monarchs who ruled Fascist Italy, Vichy France, General Franco's Spain, the Balkan countries and Finland.

In that same Spring came news of disasters in the Middle East. A single German division under General Erwin Rommel, sent to Libya to rescue beleaguered Italian forces, pushed the British Eighth Army tottering back to the Egyptian frontier and threatened the Suez lifeline. Farther east in Iraq, the anti-British general, Rashid Ali, seized power and cut off the oil pipeline to the Mediterranean.

In the Far East the news was equally catastrophic. 'It really was a depressing time,' wrote former Foreign Secretary, Lord Avon, in his memoirs. The US Pacific Fleet had been destroyed at Pearl Harbor, two formidable British warships, HMS *Prince of Wales* and HMS *Repulse* had been sunk off the Malayan coast and Hong Kong had been over-run by Japanese troops on 15 February. Singapore had capitulated with 62,000 British and Colonial soldiers taken prisoner, half of whom would die while prisoners of war, and their slaughter had already begun. For example, when twenty-five Australian Army nurses and sixty-five English soldiers surrendered to the Japanese on the Malayan coast, they were marched to the beach where the soldiers were bayoneted and shot; the nurses were ordered to wade into the sea, and when they were waist high, machine-guns fired on to their backs until they sank into the bloody water. Only one of them, Sister Vivien Bullwinkel, survived. Incidentally, she did in fact return to that beach on Banka Island in 1993 to unveil a memorial to those nurses who had died there. She donated the bullet-riddled uniform she was wearing when she was shot to the Australian War Memorial museum. The Japanese officer who ordered the shootings committed suicide rather than face justice. Sister Bullwinkel died aged 84, in July 2000.

The fortunes of Britain and her new ally, America, seemed hopeless. Indeed, so bad did the prospects for the Allies look that some British cabinet members, who knew more than their colleagues of the peace proposals brought by Hitler's Deputy, Rudolf Hess, when he flew solo to Britain in May 1941, wished that the British government had accepted those terms. In making that dramatic solo flight from Germany and parachuting to land close to the Duke of Hamilton's home in Scotland, Hess's mission was a genuine attempt to negotiate an end to the war and it was enthusiastically supported by eminent politicians and statesmen in Britain, including, as recent research alleges, the Duke of Kent, a younger brother of the reigning monarch, King George VI. Curiously, once the Nazi's peace mission failed, the Duke was killed in a mysterious air crash, about which all the official documents are said to have been 'lost'.

On the evening Hess dropped like a bolt from the blue, the Luftwaffe raided London in force yet again, killing 1,436 civilians, more than on any other single raid on Britain. When Churchill toured the rubble-strewn streets the next day, he was greeted by crowds shouting, 'Give 'em it back, Winnie'. From newspaper reports of Churchill's reception, it seemed as though morale in the East End was holding, but the government knew well enough that nationwide it was not good. When Churchill waved his cigar at housewives searching through the rubble of their houses in Manchester and beamingly shouted 'We can take it!', one of them looked up and shouted back, 'Ay, maybe you can but we're the ones taking it 'ere.'

In some quarters morale had reached such an all-time low that Churchill took the regular pep-talk slot of novelist J B Priestley on the radio after the nine o'clock news to broadcast an urgent appeal to the nation calling upon the country not to despair. 'We must remember,' he said, 'that we are no longer alone. We are in the midst of a great company. The whole future of mankind may depend upon our conduct and our action.'

But what action were they to take? The British Army, defeated in France, had left most of its equipment behind on the beaches of Dunkirk and was far too weak to tackle a major battle. Churchill considered all possible means of striking back at the enemy. Unknown then to the public, he was toying with desperate ideas, even considering the possibility of using 'weapons of mass destruction' – bacteriological and chemical warfare.

In fact, it was early in 1942 that a certain Dr Fildes, Director of the Biology department of the government's secret research station at Porton Down in Wiltshire, was searching Britain for a firm that could supply five million small, linseed oil cattle cakes. These cattle cakes were then to be impregnated with anthrax bacillus and possibly dropped on the German plain, by bombers on the way back from Berlin. They would be picked up by grazing German cattle and thereby infect and kill thousands, perhaps millions, of German men, women and children.

Another idea which Churchill asked his scientific advisers to consider was the use of poison gas. This had already been seriously discussed as a means of drenching any German troops assaulting the southern beaches of Britain immediately after the fall of Dunkirk. In a memo to his Chiefs of Staff he wrote: 'I want the matter considered in cold blood by sensible people and not by that particular set of psalm-singing, uniformed defeatists which one runs across now here, now there.' On this possibility, Wing Commander W E V Malins recalled, in a letter to the *Daily Telegraph* on 6 January 1997, how pilots had been trained in the spraying of gas from Lysander aircraft since as early as November 1939. Fortunately Churchill was dissuaded from using gas in 1940, perhaps because he was informed that Germany could retaliate with more deadly nerve gases including Soman and Sarin, later refined into Tabun.

The Soviet Union was in desperate straits too. Those early months of 1942 had brought the Red Army to the brink of defeat with serious setbacks in the Ukraine and in the besieged city of Leningrad. There, in January 1942, four thousand people a day were dying of starvation and German bombardment. Stalin had his commanders on the German front captured and shot. Spring brought no relief. Melting ice revealed decomposing corpses. Epidemics were feared. In May Germany captured three Russian armies. On 20 May Soviet Foreign Minister Molotov hastened to London in an uncompromising mood to see Churchill. Something just had to be done to help Russian troops fighting desperately against a reinforced German Army. Molotov demanded a second front be opened by the Allies in Europe (the Balkans or France) to draw thirty or forty divisions off the Eastern Front. But anxious as Churchill was to help the Russians, he could only emphasise the real drawbacks of a premature landing in Europe with inadequate strength. It would inevitably result in the establishing of a weak bridgehead which would soon be overwhelmed by German forces. Such a fiasco would bring no appreciable help whatsoever to the Russians which, if they were defeated, would mean the Western Allies would lose an eight million-strong Red Army.

Nevertheless, on walls amidst the debris of bomb-shattered houses of English industrial cities and ports, workers in the Communist Party daubed in large letters 'SECOND FRONT NOW'. To invade anywhere on the continent at that time would undoubtedly have needed a greater naval and merchant fleet than the one which was already rapidly diminishing thanks to the German U-boat campaign. Furthermore, Intelligence reports indicated that the Allies could not count upon much help from an uprising against Hitler on the continent before they had absolute numerical superiority. There was no real opposition to Hitler in Germany either. The cheering crowds in Berlin whenever Hitler spoke were proof enough of that.

So once again it came down to an air offensive. But even this seemed doomed to failure, according to an official enquiry into the effectiveness of Bomber Command's recent operations against targets in Germany. Mr Butt of the War Cabinet Secretariat and a select team had examined 650 photographs taken by night bombers on their bombing approach to targets and studied summaries of operations and other pertinent documents before producing shattering conclusions. They revealed that on most night operations about one third of the aircraft returned without having found their primary target, and of those crews claiming to have attacked the target only one third had come within five miles of the aiming point. The worst failure was against crucial targets in the Ruhr Valley, centre of German industrial production. On these operations Butt found that only one in fifteen aircraft reached the target. In short, many of the aircraft hitherto credited with attacking the target dropped their bombs in open country.

What came to be realised also was that even during training by daylight it was difficult enough to keep a bomber straight and level enough to hit a precise target area. To attack a precision target at night in a foreign country depended first of all upon navigating to the exact location, and recognising targets such as factories, railway marshalling yards or military sites especially when the aircraft was being buffeted about by anti-aircraft fire and a pilot's efforts to avoid being hit. A slight swing of the bomber could throw the bomb load way off the target.

It was in such a critical war situation on 22 February 1942 that Air Marshal Sir Arthur Harris was appointed to be Commander-in-Chief of Bomber Command. His was an unenviable task. He knew full well he would get little support from politicians who lacked faith in the capability of Bomber Command's offensives. Harris though had faith enough in his men. He knew they could and would respond to his leadership despite all their losses. Quickly he convinced Churchill that a new form of air offensive – saturating the target area with massive bomber formations – could force Germany to divert fighter aircraft from the Russian front and keep large numbers of men and guns on anti-aircraft duties in Germany. But in reality these were only arguments to convince the Prime Minister. Harris was one of those air strategists who still today believe that wars can be won from the sky, if necessary by terror bombing civilian targets.

So it was that on 29 May 1942 Harris was ready to mount a raid on such a 'vast scale' that would swamp the defences and reduce the loss rate. By dragging in every possible bomber aircraft and crew from the squadrons and training units, 1,046 bombers were standing by ready to attack On the night of 30/31 May 1942, Cologne was buried under a mound of ash and rubble. Reports showed that 469 citizens were killed, and 45,000 made homeless. Churchill was jubilant. This support suited Harris. He was sure now that terror bombing was the way to bring the war quickly to an end. 'What we want to do in addition to the horrors of fire is to bring the masonry crashing down on top of the Boche and to terrify them,' he said.

And so a new reign of terror over the Reich began, though terror was everywhere. On the very same day as the Cologne raid, Gestapo Chief Reinhard Heydrich lay dying from bomb wounds delivered by assassins flown to Czechoslovakia by the RAF. As part of reprisal punishments, 3,000 Jews were rounded up for slaughter and killed in the small village of Radziwillow. Ten days later, when Heydrich died, 199 men in the village of Lidice, six miles north of Prague, were shot; sixty-six women with their children were taken to Ravensbruch concentration camp and killed. But massacres by the SS were happening all over Europe then. Terror, in other words, was not confined to one side.

For Bomber Command a relentless battle was now joined in the skies over Germany and, except for one brief period of atrocious weather in the winter of 1943–4, there was little respite for aircrew, and for the stoical citizens of Germany as city after city faced the fury of massive nightly bomber raids. Both Harris and General Ira Eaker, commanding the USAAF, now felt sure of their campaign for they were following the 'Point-blank Directive' given to them after Roosevelt and Churchill had conferred with the Combined Chiefs of Staff at Casablanca in February 1943: 'Your primary object will be the progressive destruction and dislocation of the German military, industrial and economic system and the undermining of the morale of the German people to a point where their capacity for armed resistance is fatally weakened.'

The primary objectives under this directive were really to be sub-marine construction yards, the aircraft industry, transportation, oil plants and other targets in the enemy war industry. But this was where Harris's interpretation of the Directive differed from that of his boss, Chief of the Air Staff, Sir Charles Portal, who wanted Harris to concentrate more on the destruction of oil plants and told him quite firmly that an air offensive against oil gave the Allies the best hope of victory in the next few months of 1944.

Harris, for his part, argued that it would be more effective to stick to his plan for the destruction of sixty German cities by devastating an average of two and a half cities each month. For the months of October, November and December 1944, Harris partly went along with Portal's instructions and launched some massive daylight raids on oil plants and chemical works in the Ruhr. But the destruction of German cities was never far from Harris's thoughts. Portal was angry and told Harris he could have done much more towards the destruction of German oil plants. 'I am profoundly disappointed that you still appear to feel that the oil plan is just another panacea,' he wrote in a long, condemnatory letter to Harris.

Harris once again explained the difficulties and wastefulness of precision bombing: 'If you miss an oil plant you hit nothing, and by their nature they are easy enough to miss. If the Germans were asked today, "Oil plants or cities?" they would say "Bomb anything you fancy but not the cities."' Harris believed that they could always be sure to hit one vital component of all plants whether oil or chemical and that was the workers themselves. Again and again he maintained that the aiming points for bombing raids should not be on precise industrial sites but bigger targets such as the centre of cities where the workers lived. And, therefore, the focus of Bomber Command's efforts should be on that part of the Casablanca Directive: the breaking of civilian morale.

By 1943 it was openly being admitted that the Hague and Geneva Conventions, which had set down an agreed civilised form of warfare intended to protect civilians and prisoners of war, were no longer being observed. It was now total war which had no place for civilised conventions. It was just one nation's people against another's. War had long since been barbarised. For seventy-six nights in succession, London had endured mass incendiary raids as German bombers fought to break the back of English morale in the heaviest aerial attacks known in warfare. And it was on one of those nights that Sir Arthur Harris had looked out upon an ocean of fire spreading over the heart of the city around the lofty dome of St Paul's Cathedral standing out defiantly against the flaming inferno, and turned to a fellow officer to remark quietly: 'Well they are sowing the wind.' He then added the last few prophetic words. 'They will reap the whirlwind.'

That retribution was about to be delivered tenfold. This policy was clearly presented in a paper to the Prime Minister by the British Chiefs of Staff: 'As our forces increase we intend to pass to a planned attack on civilian morale with the intensity and continuity which are essential if breakdown of that morale is to be produced – we believe that if these methods are applied on a vast scale, the whole structure upon which the German forces are based will be destroyed.'

In June 1943 British bombers launched 'Operation Bellicose', a series of shuttle bombing raids, in which bombers struck at targets in the deep south of Germany before flying on to airbases in Algeria where they refuelled. On the return trip they again bombed targets in southern Germany such as the Friedrichshafen rocket assembly plants.

By the middle of 1943, Bomber Command was ready for the most gruesome task of aerial bombardment ever known to man, the operation with the ominous code name 'Gomorrah'. Its aim – to 'obliterate' Germany's second largest city, Hamburg.

Hamburg, one of the world's finest ports, boasted the most extensive shipyards in Europe where half of all German submarines were built. With a population of almost two million people, the city housed 3,000 important industries, most of which were engaged in armament production, and many petroleum and oil refineries. Not surprisingly, next to Berlin it was the most heavily defended city in Germany and Occupied Europe. Consequently, when Harris was called upon to 'take out' that city, he realised the task would require 'Maximum Effort'. So it was that on the night of 24/25 July 1943, a force of 800 RAF heavy bombers followed alternately by USAAF bombers, showered upon the proud city of Hamburg thousands of high explosive bombs, stick incendiaries, liquid incendiary bombs, phosphorous canisters and incendiary flares. Again and again the bombers struck over a period of ten days.

The intense heat from rapidly spreading fires rose quickly creating drafts of cooler air rushing in to feed the flames at the bottom producing a phenomenon known as a 'firestorm' – a fiery storm unprecedented in history, rearing thousands of feet above the stricken city. Winds caused by the fire even uprooted trees, and no one caught in that swirling draft could survive. Bodies were shrivelled to tiny corpses in the intense heat.

Nor could any force extinguish that cauldron of fire. High Explosive bombs wrecked all the public utilities – water, telephone and electricity mains. They were totally out of service. In those terrible ten days of July 1943 Allied bombers gutted more than 6,000 acres of Hamburg. In comparisons sometimes made, the Luftwaffe's bombing of Coventry in 1940 devastated 100 acres.

Immediately after the Hamburg holocaust, a wave of utter terror radiated from the city striking fear as never before into the hearts of residents in all major German cities. Here could be a grim taste of what might be about to come. The first signs of panic hit the Nazi High Command, as Reichsminister for Armament Production, Albert Speer, at his home in Heidelberg, said to this writer: 'We all thought that further immediate attacks of the same massive force like those on Hamburg or Cologne upon another six German cities would cripple morale especially of those in armament factories, and I made a report to Hitler saying that a continuation of such attacks might bring a rapid end to the war.'

The German High Command was very worried indeed. Feldmarschal Erhard Milch, who had built the secret pre-war Luftwaffe and had commanded the bombing of London in 1940, was even more forthright: 'The situation is much blacker than Speer paints it. If we get five of six more attacks like these on Hamburg, the German people will just lay down their tools, however great their willpower. There can be no more talk of sending night fighters to the Eastern Front.'

Harris's bombers had got through to Hamburg in July by confusing the radar eyes of German night fighters by aircraft dropping bundles of metal foil and metallised paper acting as decoys producing conflicting echoes on defensive radar screens. The main attacking stream of bombers was thus covered by a blanket of tin-foil reflections.

It looked as if the bombers had the defences beaten, and for the next few months Harris kept up his heavy attacks on Mannheim, Munich, Hanover, Stuttgart, Frankfurt and the Ruhr towns with 'acceptable losses'. Then, on 30 March 1944, the RAF launched its most disastrous raid of the war.

Under a cloudless moon, 750 Lancaster and Halifax bombers set out deep into the heart of Germany to 'obliterate' the historic city of Nuremberg. They flew into a 250-mile dog-fight in which German Air Force night fighters easily picked off their targets in the moonlit sky. Instead of striking a mighty blow at German morale, the raid turned into the RAF's heaviest defeat, with 170 bombers destroyed and over 500 aircrew killed in one night. Surprisingly though, some pilots like Joe Hitchman for example, who would not allow any of his crew to carry lucky charms, reported back to base as having had a comparatively uneventful mission. Ironically, his Halifax was called 'Friday 13th'. It completed 128 missions and was later 'reborn' for display in the Yorkshire Air Museum, Elvington. Joe Hitchman was there to see it.

The heavy losses of that Nuremberg raid did, however, bring to an end, for a few months, Bomber Command's tactics of massed and concentrated attacks against major targets. Furthermore, the long awaited Second Front was about to be launched on 6 June 1944 and Bomber Command had urgent demands upon them to wreck French road and rail networks to hinder movement of German troops and armaments. These demands came at the same time as Germany was about to launch its own kind of terror bombing. It was also on 6 June 1944 that German OKW (Wehrmacht High Command) had given orders for the launching of one of the war's most terrifying weapons, the flying bomb, a cheaply built pilotless plane with a one-ton high explosive warhead. It was propelled very fast by a jet device. The public soon got used to hearing the deep resonant roar of its engine and also to the sudden frightening silence at which people hurled themselves to the ground knowing that the cutting out of the engine was the signal for the flying bomb to nose-dive earthwards and explode on impact.

Fortunately for Londoners on that 6 June, the flying bomb – shortly to be christened the V-1 by Goebbels – could not be set up on its launching ramps in time because trains carrying essential steel catapult rigs could not get through to the sites on the Channel coast for six days because the French road and rail networks had been so devastated by bombs. It was only a temporary reprieve.

Late in the evening of 15 June 1944 London reeled under the bombardment from no fewer than 244 flying bombs. Now Bomber Command really did have to forsake the bombardment of cities and concentrate on the bombing of V-1 launching sites and on military targets. Casualties in London from flying bombs were high – 6,184 civilians were killed and 17,981 seriously injured.

Then a second threat drew near from an even more terrifying weapon – the long-range rocket. Thrust vertically into the air by jet propulsion, it rose six miles then, flying in a gigantic parabola, it fell two hundred miles away from the launching point. Travelling faster than the speed of sound, it was impossible to shoot down and exploded on its target without any warning whatsoever.

On 7 September 1944 Hitler launched hundreds of this much feared, long-range rocket against London and revived all the terrors of the Blitz. The launching sites now became priority targets for both RAF Bomber Command and the USAAF as Allied Armies fought furiously to reach the launching pads which lay in the area around the Hook of Holland within two hundred miles of London and sixty miles of the Allied front line. Despite all the efforts of the Allied bomber offensives, these V-2 Rockets killed 2,724 Londoners and seriously wounded 6,476.

Churchill, fearing the utter destruction of London, was then again prepared to use poisonous gas or the anthrax bombs brought from the United States in March 1944 and of appalling potentiality comparable with the atomic bomb. Fortunately he was discouraged from using either of these weapons and the rocket bombardment of London and Antwerp ceased when the Allied armies overran the launching sites.

Now both the USAAF and the RAF could revert to their bombing tasks of the 'Point-blank Directive'. Harris, however, still believed that saturation bombing of cities could bring an end to the war with minimal loss of life for infantry battalions. Consequently, late in 1944, when many German cities were already reduced to rubble, Harris refused to switch Bomber Command's main effort away from terror bombing to oil targets favoured by Sir Charles Portal, Chief of the Air Staff.

The bombing terror, it must be said, was not confined to the citizens of Germany. It was also known all too well by bomber crews themselves. 'We all felt stark terror from time to time and in different ways,' said one of the most decorated of those crews, Group Captain Hamish Mahaddie DSO DFC AFC and Bar. One cannot imagine how terrible it was for those young airmen above the heavily defended area of the Ruhr. 'Time and time again I saw the ghastly spectacle of our comrades falling from the sky like flaming comets as the concentrated flak took its toll,' wrote rear gunner Ron Smith DFM. As the war dragged on, the Allied Bomber Offensive built up to a crescendo with Pathfinder squadrons often preceding the Main Force attacking oil and chemical plants as well as creating chaos in cities which American British and Russian armies were about to assault. Amongst these targets was Dresden.

It is well known that the bombing of this city was the cause of very much subsequent criticism of terror bombing. Harris was made the scapegoat for the decision not reached by him alone but by the Chiefs of Staffs and Commanders of Allied Armies. US General Marshal indeed asserted that Dresden was bombed at the specific request of the Russians. In fairness to them all, however, we must remember that the war at that time, 13 February 1945, was far from won. Allied Armies had not yet crossed the Rhine and German resistance would be even more stubborn once battles were fought in the Fatherland itself. Fighting would be ferocious and casualties high. In the Spring of 1945 it was clear that something drastic was needed to bring Germany to a state of collapse. Air power did seem to be the only way to force Germany to that capitulation decision of 'unconditional surrender'.

So it happened that on the night of 13–14 February, as part of an Anglo-American plan, 255 British bombers hit Dresden starting multiple fires. Three hours later 529 RAF bombers battered the city's railway marshalling yards and fanned the fires into a firestorm which raged all-consuming over eleven square miles of the city. The next morning 450 bombers of the USAAF set another part of the city ablaze for seven days and nights. A fireball rose above the city causing terrifying drafts which sucked in men, women and children.

Worse was to follow. On 15 February, a mere thirty-six hours after the first raid, a further 200 USAAF bombers attacked Dresden again. The death toll of those raids can never be calculated exactly but 135,000 people were officially identified as killed. But who knows how many lay incinerated beyond recognition under the mounds of rubble?

The inscription on a mass grave in Dresden reads: 'How many died? Who knows the number?'

Now it became terror upon terror. Horror escalated, creating even more terror. For instance, on 24 February the whole of the RAF and USAAF air power was committed to the execution of a deliberate terroristic operation, 'Clarion', attacking railways, roads and bridges all over Germany, bringing the war even to the smallest market towns in order to create a general collapse of morale. And on that same night a raid on Pforzheim, deep into Germany, raised not only a firestorm killing 17,000 people, but resulted in immediate brutal acts of revenge which only received publicity some fifty years later amongst most remarkable ceremonies of reconciliation.

It all began two weeks after the Pforzheim firestorm when John

Wynne's Flying Fortress was hit and ablaze close to that ruined city and not far from the Franco-German frontier. He ordered the crew to bale out, but he was trapped in his cockpit by a tangle of oxygen equipment and, though he had managed to stand up, he could not reach the emergency escape hatch. Realising the aircraft was diving rapidly, he reached for the controls and steadied the bomber. Eventually the fire went out and Wynne miraculously flew the bomber back to base in England. There he notified relatives of all his crew that they had baled out and would probably be safe as Prisoners of War. At least he thought they would.

The six men unfortunately were captured and marched through Pforzheim, where crowds hurled rubble at them, to the nearby Huchenfeld village school where they were placed under guard. There they took off their flying boots, collapsed on the floor and slept. Very early the next morning they were suddenly dragged from their beds, still half asleep and marched bare-footed towards the church. As they passed a barn, one of the crew, Tom Tate, caught sight of ropes draped over a heavy beam. 'They are going to hang us,' he said to himself. No sooner had the thought struck than he turned and barged rugby fashion through the mob and ran bare-footed, weaving his way into a nearby wood where he hid buried under dried leaves. Later he gave himself up to a German army section who protected him. Whilst he was awaiting transportation to a Prisoner of War camp, a woman from the village brought a pair of boots belonging to the husband she had just lost in the war. It was a brave act for she could have been imprisoned for helping a POW. When Tate was taken to the railway station to be put on the train for the POW camp, another mob threatened to take him from the soldiers. Two guards cocked their rifles and pointed them directly at the leaders of the mob. Just at that moment the train arrived and Tate and his guard climbed quickly aboard.

Tom Tate did not know then what had happened to the rest of his crew. They had been marched to the churchyard and shot. Another airman who had run with Tate had been recaptured and shot in the churchyard too.

After the end of the war, when their murders were being investigated by the War Crimes Commission, Tom Tate was brought from England as a witness. Evidence revealed that these young murderers were not part of a spontaneous mob but teenage members of the Hitler Youth battalion who had been ordered by their Pforzheim Nazi commanders to don civilian clothes and shoot the aircrew in cold blood. The Nazis who ordered the shooting were condemned to death and the Hitler Youth given lighter sentences because of their age.

And that might have been in the end of the story had not the plane's pilot, John Wynne, then a sheep farmer in Wales, heard about the fate of his crew. He was horrified, but gradually bitter hatred was replaced by a totally different emotion, a desire not for revenge but for reconciliation. As a first step towards that end he sent the village flowers and trees and arranged visits from his small village school to the one in Huchenfeld. The best gift of all he sent to those children of Huchenfeld was a beautifully carved Welsh rocking horse that he christened '*Hoffnung*' – Hope'.

The villagers of Huchenfeld, who had endured their guilt for years, invited John Wynne and his wife Pip to be guests of the village for the presentation of the rocking horse to the school. He was amazed at his reception. Over a thousand residents turned out to welcome him to what amounted to an enormous street party.

Here the story of murder and reconciliation took another curious turn. In the mid-1990s Tom Tate was sorting newspapers when he came across a Saga travel magazine which fell open at an article telling of 'the village that wanted forgiveness'. He was astonished to read that a retired pastor from East Germany had come to live in Huchenfeld and, learning of the murder of the RAF aircrew, had resolved to erect a memorial plaque to their memory on the church wall. The plaque is inscribed with but two words: 'Father forgive'. Subsequently in a service of reconciliation, a clergyman from Coventry, a city devastated by the Luftwaffe in 1940, came face to face with a German crying inconsolably. When the clergyman tried to comfort the distressed man, he looked up and said: 'You don't know what it is like for me. You see I was one of those who shot the airmen.'

Now relatives of those airmen have forged strong links of friendship with the villagers of Huchenfeld, and they vow to do what they can to prevent the future repeating the mistakes of the past. They all agree with the words of John Wynne in handing over the rocking horse called 'Hope' to the kindergarten children: 'Our future shall ride upon her back.'

Let us all hope we *have* learnt from the mistakes of our past. There are not many left now who lived through the infernos of those devastated cities or the shrapnel-slashed hell in their fragile bombers above blazing city ruins. Fewer still remain of those who survived that first thousand-bomber raid on Cologne which began those years of absolute terror. Even those who were there are apt to forget. Perhaps people need to be reminded of what the gruesome terror of war does entail. Then possibly other ways than utter savagery might be found to solve international arguments. Sadly, recent experience suggests that we have not yet learnt enough and if this is true, we could be faced one day with a far greater catastrophe than ever was the terror bombing of the Second World War.

Eric Taylor
2004

1. The Gathering of Eagles

'This raid, instead of being the costliest
in history for the enemy, could be the
costliest in history for us.'
Briefing Officer, Bomber Command

Saturday, 30 May 1942

It was a day that started like yesterday and the day before that.

Across the airfields of England's eastern counties a damp May
mist drifted. It swirled across the main runways, round the
perimeter tracks and the dripping green hangars. On the horizon
thunderstorms muttered darkly to each other, and in the early
morning sky dark clouds formed up like herds of grey elephants
pushing and shoving each other until they completely blotted out
the lighter patches beyond.

After breakfast the mist gave way to a cold, unrelenting rain
which seeped under doors and window frames; it bounced off the
wings of the big, dark bombers that stood waiting silent and
sinister in a thousand dispersal bays of fifty-three airfields.

In the overcrowded RAF messes, 6,000 aircrew waited and the
nervous tension rose perceptibly. Men who had never smoked
before accepted cigarettes. They gazed through the steamed-up
windows at the faint silhouettes of buildings lit up by spasmodic
cracks of lightning which flashed through the menacing gloom.
Endless rubbers of bridge were begun and men wandered aimlessly
from one room to another, sometimes exchanging words about the
worsening weather and the possibility of the operation being
'scrubbed' again.

They were an odd mixture. Some had already been through the
'sausage machine' of the first ten operations. Others were
completely raw, not even properly trained, and a few were nearing
the end of their thirty-op tour. And they waited, acting their parts,

27

some more convincingly than others, maintaining a guarded neutrality with the secret enemy – fear. They all knew something big was on but they did not know exactly what. Slowly the rumour started to circulate that they were destined for some suicidal mass daylight raid.

Jim Davidson, a veteran, heard the story at RAF Croft, on the Durham/Yorkshire border, but he was not particularly impressed or worried about the prospect. Two years as a rear gunner had conditioned him to accept the odds against survival. There was nothing to be done about them, except to look well after the efficiency of his guns and turret.

Jim was a tall, well-built, sandy-haired young Scot, displaying an image more of a ghillie than the glamour of an air-gunner. He did not look the kind who would panic in an emergency: if things got rough, you would expect him to pull out his pipe, pack it methodically and then give his considered judgement – except that in his job there never was time or space for that sort of thing. He was concerned less with the rumour of the raid than with keeping reasonably dry and warm in the primitive living-conditions afford by RAF Croft, new, muddy 'satellite' airfield to Middleton St George in County Durham.

Satellite airfields were popping up like mushrooms all over the country at that time in order to cater for the increasing number of squadrons arriving from all over the world and for the rapidly expanding Bomber Command. They were built for utility rather than comfort. The essential features were got ready first – runways, dispersal areas and a perimeter track. Next, in order of priority, came the administrative buildings, squadron offices, crew rooms and various messes. Last to be considered seemed to be the provision for aircrew comfort off duty.

Jim Davidson lived in a cold, damp Nissen hut where, in winter – winters were long in County Durham – rivers of condensation streamed down the metal walls. When it rained – 'and when wasn't it raining that spring?' – great gusts of wind would hurl it at the tin roof, beating it like a drum. Group Captain Tom Sawyer DFC, Davidson's Commanding Officer at that time, remembers how the same effect of heavy rain was achieved by aircrew coming home late 'with a skinful of beer and peeing great jets on the sides of the huts, close to where their friends' heads lay abed. It sounded as if it was raining four-inch nails. And if they had retired earlier than the revellers, they were not amused.'[1]

Davidson had come to Croft with 78 Squadron to be converted from Whitleys to the four-engined Halifax in time to take part in 'this big raid', and he was not at all impressed with what he saw. Locals had christened it RAF 'Sinking-in-the-Ooze', and the comment of incoming aircrew peering from the back of the truck that brought them from the railway station was invariably the same: 'Bloody Hell! What a dump!' But they made the best they could of their conditions, stealing coke for the stove and using greatcoats for extra blankets.

The British public, then strictly rationed, misguidedly thought that RAF flying crews lived off the fat of the land, cosseted with every comfort that wartime Britain could provide – 'Why, they even have a real egg for breakfast every morning!' But the reality was far from this, especially on the new airfields. Sergeants and officers lived in separate Nissen huts, and the only concession to comfort and rank for the officers was that they had only ten beds to a hut whilst the sergeants had twelve; as an additional luxury the officers had three tin wash-basins.

When Jim Davidson had entered the Nissen hut at Croft, with his spaniel dog, Whisky, he found the RAF police and the adjutant going through the personal belongings of aircrew who had been in the beds the previous night. They would not be coming back. They had gone for the 'chop'.

He had sat for a moment on his hard bed remembering when he had gone off to boarding school for the first time and was dumped miles from anywhere. And the same thoughts ran through his mind: 'Well, this is it. What have I let myself in for?' He would just have to wait and see.

Another Scot, David Walker, was known to his friends as a cheerful chap who was rarely put out by the sudden and unaccountable changes of routine that service life involved but on that Saturday, as he sat alone in the 44 Squadron's Mess at Waddington waiting for news, he could not help musing on the fact that it really was a strange sort of way to be spending a twenty-first[2] birthday.

He should have been celebrating with Barbara, his pretty, dark-haired girlfriend in Lincoln. He smiled at the thought of how she had introduced herself jokingly with: 'Ny name's Barbara and I'm a "Yellow Belly". Do you want me to prove it?' And she had made as if to pull up her blouse at the waist before explaining, in a burst of laughter, that all real Lincoln folk were called 'Yellow Bellies' due to the yellow waistcoat soldiers of the Lincoln Regiment used to wear.

That Saturday David and Barbara had planned to go dancing at the Montana Ballroom; instead he would be bringing death and misery to hundreds of people like themselves in Germany. He did not like the idea one little bit.

'Don't you know there's a war on?' People were quick to use the old cliché as an excuse for anything that was not going exactly as planned. But he had never felt the same way about bombing since he had helped with the rescue work on the Waddington NAAFI when it was hit by German bombers. Whilst they were trying to ease a young girl's body from the pile of masonry and timber, he had gently taken hold of her head with both hands to steady it. To his horror, as they all lifted together, the young girl's head came away from her shoulders and lay detached in his hands. His fingers went limp, and the dusty blonde head fell with a sickening crack onto the bricks. It then rolled down to come to rest at his feet. 'And this is what I am doing to others in Germany,' he had said to himself. The guilt lay heavily upon his conscience. That experience and the events that followed were to lead David Walker to a destiny that he had never for a moment imagined.

Coming from a family of long-standing members of the Church of Scotland, he had been a Sunday School teacher and President of the Church's Youth Fellowship. On Saturday evenings he used to stand with a group at the corner of Inverness town hall and give public testimony to his faith. He was filled with religious fervour and wanted to be a minister. When war had broken out in 1939, he was not sure what to do – he was partly inclined to study medicine whilst another part of him urged him towards the Church.

He did neither. Instead he applied to join the Air Force as a pilot. There was a long waiting-list, so he accepted signals training. After surviving thirty operations he realized that wireless operators had a much better chance of staying alive, so he never applied again. 'Let someone else drive,' was his reply whenever the subject was raised. He did not want to change things in case it changed his luck.

That was why he kept the ivory Buddha on the chain around his neck. Although he was a devout Christian, his father, who collected antiques, had given him one of these Buddhas to wear for luck on his first trip. After that he would not be without it. He did not think that he was superstitious or that certain objects had power of salvation. It was just that he did not like the idea of change when things were going all right. In fact, during the whole of that first tour of thirty operations he had never once feared that he would die. He had met other men who had said, 'So long, David. I don't suppose I shall see you again.' And no one ever did see them again. 'It seemed to be true,' said David, 'that once men started talking like that they did not last long, and the men who lasted longest seemed to be those who did not allow themselves to think about the statistics – a five per cent loss rate for each operation, which brought your number up very quickly.'

David had talked about all this to Barbara, and she knew whenever he was flying on a night operation because whenever he did an air test prior to an op he would always swoop down and 'beat up' the glass dome of the office where she worked at the Ruston and Hornby Iron Works, making tanks and submarine engines. In this way Barbara and her irate boss would know that she would not be seeing him that evening – which was a pity on this particular day for she had saved a precious and rare tin of salmon for his twenty-first birthday tea. Now there would be that agonizing wait until she could telephone to ask if David Walker's Lancaster was back.

Not all the Waddington aircrew were lucky enough to be allocated the new Lancaster. Experienced pilot Henry Maudslay, an old Etonian who would later be remembered for his part in the Möhne Dam raid, had to make do with an old Manchester which had been cannibalized for spare parts to repair other damaged Manchesters. But if that bothered Henry, he was not the man to show it; he took everything as it came, calmly.

The types who never 'flapped' took the waiting phlegmatically too. At RAF Station Skellingthorpe, one of them, the newly promoted Flying Officer Manser, stood by. He was to fly an old Manchester bomber that he had brought over from Conningsby to be part of the 50 Squadron Force detailed for the night's operation. It was to be his fourteenth. It would also go down in history as one in which valour of the highest order was displayed without regard for personal safety.

To most of his fellow aircrew, Leslie Manser was something of an enigma. He might have been waiting for a training flight for all the emotion to be seen in his face. It was not that he was a hardened veteran – he had celebrated his twentieth birthday just three weeks earlier – but he was recognized as a skilful pilot and an extremely competent captain. His crews all had faith in him.

Earlier that day he had air-tested the Manchester, a dirty machine that had been relegated to training duties for many months, and he had signed Form 700 to say that he was satisfied with its airworthiness. Maybe he was influenced by the fact that he knew that 'maximum effort' had to be made to get every available aircraft into the air. But nevertheless it must have satisfied his own high standards for he would not otherwise have risked the lives of his crew. Under normal circumstances it clearly would not have made the raid, but Herculean efforts had been called for to have every aircraft possible ready and so ...[3]

The Manchester was a poor aircraft anyway. It was originally designed to take four Rolls Royce Merlins, the engine which powered the Hurricane and Spitfire, but when it became clear in 1938 that there would not be enough Merlin engines to go round, as the fighters had priority, Rolls Royce suggested that the Manchester should be powered by two Vulture engines. This was done, but its performance was inadequate; it had a very poor rate of climb and could not reach the same height as the older Hampdens when fully loaded. Nobody liked them. For instance, when Guy Gibson went to take over a Manchester squadron, 106, he was greeted by a friend with: 'You're a clot. These Manchesters – they're awful. The actual kite's all right but it's the engine. They're fine when they keep turning but they don't often do so. We've had an awful lot of prangs.'[4]

Manser's 'kite' was also in desperate need of a good servicing. It had lacked the care that operational aircraft received and had been modified so that some essential features were missing; the mid-upper turret was not there, and the escape hatch had been permanently screwed up. Perhaps the best that could be said for this particular bomber was that it had at least satisfied the basic and rigorous standards of Leslie Manser. Which was a pity, for that Manchester would kill him soon ...

In another Manchester crew, of 49 Squadron at Scampton, was Sergeant Eric Clarke,[5] who was well aware of the grim reputation Manchesters had. He had had too many scares in them for him to be altogether happy. At that time the regulations said that no pilot could get airborne unless there was a wireless-operator with him.

Consequently when any Tom, Dick or Harry pilot wanted to air-test one of these new Manchesters, they would grab any wireless-operator handy at the time, and Eric Clark had been handy just too often for his peace of mind. And he had learnt that Manchesters were pretty dreadful machines.

After eleven operations in Hampdens and one in a Manchester, he was conscious of the number thirteen. It always seemed to be cropping up. It had dogged him throughout his service. He had been sworn in on the thirteenth, posted to 49 Squadron on the thirteenth; his first op was on the thirteenth; the Squadron numbers 4 and 9 added up to thirteen. Now another thirteen was coming up. This next operation – his thirteenth.

But he was not superstitious. Thirteen was not unlucky for him. Or so he thought.

Scot Flight Lieutenant Doug Henderson DFC took the waiting all very calmly too.[6] He was used to rumours and not alarmed. 'So what did we do? We had another wee drink and another.' Forty years on the 'wee drinks' killed him, a casualty of war as surely as if he had been killed in action.

In those days, when Doug Henderson was on one of those rain-sodden Yorkshire airfields at Pocklington, from which flew Australians, New Zealanders and Rhodesians as well as RAF crews, pints flowed freely. Every night the off-duty aircrew bussed into York and to Betty's Bar. There, and in other smoky pubs of the ancient Roman city, off-duty crews 'made whoopee', living only from raid to raid, thinking only of the next one when one was over. At week-ends they would wander through the narrow Shambles, eyeing the girls from Rowntrees (the Quaker firm said to be making shellcases instead of chocolate boxes), along the river, around the Minster and back again to some friendly bar where their voices echoed familiar lines: 'Christ! I thought we'd bought it. There we were, down to a thousand feet when ...' whilst someone at the fringe of the group would be going through the motions of playing a fanfare on a trombone – which meant he was 'blowing his own trumpet', or 'shooting a line' as the RAF types called it then.

Today traces of those days can still stir the memories of white-haired men sporting 'Flying Officer Kite' moustaches who gather occasionally in the cellar of Betty's Bar, where names of those long-dead flyers are scratched alongside photographs of young laughing aircrew. For a few nostalgic moments they relive those 'nights on the town' that released the tension between operations.

However, life in York at that time was not 'all beer and skittles', as Doug Henderson himself had witnessed. Almost a month to the day prior to the Cologne raid, York had suffered a battering from the Luftwaffe bombers, part of a 'tit for tat' policy of retaliatory raids in which the British and German commanders were indulging. The RAF had burnt half of the medieval cities of Lübeck and Rostok, and Hitler had ordered Goering to attack cathedral cities of similar historical importance. Consequently in April 1942 Exeter, Norwich, Bath and York were bombed.

The first salvo of bombs had landed on York railway station just as the crowded 22.15 express had steamed in, crowded with weary servicemen laden with kitbags, packs and rifles. These men were not going to lose their precious seats on account of an air-raid warning in provincial York, so they stayed put despite the loudspeaker warnings to leave the train. But not Doug Henderson. He was already standing in the half-open door ready to leap onto the platform and race for a taxi. Already he was cutting it fine to be back on base by 23.59 hours, after a week-end in London.

It was fortunate for him that he was at the ready, for the first 250-pound bomb came crashing down to explode at the far end of the station as his feet touched the ground. He raced through the smoke and flying debris in record time, past the barrier where the red-capped Military Police used to stand to apprehend absentees and out onto the grassy bank of the old moat by the city wall before the next wave of bombers came in.

That night, when the York railway system, the pride of LNER, was reduced to fire-blackened ruins together with the ancient guildhall and 8,000 homes, Flight Lieutenant Henderson discovered for himself what it was like to be bombed. He saw for the first time the frightened, smoke-blackened faces of men and women and the panic-stricken, tearful faces of children. Over 300 York civilians were killed or seriously wounded that night. The picture stayed with him. It was always with him as he flew over Germany dropping his own bombs. It was to be with him all his life.

At RAF Linton-on-Ouse, seven miles from the ancient city of York, the tannoy crackled into harsh metallic life quite early that morning. 'All members ...'

'Rusty' Hudson heard it as he lay back on his bed with arms behind his head gazing at the ceiling. He suited his nickname well, for he had a rust-coloured nose which matched a chin so red that it looked like a boil about to come to a head. 'Rusty' seemed to suit his nature as well as his appearance: in the officers' mess they knew him as a typical 'one of the boys' type who joins in everything. Jackie Barton, his girlfriend, knew him better, and she was worried.

She had met Rusty on his first and last visit to York's School of Ballroom Dancing. She had partnered him in the waltz and, having mastered the straightforward 'one, two, three' (which he had to mutter to himself as he went along for he had not much sense of rhythm), he had not bothered to go again. But he had seen a lot of Jackie, a slim eighteen-year-old with dark hair and a bright smile, beginning her first year as a student nurse at the County Hospital. Together they had plenty to talk about. Rusty, never very good with small talk or casual conversation, found that Jackie was a good listener. He could talk to her enthusiastically about his future as a dentist. Already he had two years behind him at the Turner Dental School of Manchester University and looked forward to having his own practice after the war. He had an old but reliable Matchless motorcycle, which his father, also a dentist, had bought him. Consequently whenever Rusty was free he would ride down to the hospital to pick her up. They were a well-matched pair in every way, and it was natural for them to confide in each other. But it was not until early one morning after a nurses' party, when Jackie and Rusty were lying back on a couch in a quiet corner, that she learnt of his secret fears, the nightmares and the dread of finally 'going LMF'.

It was a cruel procedure in every way. Men who had done a full tour of ops and were well into their second could suddenly find their stock of courage had run out. They could stand no more. Despite having volunteered in the first place and done a splendid job, they could be court-martialled, stripped of their rank and flying brevets and thenceforth employed in the lowest grades of trades. Across their documents would be stamped 'LACK OF MORAL FIBRE'.

All you had to do was 'boomerang'* once too often.

---

* Come back with engine trouble, aborting the raid. See also Chapter 8.

Rusty Hudson had five trips to go, so he was close to finishing his tour. But each trip it got worse. On the last trip he had turned back with 'engine failure' when there was not much wrong with it. Those who knew him recognized the signs. He would smoke a cigarette in a hurry and then light another. By his bedside in a tin box were letters he had written that someone else could post if he did not get back one night. And the feeling grew stronger on each trip that this would be his night for the 'chop'.

He felt better away from the station with Jackie. Now with the tannoy announcement he felt trapped, desperate to talk to her – and he would.

Alongside the A1 at Alconbury Weston, a little to the north of Huntingdon, former civil flying instructor and RAF Volunteer Reserve pilot Jack Wilson, a cheerful enthusiast from Dublin, was one of the few this Saturday morning who was really looking forward to his first operation. He had volunteered to come off flying instruction, where he had earned his Air Force Cross, and was eager to hit back at Nazi Germany.

Happily married now for three years and with a two-year-old daughter, he loved his flying but felt he ought to be taking his fair share at the sharp end of the war. Christina, his wife, realized there was no point in raising objections; she knew exactly how he felt. In May 1942 Christina Wilson[7] was living in Northampton with young Deirdre, thirty miles from Alconbury; she would have liked to have lived with her husband in married quarters or in rented accommodation close to the camp but the RAF did not look with favour on wives who lived in the close neighbourhood. It could have been bad for morale and administratively difficult to have so many young widows together. And so for a little time Christina made do with the occasional week-end visits; then in 1943 they took a cottage close to the camp. There, in the garden, Jack would relax before going off to get ready for a raid. And it was from there that she was to see him go off on his last.

On this particular week-end Jack had telephoned to say that he would not be coming to see her, and she sensed from his guarded speech that soon, very soon he would be flying on a raid – his first. And so, like so many other wives and mothers, she began to live from one night to the next morning, waiting anxiously.

For his part, Jack was not in the least worried at what the day would bring. As his wife said many years later, 'He was raring to go, full of that patriotic fervour and determination.'

And so the eagles gathered. By this time few knew what was going on but everyone knew it was 'something big'.

Quite by chance, at RAF Honington that day was twenty-one-year-old Ken Pexman. He was there for re-training as a bomber gunner after being a gunner in one of the early RAF fighters, the Defiant, which had a machine-gun mounted behind the pilot to fire backwards. At first it had given the Luftwaffe fighters who approached too close a nasty shock. But once they got the measure of this unusual machine they found it could be attacked with impunity from below, and the Defiant was withdrawn from service. Ken Pexman had been given the choice of transferring to Havocs or being retrained for air-gunner duties with heavy bombers. He chose the heavies.

But before going on bombers he had one special request to make. He wanted to get married. Leave was granted – seven days. It was a typical quiet wartime wedding with Ken in his best wartime blue uniform, buttons sparkling, at St Hugh's Church, Scunthorpe. The honeymoon was spent locally and Ken was really happy. Or so it seemed. He bid a cheerful good-bye to his wife, Mabel, and to his family. He was doing all that he ever wanted to do – flying. He certainly did not look like a man with a premonition that he would never see his twenty-second birthday. However, this is what he felt himself and had confessed only to his brother Max.[8]

Ken had been keen to fly since he was a boy at Scunthorpe Secondary School. It appealed far more than the prospect of following his mates into the steelworks whose blast-furnaces lit up the evening sky near home. However, when he first left school he was too young to join the Air Force and he took a job as wages clerk in the steelworks. But he never lost that first boyish enthusiasm for flying, so that when his call-up papers eventually arrived, he volunteered for aircrew. His parents raised no objections, even though they realized full well the risks involved. After all, argued his father, it could be no worse than the blood and mud of the trenches he himself had endured with the 10th Lincolnshire Regiment on the Somme in the First World War. Eventually his mother learnt to live with the fear of the telegram boy riding down the street to deliver the dreaded Air Ministry message.

Now, for the time being at least, Ken Pexman could look upon all the activity going on around him in an interested but detached sort of way. It had nothing really to do with him. His conversion training would be starting when this raid was over. Or so he thought.

In almost the same frame of mind was former jockey Vic Mitchell, who had arrived at RAF Finningley OTU two weeks earlier to complete his air gunnery training. He too, in those last few days of May, was struck by the contrast between the furious activity in the hangars and the listless inactivity in the messes.

Out on the dispersal areas fitters sprawled over engine nacelles, electricians, instruments specialists and radio mechanics checked and re-checked for faults. Tractors towed trains of trolleys loaded with bombs to the waiting bombers standing with bomb doors open. Then they were manhandled under the gaping belly where armourers very carefully checked the switches and crutches before starting to winch up the heavy load. They sweated not only with the physical effort involved but also perhaps from anxiety. They knew it was highly dangerous work. Bombs could and did fall. Indeed, when one 4,000-pound 'Cookie' blast bomb fell and exploded at Scampton on another day, it killed all the armourers, totally destroyed six Lancasters and severely damaged five others.

'Bombing up' was no easy job. Ground crews had a hard and hazardous job; deaths and severe injuries were not uncommon when a 'maximum effort' raid pressure was on.

Corporal Alan Smith recalls how his section were standing back from a Halifax they had just finished servicing at Leeming when the rear gunner decided to test his Browning guns into the ground and almost shot both legs away from aircraftsman Alan Waters. 'His left calf was completely cut away and he had a hole as big as my fist in his right shin.'[9] On another occasion the photoflash flares fell from the bomb rack and ignited under the bomber. Corporal Hill dashed under the bomber already tanked up and bombed and began flinging the spluttering flares away before the aircraft caught fire, earning a mention in Despatches. On another raid Alan Smith had a 'close shave' when ninety incendiary bombs showered down upon him due to a sudden surge in the current which triggered off the release bar. He risked going up with the bomber in one big bang by staying long enough to fling the ignited ones away.

Supervising all this technical activity was the ubiquitous flight sergeant, a man held in the highest regard by all aircrew. It was no wonder that they would often take 'Chiefy' and his team down to the local pub for a pint to show their gratitude for the way his team serviced their bomber.

Amid this highly organized bustle at Finningley, Mitchell was struck by something which seemed rather strange and remarkably casual – the last minute 'crewing up'.

Around a NAAFI tea wagon men would be smoking, eating sausage rolls, sipping mugs of tea, and would start chatting with the words: 'Are you crewed-up yet?' If the reply happened to be, 'Not yet,' there might follow an invitation, 'Would you like to join us?'

Mitchell remembers that eventually there seemed to be one particular group that nobody wanted. 'The Awkward Squad' they called them, and so they formed their own crew together. On this memorable day when the big 'buzz' started, there were no further aircraft available, but they were now determined to be part and parcel of the raid wherever it was going, and they pestered all and sundry until someone said there was an old Wimpy at the other side of the airfield that might be a possibility. Fired with new hope, they sought the flight sergeant, who said the aircraft was unserviceable but that he would 'have a go'. Urged on by 'the Awkward Squad', the mechanics worked on patiently until indeed they did get the old lady airworthy. The crew were delighted.

What was going on? No wonder Vic Mitchell at Finningley was puzzled. Someone was scraping the barrel. Even 'the Awkward Squad' now had a kite on this dull May day.[10]

Aircraft and men were being brought into the operations at very short notice – 'maximum effort' this time really did mean *maximum*.

Only two days before the Cologne raid, Fred Simpson,[11] a sergeant engineering specialist, was working with a ground crew section servicing Halifax bombers at RAF Leeming on the Yorkshire/Durham border and he was not finding it at all to his liking. But being a regular airman and the type of man he was, he saw no point in moaning. He did something about it. He applied for aircrew duty as a flight engineer expecting that after a few weeks of waiting and then further conversion training he would become aircrew. What he did not expect was to be put immediately onto aircrew duties and onto ops as well. By temperament and training, Fred Simpson was ideally suited for the job.

As a strapping, fair-haired young lad of fifteen he had decided to bring a bit of excitement into his life as a trainee fitter by joining a Territorial cavalry unit, the Yorkshire Hussars, and he began his service career — like his future boss, 'Bomber' Harris — as a bugler. For the next $3\frac{1}{2}$ years he enjoyed being a week-end soldier and a weekday engineer apprentice. But by the time he was nineteen he found he could enjoy the best of both worlds — service and engineering — if he joined the RAF as a fitter.

Thus on 11 February 1937 he reported to Uxbridge Recruit depot for his initial training. He was a very smart recruit, particularly at 'squarebashing' and was picked out for the King George VI Coronation parades before being posted to No. 3 School of Technical Training at Manston, a station which was to feature dramatically in his life later on. 'It was not really an ideal place for a fit young technical training student. There were too many distractions with Margate on one side and Ramsgate on the other, each packed with lively, pretty young girls at holiday time bent on getting the most from their two weeks by the sea.' However, young Fred scraped through his course successfully and went on to further training at Northcoates. From there he went to France shortly after war broke out in 1939 and served for a spell in the Advanced Air Striking Force.

Returning to Britain before the Dunkirk evacuation, Fred embarked once more on Technical Training at RAF Henlow, where two significant events happened. First of all he met a girl called Dorothy and married her on 11 February 1941, and secondly he got a call across the workshop from 'Chiefy' to say that there was a new trade open to him, an opportunity to remuster to flight engineer.

Twenty-four hours later he was on his way to an air gunners' course — engineers had to be able to work the guns at that time — and that was followed by a course on the servicing of the new Stirling bomber at the Short aircraft factory. Then, with the typical forces flair for cock-eyed postings, with all his training on Stirlings behind him, he was posted to a Halifax squadron. It did not surprise Regular Airman Fred in the least. In any case, Leeming, where No. 10 Halifax Squadron was stationed at this time, was near enough to his home town of Middlesborough for him to get back to see his wife and baby, Bill, on a forty-eight-hour pass.

He was finding it no easy matter in those days supporting a wife and baby on what he earned. As a flight engineer he was paid 10 shillings a day, and on the week-end of that momentous raid the Durham miners were on strike because eighteen-year-olds were getting only 9s.8d. a shift. They agreed to go back three days later for an extra 2s.6d. a shift – a little more than Fred's flying pay.

He was so short of money on one week-end when home on leave that he lacked enough to buy a pint, so he put the baby in the pram and wheeled it around to every relative and friend who lived nearby. Naturally, as was the custom then, they all slipped a piece of silver into the baby's little clutching hand. When he got home there was 28 shillings in the pram.

At Leeming Fred Simpson had got to know the Halifax well, and several times he had been asked to go up in the Halifax, which was being air-tested. It was on one of these occasions that he met the new Flight Commander, Squadron Leader Tony Ennis, and discovered what he already thought to be true – that flying was much more fun than the frantic non-stop work of the servicing bay.

He could not have chosen a more opportune time for applying for flight engineer aircrew duties, for Tony Ennis, still a comparative newcomer to the station, was getting his own crew together and he liked what he had seen of Simpson. With the pressure of this 'maximum effort' raid there was no time to spare, so on Saturday 30 May 1943 Fred Simpson was in the new crew of Tony Ennis, with Australian Ben Gibbons as navigator, Pilot Officer Simpson as wireless-operator and tail gunner Sergeant Bertram Groves.

How would they work out as a team? There would be little time to find out, for this would be the first and the last time they would fly together.

Another ex-apprentice with Fred Simpson at Leeming was John Macfarlane,[12] a stocky young flight engineer/air gunner also from Middlesborough. Together they were a pair of jokers. On one occasion they got into the briefing room before anyone else and put the route-marking wool right across the map from Leeming to the 'Big City', Berlin, just to hear the groan that would go up when the curtain was drawn back. Mac used to say that, once the glamour had gone out of flying, aircrew did not worry much about what they did as far as petty rules were concerned. They would, for example, just walk out of the camp and hitch-hike home if no ops were on for the night. The camp was alongside the A1, and aircrew were always sure of a lift in those days. Next morning there would be the early milk train back.

Sometimes Fred would borrow his father's car, and they scrounged petrol from wherever they could by various dodges. Once they got hold of a big can of paint-stripper and poured it in the tank. It went like a rocket but unfortunately they spilt quite a lot down the side of the car, and it lifted all the paint off. His dad was not at all pleased.

Thus Mac and his pal Fred, and many aicrew like them, lived for the day and, as their commander, Harris, once said: 'They let off steam in an atmosphere of eat, drink and be merry for the next time we shall most certainly die.'

During those last two days of May, though, they had no opportunity of going out, for all were confined to camp. There was even a broad strap and lock around the civilian phone near the guardroom. No one, it seemed, was going to get to know what was going on.

As they waited for the night's operation, John Macfarlane entertained or irritated his fellow sergeant in the mess by reading poetry. The poetry of death. 'He was cocking a snook at Fate, I suppose,' was how a friend explained this perverse sense of humour. 'One of the poems he read was Yeats' "An Irish Airman Foresees His death".'

Whether John Macfarlane was tempting Death or not, he was, at the same time, taking out an insurance policy in pinning to his vest his lucky charm, a little man made out of beads that his mother had bought at a jumble sale, and in his wallet was his lucky threepenny bit.

And so they waited, in one way or another, on those fifty-three bomber stations that spring day forty-four years ago now. They knew that 'something big was on', and that knowledge, with all its implications, divorced them from the outside world. That world of homes and meals, of girls and beer, no longer existed. No past. No future. Only now. Even the fighting war meant little to them: the British Eighth Army resisting Rommel in the Western desert ... Tobruk ... convoys in the North Atlantic ... the battle for Kharkov.

News in the papers was not for them. For, in a way, they knew they were the condemned men, these youngsters with the Brylcreamed short-back-and-sides and the slightly absurd 'Flying Officer Kite' moustaches. They knew that soon they would be setting out on some momentous raid. And then ...

Some, like Roland Winfield, a medical officer[13] at Oakington, had come to terms with it all – as we shall see – adopting a philosophy that the cause for which they were all fighting was far more important than the preservation of their own lives. Accepting this attitude had brought peace of mind.

Others were not quite so calm or philosophical. The waiting was nibbling away at their nerves, and as the hours and minutes ticked away on the mess clock some would curse and cry out: 'For God's sake, send us or call it off!'

2. The Great Dilemma

On that morning in May, Air Marshal Sir Arthur T. Harris ('Bomber' to the Press, 'Butch' to his aircrew, 'Bert' to a few close friends) was painfully aware of his dilemma and the odds against the great operation he had planned for his 'boys' as he walked at a leisurely pace over to the nerve centre of Bomber Command Headquarters – 'the Hole' – a spacious operations room, seventy-five feet underground, deep in rural Buckinghamshire near the village of Walters Ash.

Unlike many wartime headquarters, this was purpose-built and new. It had opened in 1940, just two years before Harris had been appointed Commander-in-Chief. From the air it was difficult to locate hidden among the beechwoods of the Chiltern Hills, its buildings separated into patterns that looked like small country housing estates. Indeed, the Luftwaffe never did find the site, and it survived the war unscathed to fulfil a major post-war role with the RAF Strike Command.

Tucked away in the Chiltern Hills, the Headquarters was conveniently close to Prime Minister Churchill's house at Chequers and readily accessible from London. Harris lived on the site and would often walk through the woods before attending 'Morning Prayers', the routine nine o'clock target-choosing conference.

He was a broad-shouldered, bulky man, generally regarded as remote and grim; a man who could freeze an Eskimo with a look; a man of explosive temperament whom you would think twice about disturbing. Junior officers on his staff feared but admired him and were never quite sure what was going on in the mind behind that poker face. 'Like most "copper-knots" he had a fairly short temper and was very outspoken and indeed rude when he so chose,' was how one of his most famous subordinates, the future Air Vice-Marshal 'Pathfinder' Bennett, was to write.[1]

This morning Harris's pace was slower than usual, for he was wrestling with a problem as he walked between the dripping beech trees, wondering still about the night's target but knowing one thing for sure: a decision would have to be made, one way or the other, today. The air armada would have to attack or disperse.

But to mount the operation in such unfavourable weather conditions could be courting disaster, for Harris was about to do something which no commander in history would have chosen to do – to risk the whole of his front-line strength, the whole of his reserves and all his training backing, in one battle.

It was a bold venture, needing audacity and courage. Harris was well endowed with both. He had already achieved a remarkable logistic feat in assembling over one thousand bombers. Many were now equipped with the new and revolutionary navigation and blind bombing devices which should ensure maximum concentration of the force over the target area. Here, now, was the opportunity – which might not come again – to deliver a blow which could prove once and for all the war-winning potential of Bomber Command.

Already the new strategic bombing offensive was underway. The directive of 14 February had given him four primary targets to 'blot out': Essen, Duisburg, Düsseldorf and Cologne.

Now he had the opportunity to carry out part of that plan: to destroy completely by fire one of Germany's biggest industrial centres, to erase from the map of Europe, in one night, a major German city.

Unusually bad weather for May, though, was frustrating him. Thundery conditions and heavy cloud prevailed over Germany on the day originally planned for the raid, 27 May, and so Harris had postponed the operation for twenty-four hours. The next day the weather was no better, and again the operation was put off for a further twenty-four hours. On the third day, Friday 29 May, bad weather had forced yet another postponement.

Now, on Saturday 30 May, the weather looked equally unfavourable. It would not have been such a criticial factor for one of the recent routine raids with about 200 aircraft taking part, but to put a thousand bombers in the air all heading through thick cloud for one target would be inviting a catastrophe on an unprecedented scale. It was not just the risk of collision over the target area that worried Harris but also the high risk involved in landing the force after the raid, on home bases hidden by heavy cloud. The landing after the raid was always a hazardous part of any operation, as the Luftwaffe had found when in the month of the 1940 Blitz on London they had lost 250 bombers from crashes on return to their own airfields. General Kesselring had harangued the Luftwaffe leaders, saying that even the entire resources of the Reich could not stand that rate of loss. Neither could the RAF.

On the other hand, Harris knew for sure that to delay the operation again would give more time for the opponents of Bomber Command to persuade Churchill to break up the force and disperse its aircraft to support the Army in Africa, and the Navy in its battle with the German Atlantic submarine fleets. Already he had had a taste of things to come when the Admiralty had withdrawn its support for the 'Thousand Plan', and with it 250 bombers at the last crucial moment.

'Typical Admiralty bloody-mindedness!' Harris had said and then stubbornly set about raising the extra aircraft from Bomber Command itself, calling for 'maximum effort' to bring into service aircraft relegated to training and scratch crews from staff and instructional duties, scraping the barrel. In a way the weather helped him – giving extra time for the force to be assembled, but now time was running out, for the night of 30/31 May would be the last on which conditions of moonlight would be suitable.

Such was the situation at ten minutes past nine on the morning of 30 May 1942, when Air Marshal Harris walked into the high-ceilinged operations room for his 'Morning Prayers'. The hum of voices quietened but the atmosphere was busy with officers monitoring a constantly changing mass of information.

Harris sat down at his desk, nerves taut as fiddle strings, for the meteorological report. He listened carefully but with apparent indifference, no sign of feeling showing on his face. He would be fifty in a few weeks and he usually appeared younger, but not today: strain and fatigue lined his face. In the past several days he had worked well beyond midnight yet was up at six the next morning.

The meteorological officer, Magnus Spence, delivered his forecast in an equally emotionless voice, stressing his points meticulously, as a schoolmaster might to a class of slow learners. It was not a good forecast: the same old story of storms and heavy cloud formations over north-west Germany. And then, unexpectedly, there came a glimmer of hope: 'In the south, cloud formation could break up.'

Harris looked at Saundby, Deputy C. in C., and the met. officer continued, 'There is a fifty-fifty chance that the cloud will clear from the Cologne area by midnight. The home base will, on the whole, be clear of cloud.' That was it. The met. officer stopped speaking and stood with his hands clasped in front of his body. Faces were grim. There was a sudden tension as each man glanced at his companion.

Now it was up to Harris. He sat back in his chair, staring at the charts.

The big question still unresolved was: would the weather hold long enough for the thousand bombers attacking the city to get in and out within the ninety-minute concentration? If the break in the clouds held, there would be no problem, but if the break did not, the worst could happen.

Harris sat motionless, still staring at the charts. Watching him was Dudley Saward[2] his chief radar officer, who recalls the scene vividly: 'Slowly his forefinger moved across the Continent of Europe and came to rest on a town in Germany. The pressure of his finger bent the end of the joint and drove the blood from the top of his fingernail, leaving a half circle of white. He turned to his Senior Air Staff Officer, his face still expressionless: "The Thousand Plan tonight."'

Other men might have hesitated more, might indeed have played safe. Not so Harris. The experience of a lifetime had conditioned him for this very moment. For he was a fighter born and bread. Once he had got his teeth into something, he would not let go, come hell or high water. If ever there was a case of the right man, in the right place, at the right time, this was it.

Harris came from a classic imperial background. His father was an Indian Civil Servant, but he himself was born in Britain in April 1892 whilst his parents were on leave, and then went out to India. At the tender age of five he was sent home to a boarding school, Allhallows, where he had to learn how to fend for himself. Only boys who were physically robust and mentally tough could hope to survive the rigours of that Edwardian public-school regime. Harris learned quickly two basic lessons of life: how to deal with a bully ('If a number of you get together, however much smaller, you could always give any bully a hell of a time – and he left you alone'[3]) and that attack is always the best method of defence. He was to remember those two lessons many times later in life when confronting opposition. But along with his growing independence there was also a caring for others who were not so capable of looking after themselves.

With his tough, wiry physique, Harris excelled on the sports field and also in the training exercises of the Officers Training Corps. He was the first cadet at Allhallows to win his War Certificate 'A'. Even at that early age he strove for excellence.

His father, who came from a family with high-ranking military connections, wanted young Arthur to join the Army, but the young man had other ideas. Something had happened, quite by chance, in his last year at Allhallows which had changed all his previous ideas on a military career. He was given a free ticket to a play in which a Rhodesian planter came back home to marry his 'society' fiancée but found her so boringly snobbish that he married the pretty young housemaid instead, whom he thought would be far more suited to be a farmer's wife. The whole idea of Rhodesia took a firm hold of Harris's imagination. There was a land of opportunity, where class, school and family did not matter a bit. You were simply what you were. He too would be a farmer in Rhodesia.

There was no shifting him once he had made up his mind – a trait of his character which would be remarked upon many times in his life. There were many rows with his father but a few days before his eighteenth birthday young Arthur Harris, travelling on a second-class ticket, sailed from Tilbury. He was on his way, regardless of opposition, determined to make a life for himself.

Once in Rhodesia he took rough and tough jobs, gold-mining, driving horse-drawn coaches, all the time learning how to deal with people in all walks of life. And he grew into a tough, independent, self-confident Rhodesian. Forty years later he was proudly to write: 'I was, I still am, a Rhodesian.'

Then came the Great War – as they called it then – and in August 1914, 'like all the other damned fools', he rushed to volunteer for the army. But even at that early stage of the war he was not quick enough off the mark. There was only one place left to fill in that 1st Rhodesian Regiment – bugler. Determined not to be disappointed, young Harris picked up the bugle and blew a blast that nearly took the adjutant's head off. He was in! But he did not know what he was in for. The regiment was ill equipped with old Canadian rifles and seemed to spend most of its time marching from one part of Africa to another. 'And how we marched! We marched and we marched and we marched, and God knows how we marched, as far as I was concerned I'd already marched too far!'[4]

Fortunately for Harris and eventually for Britain, the German South-West African Campaign ended in July 1915, and the regiment was disbanded, leaving him in Cape Town with his bellyful of marching and a determination to find some way of going to war in a sitting position. 'I swore I'd never walk another step.'[5] Along with 300 other disbanded soldiers he went along to the shipping office to get a passage to Britain, to join something there – preferably the cavalry. But cavalry recruitment had stopped. He tried the artillery. They also were full. And then he remembered the advertisement calling for volunteers for training as pilots with the Royal Flying Corps. Another sitting down job! He applied and was laughed away. Six thousand other young men were on the waiting list above him.

What did Harris do? He got a note from his father to one of his high-ranking uncles at the War Office and walked past the supercilious second lieutenants who had barred his path the previous day. His Uncle Charlie was away somewhere at a meeting, but one of his minions took charge of Arthur Harris and walked him down the corridor for the customary 'short arm inspection' – 'Drop your trousers, cough, lift your arms.' The old medical officer asked a few questions, discovered he had marched for six months and thought that was good enough to qualify him as fit for flying training. Once again Harris had got his way. He was going to war in a sitting position!

By 6 November 1915 he was appointed a second lieutenant, then sent to the Central Flying School, where he qualified for his pilot's wings fourteen weeks later.

At his first squadron he introduced practice night flying, believing that proper training to meet every situation was essential to efficiency. 'This matter of proper training was to become a fetish with him in later life, and to which Bomber Command in World War II was to owe a great deal of its success. It was also at this time that the possibilities of the use of aircraft by night as offensive weapons were first sown in his mind,' one of his Bomber Command staff officers was later to write.[6] Soon he was flying fighters in France.

At first no one seemed to know how to make full use of aircraft in wartime, but then the idea of a bomber was born and with it a vision of a new way to victory: the destruction of an enemy's cities and industrial capacity from the air.

Yet the man and this vision might never have come together at High Wycombe in 1942. It was all a matter of chance. 'I only drifted into the RAF after the Great War,' Harris was later to recall.[7] Drifting or not, he made the most of his experience during those inter-war years.

In 1919, policing in India with obsolete and worn-out aircraft, he was visited by a general. Never afraid to speak his mind, Harris caustically referred to his maintenance resources as a 'ball of string'.

Then, in 1922, in Iraq, where the RAF were responsible for internal security, Harris acquired a reputation for unorthodox direct methods to gain his ends. His aircraft, he said, were being wrongly used. Instead of ferrying beer to the troops, they should have been dropping bombs. To prove the point, he had a large hole cut in the nose of the Vernon aircraft, then a bomb sight and bomb racks fitted. Next came squadron practice. Out in the desert they drew a large circle, stuck a red flag in the middle and in the early hours of the morning would practice dropping 28-pound bombs from 1,000 feet. Very soon, with much more practice, they were hitting within ten feet of the target.

Satisfied with this accuracy, Harris then went to see the area commander, Sir John Salmond, and proposed that his squadron should change roles with the DH Squadron currently engaged on frontier bombing tasks, because the Vernon could carry a heavier bomb load and could guarantee to hit the target more accurately. To clinch the argument, he suggested a bombing competition: if Harris's bombing claims proved valid, the squadrons should change roles – Harris's bombing, the other carrying beer there and the casualties back. The well-practised No. 45 Squadron won convincingly, and the roles were changed. Soon Harris was bombing Turkish troops and truculent civilian tribesmen into submission. And not only by day. By night he could induce far greater fear in the families of tribesmen. As Harris was to recall years later: 'You could just imagine what they would think if they heard us over them in the darkness – you know – By Allah, they can ruddy well see us in the dark too!'[8]

Bombing civilians by night was seen to be an effective way of shortening a war conflict and saving soldiers' lives. He found also that, by burning down villages with small incendiary bombs, raiding tribesmen would be 'taught a lesson'. The principle of long-range night bombing was established. He had no qualms about civilians getting killed; winning and shortening the war were what mattered.

The idea that the bomber would decide the next war by paralysing the enemy's civil and industrial life was now being vigorously asserted by Lord 'Boom' Trenchard, Chief of the Air Staff. Civilians would have to be bombed.

'Such objectives,' wrote Trenchard, 'may be situated in centres of population in which their destruction will result in casualties to the neighbouring civilian population, in the same way as the long-range bombardments of a defended coastal town by a naval force results in incidental destruction of civilian life and property. The fact that air attacks may have that result is no reason for regarding the bombing as illegitimate providing all reasonable care is taken to confine the scope of the bombing to the military objective.'[9]

Already, with that final part of the sentence, the Air Ministry and politicians were providing the gloss that would be put over the future bombing of Germany. Then, though, Harris was more concerned with practicalities than politics, with training his crews to a high standard of efficiency. And what was asked of these crews by the government? Air displays!

In 1930 Harris had a break, one of the most enjoyable in his long service life. He was put in charge of what he was to describe as an entirely useless station of aircraft: flying-boats. Enjoyable though it was, he was not entirely happy: 'I knew I was wasting my time.'

He never wasted time again. The next posting was to the Air Ministry, first in Operations and Intelligence and then as Head of Plans, experience valuable in preparing him for his ultimate task, in 1942, as Commander-in-Chief Bomber Command, for there at the Air Ministry he was dealing with grand strategy problems and gaining insight into the ways of fighting what he was to call 'the dead hand of bureaucracy'.

In the mid-thirties at the Air Ministry the bomber came to dominate British policy, for the exponents of air power had now convinced most politicians that the decisive battles of a future war would be fought in the skies above the cities of the warning nations. In 1935 Italy invaded Abyssinia and resigned from the League of Nations, and Germany re-armed so that her Air Force was greater than Britain's and was expanding to 20,000 first-line aircraft. Panic bells were ringing in Whitehall. Even the staunch pacifist Ramsay MacDonald, heading the National Government of the day, was moved to order an expansion of the RAF. The new Conservative Government upgraded the scheme and gave priority to the heavier bombers. Harris, at the Air Ministry, was given the job of preparing the blueprint of the bomber force he was to command from 1942 to 1945. Fortunately, his insistence on having a strategic bomber force began to be accepted, and specifications were laid down for a four-engined Halifax bomber and twin-engined Manchester (the prototype for the superb four-engined Lancaster) and the Stirling. Thus Harris was part of that planning team responsible for the giant bombers he one day was to command.

In 1938, when British forces were fighting an Arab revolt in Palestine, the new Air Officer Commanding, Air Commodore Sir Arthur Harris, chafing at restraints imposed by politicians, said, 'My advice to all young commanders is this. Whenever you see any prospect of being called out in aid of the civil powers then get to hell out of there. If you fail by being too soft – you'll be sacked. If you succeed by being tough, you'll certainly be told you were too tough and may be for it.' Prophetic words indeed. But that time was yet to come.

With the outbreak of war Harris was sent to command No. 5 Bomber Group at Grantham. Rarely had he been so depressed. He saw there 'a skeleton formation with not enough meat on the bones to prevent a rattle which would be audible to the enemy.'[10] 'I had come to make bricks and there was no need for my predecessor to advise me on the lack of straw.'[11]

Fortunately for Britain, there was the 'Phoney War' from 3 September until 10 May when there was no fighting on the Western Front, and for those four months there was no effort by aircraft from either side to attack an inland target. Ironically, when two RAF aircraft did bomb Mönchen-Gladbach, the only person killed was an Englishwoman, wife of a former German prisoner of war.

During this breathing-space Harris analysed Number 5 Group's shortcomings and, though he could do little to increase the number of front-line bombers available, he could do a lot to increase their effectiveness. He insisted on improvements to rear gun turrets of bombers: Hampdens were modified and the Halifax came into service with a much more effective tail-gun turret than would otherwise have happened. When these aircraft were later in action, these tail-gunners were really needed, for the losses in the main came from night fighters.

But at this stage of the war what were they needed for? The feeble expedient of dropping leaflets. Though Harris's aircraft were not used for this, he recalls with heartfelt scorn that, 'The only thing achieved was to supply the Continent's requirements of toilet paper for the five long years of war. You have to think what any man of sense would do with what was obviously an enemy pamphlet.'[12]

Whilst Harris was at No. 5 Group, the Avro Manchester arrived, and with it came from the Minister of Aircraft Production, Lord Beaverbrook, a 'No Modification' order. Harris was livid. He had found the Manchester defective and deficient in many ways. Typically, no punches pulled, Harris wrote about the new Manchester: 'As matters stand at present the first twenty can never be used for operations (otherwise than for the purpose of throwing away crews!) and urgent steps must be taken to put right the shortcomings!' Thus he was helping to build up a bomber force of a size and capability that could take a substantial offensive against Germany.

With the fall of France, Harris returned to the Air Ministry as Deputy Chief of the Air Staff. And did the inmates know he was back! One of the first things he did was to cut them down to size – by forty per cent. 'As the missive crept round the corridors you could almost hear the wails of despair with which the bureaucrats in the building greeted it.'[13] Much to their relief, however, in June '41 Harris was sent to America with a mission to expedite delivery of war stores and equipment. Once there he got on famously with Roosevelt and Hopkins. He chased around factories helping to speed up deliveries, and down in Texas, where air-crew flying training schools gave initial training to RAF crews, he fostered a splendid atmosphere of co-operation.

And then, at last, came the posting for which his service had really conditioned him: Chief of Bomber Command.

On 23 February 1942 Air Marshal Sir Arthur Harris drove up to the main gates of Headquarters Bomber Command at Wycombe and entered that special loneliness that belongs to high command. A loneliness without privacy. He was taking up his post at a gloomy time of the war when Nazi Germany lorded it over Europe from the Atlantic to the Black Sea, from the Arctic to the Mediterranean, and he knew that it must be many years before an Allied army could breach that 'Fortress of Europe'. On his shoulders would fall the weight of other men's failures and of their despair. But Harris was not dismayed. He was ready to do battle – with both the enemy and bureaucracy. He knew that the Cabinet's faith in Bomber Command had dimmed but he still clung fast to his faith that it was potentially a decisive weapon. And it was indeed the only weapon at that time with which to strike directly at Germany itself.

Unfortunately, there was in Germany an adversary fit to parry whatever blows Harris was about to deliver. Albert Speer was also a new boy, a brilliant architect newly appointed Minister for Armament and War Production. He was thirty-six, energetic, outspoken and with a remarkable talent for organization and improvization, a man who quickly saw what was needed and got it done without fuss. Immediately he immersed himself in tackling the problems ahead, for whilst Harris was planning to devastate German factories, Speer had to waken them up.

At the time of this first thousand-bomber raid when Speer came to power, Britain was geared for total war whilst German factories were still pandering to public demand for consumer goods. Aircraft production, for example, was only ten per cent higher than in 1940.

Radiating energy and enthusiasm, Speer got the German war machine mobilized to achieve a massive increase in production. Backed by Hitler's personal support, he set new targets, new priorities, allocating raw materials to make arms production the overwhelming economic priority. Short of labour, he conscripted workers from occupied territories – but he could never conscript his own German women. Hitler would not let him.[14] It went against Nazi ideology, which taught that the place of the German woman was in the home and not the factory – so in the home she stayed, along with the $1\frac{1}{2}$ million domestic servants who remained in household service throughout the war. Whilst Britain had $2\frac{1}{2}$ million women in war production, Germany had a mere 180,000.

But Speer was not dismayed. Labour was found, combed from all over Europe and put to good use so that the armaments production index was to rise steadily from 100 in January 1942 to 322 in July 1944.

This was the man and this was the situation Harris was to confront. And now, on 30 May 1942, the first blow was about to be delivered, for he had also been combing through his resources. Every available aircraft, every available crew he possessed was ready and waiting for those four words: 'Target for tonight: Cologne.'

Cologne, chosen as the first of many German cities to be 'wiped off the map of Europe', had witnessed many violent scenes in its history.

It had developed as a military outpost of the Roman Empire and soon was enjoying all the privileges of a victorious army with its own fine palace for the provincial governor and princely residences for his staff, on a hill which commanded a fine view of the river, standing proudly there as an emblem of Roman might and glory.

Then it was the turn of the Franks. They took Cologne from the Romans and turned the city into a fortress, from which eventually Charlemagne would mount his raids on the Saxons. Inside the city's safe walls Archbishop Hildebold, a friend and chaplain to Charlemagne, erected the first cathedral in 870. In it he had goldsmiths build the incomparable shrine of the three Magi. From that time onwards, Cologne became a place of pilgrimage. But that cathedral was not the one the bombers would see. The famous twin-towered cathedral was not begun until 1248, and building continued for the next 600 years, being completed in 1848.

During that time the city prospered, due to its geographic location and the mineral wealth lying close by. It was the meeting-place of roads from east and west, north and south. River traffic coming up from the coast brought goods from England which were off-loaded at Cologne for road transportation west to Aachen or east to Hanover or Berlin. Down the Rhine in huge barges from Lake Constance came goods of another kind – the exotic exports from Italy and the Indies. Again, Cologne was a convenient unloading place for further distribution. It became a Free City of the Hanseatic League, profiting from all the privileges that such a position conferred. And out of the centuries of affluence there grew a city of great architectural beauty, a motley of rich styles, Byzantine, Romanesque and Gothic, with over a hundred churches and countless monastic foundations. Small wonder it was called 'the German Rome'.

With the coming of coal and railways, Cologne grew richer still, using its wealth to embellish its fine buildings. Now it was an important junction on the main railway line from Paris to Berlin, and from London to Vienna and on to Istanbul.

True, Cologne had seen its fair share of sieges and sackings but in 1942 it was enjoying the rich variety of fare that came from the conquered countries. Its citizens were renowned for knowing how to enjoy themselves – as in the annual Carnival, to mark the end of winter. Even the Nazis, grim Puritans that they were, had not been able to dampen the average Cologne citizen's love of the good life. Although since the outbreak of the war the Carnival had been banned, this had not prevented their enjoying the same spirit in other ways.

This buoyancy was soon to take them through the most dreadful experiences war can produce. When terror struck, they proved themselves capable of enduring horrors as yet unimagined, their spirit still undaunted.

Mobilizing such forces of terror called for administrative acumen and ingenuity of the highest order. Deciding to despatch a thousand bombers to attack a German city was one thing but to be sure they all arrived at the right place at the right time was quite another. Consequently, as soon as Harris got up and walked out of the Operations Room, immediately after the target decision had been made, as was the customary routine, a session of feverish activity began.

Deputy C. in C. Air Vice-Marshal Saundby got together with his specialists to draw up the final flight plan for the operation, taking into account the very latest intelligence information: ground defences, fighter strength, 'H' hour, for opening the attack had to be calculated exactly to fit in with weather conditions and wave-timing of bomber groups, to minimize the risk of collisions. There was so much still to do and so little time. In ten hours the first Stirling would be roaring down the runway to take off.

At last all was ready shortly after mid-day on Saturday 30 May 1942 as the master teleprinter at High Wycombe sent out the first alert signal to all bomber groups informing them of the target for the night – Cologne. The accompanying instructions were terse: 'Maximum effort ... All aircraft to operate ... Full details to follow.'

Immediately strictest security measures were put into force. All outgoing telephone calls were blocked, all incoming ones intercepted. Stations and groups were now cut off from the outside world.

On the stations, speculation was rife. Everyone from the station warrant officer down to the cookhouse 'erk' knew that it was going to be 'a big one', and there were some who thought they knew even more. The aircrews conjectured idly about the target but with a rising hope that because of the weather there might not be any operation at all that night. Their hopes were soon to be dashed, for at group headquarters the operations staff were now hard at it, measuring the distance to target, computing fuel and bomb loads, preparing fighter plans and permutating waves, altitudes and speed courses to avoid collision yet at the same time achieve maximum concentration over the target area.

When all details were complete at group, the orders were put onto Form B, signed, countersigned, taken to the teleprinter room and transmitted simultaneously over secure lines to all squadrons in the Group.

The operation was on.

Now Bomber Command Headquarters were busy on another tack: certain formations outside the Command needed to know what was about to happen. Naval ships escorting east-coast convoys had to be warned that an RAF bomber stream might be passing overhead. These corvettes and destroyers tended to be sensitive about the presence of heavy bombers overhead and took no chances – especially by night when they could not tell friend from foe. Unless forewarned they would always fire first and ask question afterwards.

Again, Fighter Command, always alert to the possibility of enemy bombers attacking, had to be notified; their night fighters patrolled from dusk to dawn and had to know they might encounter home-coming bombers – maybe limping in late, off-course and with wounded aboard. Furthermore, Coastal Command's Air/Sea Rescue launches had to be at the ready for the duration of the entire operation to help aircraft forced to ditch.

As yet, however, on the station, the target was known only to the station commander, the two squadron commanders and the intelligence section responsible for preparing the details about enemy defences such as up-to-the-minute information on the movement of enemy night fighter squadrons along the route and in the target vicinity, together with reports of any new types of equipment operated by the Germans. Information as to the location of 'dummies' and similar moves by the enemy to draw the bombers away from the actual target had to be prepared meticulously for the intelligence brief for the night.

And so it was that before the general briefing a group of people on the station were in the know. Officially. But a 'buzz' could get into the air. And once a 'buzz' started, it travelled quickly. And far ...

Mrs Elizabeth Stebbing, who was working at RAF Scampton that day, was in for a shock when she went off duty late that afternoon and joined a bus queue outside the main gate. A total stranger turned to her and opened a conversation with the words: 'What a lovely day! I hear you are sending a thousand bombers to Cologne tonight!'[15]

3. A Fine May Evening in Cologne

'When the evening is spread out against the sky
like a patient etherised upon a table.'

T.S. Eliot

The weather early that evening in Cologne was fine. The late afternoon sunshine had lit up the new buds on the trees, reminding everyone that they were on the threshold of another summer – the third summer of the war, with apparently no end in sight, nothing to look forward to but separation from loved ones and the intermittent air raids.

But people were beginning to take topsy-turvy wartime Germany for granted. At first, in 1939-40, it had been exciting: victory in Poland, the fall of France, and the defeat of the British Expeditionary Force. People were intoxicated with fanfares from the radio announcing resounding German successes. In the cinemas they were treated to scenes of triumphant victory parades which raised high hopes of an early end to the war. Now the war dragged on apparently interminably, and the citizens of Cologne were adjusting, as were British citizens, to life as it was.

However, whereas in London the citizens were rationed to one egg a week, four ounces of bacon, four ounces of butter and twelve ounces of sugar, there was no such shortage in Cologne. Particular brands might be scarce and good coffee was hard to find but one could get used to the artificial kind, made, they said, from acorns. Otherwise the essentials were easy enough to find, for those who had the money. In the city, the restaurants were busier than ever, their menus augmented with delicacies from 'liberated' countries – pâté de foie gras from Brussels and Paris, smoked sausage from Poland, spiced appetizers with peppers from Romania and Bulgaria.

Even in May 1943, Goebels noted in his diary, 'The Fuhrer

simply won't approve a 110 gram reduction in the meat ration'. Speer also said that he found difficulty in cutting domestic production of consumer goods in order to increase production of war supplies. Chester Wilmot said in *Struggle for Europe*, 'In these years of adversity Churchill was able to call upon the British people to make sacrifices which Hitler dared not demand from the Germans since the Führer's popularity was built not on the promise of 'blood, tears, toils and sweat' but on the assurance of early victory in the field and continued prosperity at home.'

Thus life in Cologne throbbed faster than ever. Money and time were such uncertain commodities that those who had some to spare spent more freely than ever; dances and cabarets were packed. Beer flowed freely and there was no shortage of wine or cigarettes. Nothing went 'under the counter' as cigarettes and spirits had by then in Britain.

Men in uniform walked the blacked-out streets straining their eyes for a feminine silhouette to engage in conversation, share a table with in a bar and perhaps more. Many women, left on their own with husbands and friends away on the Eastern Front, freely admitted later with the candour that comes from a distance of forty years that for the younger ones it was exciting. 'It might seem a terrible thing today but it brought a sudden feeling of exhilaration into our lives; the excited feeling that we were still young and attractive and that it was tremendous fun for a woman – whatever her age – to be courted by a gallant young man in uniform who was likely to disappear shortly from the scene for ever and leave no complications.' So spoke Vera Veitsch.[1] It was a feeling experienced not only by women in many countries but also by the men themselves: a harmless interlude bringing a little sunshine into the grey days of the war.

People in general became more friendly. Formal reticence began to disappear as everyone had more in common – relatives away, wartime regulations to note and the unexploded bomb to talk about. There was also the companionship of the air-raid shelter, and new jobs to be tackled. Vera Veitsch offered her services as an entertainer to the German Forces, looking forward to the opportunity of travelling maybe to France and Italy. Her application was welcomed warmly: an attractive blonde singer who could dance as well was always a sure success in a garrison theatre. She did find it a little strange at first that her services seemed to be sought mainly by the SS units though. It was as if they were getting preferential treatment. And she was also surprised to find how highly regarded and well treated actresses were by higher authority. One of her friends, a tall, slender young woman with blond hair flowing down to the middle of her back, was invited with other members of the Army Special Performers to a reception attended by the Führer.

Hitler regarded himself as not only the most inspired military leader the world had ever known but also the greatest artist. He would hold large formal receptions for a few specially selected actors, painters and architects, and his special favourites would be invited over and over again. At these soirées tables groaned under the weight of what was called on the invitation card 'a modest supper'. Every delicacy imaginable was there. In the midst of all this splendour Hitler would make a dramatic entrance. Immediately all cigarettes were put out. No one was allowed to smoke in his presence. From that moment, enjoyment waned. Gradually all conversation would falter to an end, and Hitler would be left talking to a thoroughly bored and captive audience. He would lecture them for hours on end, and no one was allowed to leave. When, and only when, he had finished, guests were led away to the exits, guards everywhere along the corridors, and finally, like children who had been attending a party, they were given a present: a box of sweets or a cheap china ornament.

Cologne's theatres flourished. No stage setting could be too magnificent. Under the banner of 'Everything for our Soldiers', one musical comedy premier followed another. Cinemas, as in Britain, had long queues outside every evening and afternoon.

That Saturday afternoon of 30 May 1942, Doctor Berta Weigand-Fellinger,[2] had given herself, and her twin sister's four children, a treat. She had been to see a new film, *The Crash Pilot*, starring a popular comedian, Heinz Ruhman, at his funniest. Her enjoyment was doubled by seeing the four children slapping their hands on their knees with glee, gripping each other in terror at each mad escapade Heinz got himself into – and out of. For a short time they had forgotten their sorrow – their mother lying seriously ill in a Davos sanatorium. The children, like the people in Cologne, were living for the day and that day only.

Dr Berta herself had adopted the same philosophical attitude. Her hours were full and she just got on with the job in hand. Her husband was in the Netherlands with the Air Force Area Command, so she was on her own looking after the house and her sister's four children, and all this on top of her full-time post as medical practitioner in the Eduardis Hospital.

She felt happy though, that day. It had been a good one, a full one. In the evening she busied herself boiling two big pork hocks and sauerkraut for the next evening's meal. She wrote a long letter to her husband, taking care to paint a cheerful picture of life in Cologne, well aware of the censor, who would very quickly report anything smelling faintly of 'defeatist' talk, and then she switched on the radio for the news. Already the martial music was on, another piece selected by Dr Goebbels to prepare for his communiqués.

That news began with yet another 500-bomber raid by the German Air Force on Malta's tiny Valetta harbour where the British Royal Navy had its base. Now German convoys would be able to reinforce the gallant Afrika Corps, which had just launched a fresh and formidable attack upon the Australian and British divisions defending the fortress of Tobruk in Libya. The last bastion of defence holding up the German Army's drive to the east was crumbling. Even the British Empire's lifeline, the Suez Canal, and the rich oilfields of the Middle East were said to be almost within Rommel's grasp.

Then the newsreader turned to the Eastern Front. There, German General von Bock was said to have won a great victory over the Russian General Timoshenko's hordes attacking Kharkov. Despite the new American heavy tanks which the Russians were using, the German infantry and anti-tank units had pushed the attackers back into the River Donets. At this point Dr Berta looked across at her young friend Lieutenant Sobeck who was just back from the Russian Front, spending a few days leave in Cologne. She raised her eyebrows questioningly. Sobeck grimaced and blew a derogatory raspberry.

Already people were not so ready to believe the official communiqués. But few voiced their disbelief. Even in one's own family, to do that was dangerous. Most people had heard of cases where parents had been arrested and sentenced on evidence given by their own children. No longer was it safe to voice opinions which in any way discredited the government – even in the privacy of the home circle. Everyone feared the harsh rap on the door at five in the morning and opening to find the severe, unsmiling, over-correct man in the black SS uniform with the death's head marked silver buttons. He would come into the house, bow, click his heels and begin to ask questions.

'You had to be very careful in those days,' recalled Dr Berta, 'Of course, any intelligent person could see through the glossing over of news that was unfavourable to the National Socialist hierarchy. I sometimes listened to the BBC news from London. But not often. It was too risky. I had too much to lose, my husband in the Air Force, my job in the hospital and my twin sister's four children. Who would look after them if I were put into a concentration camp? If I listened, I should be tempted to talk, to contradict people, so I played safe. The system of snooping which the Gestapo had brought in was to blame for the fact that no one trusted anyone else. In any case, orders had been given to all Nazi Party Officials to arrest gossip-mongers at once.'

That was certainly a more drastic measure than that brought in by the British Government. At that time the Press was told to run news items headlined with such directives as 'Don't be A Bomb Bore'.

The news of what it was really like on the Russian Front came to Dr Berta that night from Lieutenant Sobeck. She heard grim reports of how the inadequately clad German infantry patrols stripped Russian corpses of winter clothing to keep themselves warm in the bitter sub-zero temperatures. But they were not all horror stories he told, for he was in a happy mood that evening, having been to the theatre. This was a real luxury after the Spartan entertainment behind the lines in Russia where to go to a cinema the entrance fee was a log of wood to provide heating. He even told a risqué story of a chorus girl with a wooden leg. Today in Cologne he had watched Ufa Palast in *Between Heaven and Earth*. It had been a marvellous evening and he wanted to tell his friend Berta about it. Consequently it was later than usual when they eventually went to bed, well past eleven o'clock.

Before retiring, Lieutenant Sobeck took a breath of fresh air outside the front door. There was a moon above but its light was diffused by mist. Altogether a peaceful scene, especially for a man back from the horrors of the Eastern Front. As he relaxed in the cool air, he mused about the play and its title, little thinking for one moment that before long their own lives would be hanging in the balance – literally between Heaven and Earth.

Not far from Cologne's busy railway goods station lived a cheerful and attractive young housewife called Klara Zarges.[3] She had eaten her simple supper of scrambled eggs with her chubby one-year-old son, Ernstchen.

Blond and dimpled, Ernstchen was a real handful for Klara, living, like so many mothers of her age, on her own whilst her husband was away on the Russian Front. Being such a lovely and inquisitive child and surprisingly mobile for his twelve months, he was into anything and everything the moment his mother's back was turned. She was, therefore, always quite thankful when evening came and she could bath him and put him to bed. In this respect he was a good boy. No fuss. He played in the bath and afterwards fell asleep the moment his head touched the pillow. What a pity, thought Klara that night, that his father was missing all the fun of playing with his son at that age.

For her it had been a day busier than usual. It was a long walk from her apartment at 23 Hirschbergerstrasse to go round all the shops for the week-end's food, for, although there was as yet no real shortage of foodstuffs, it was getting increasingly difficult to find exactly what she needed, especially certain fruits. Lemons were impossible to find. 'Use rhubarb juice,' said the radio food expert, but where do you find rhubarb juice in May?

That day Cologne city centre had been packed. There were the usual uniformed servicemen on leave and the Saturday visitors from the neighbouring small towns doing their week-end shopping too and then staying on for an evening meal, and on top of all these that day there were the punters coming in for the trotting-race meeting at Riehl.

So it was that, by the time Ernstchen had closed his eyes and fallen asleep, Klara was more than ready to relax too. But there were still one or two jobs to be done. First the black-out to be checked. The tiniest chink of light showing after black-out time was an offence punished by heavy fines or imprisonment. This painstaking observation of black-out regulations was based on the absurd belief – as in Britain – that bomber crews needed only to see the thinnest shaft of light in order to recognize a town as a target. 'Absolute nonsense,' said the former bomber pilot Gunther Rehmer one night to her. 'A small light here and there is no help whatsoever to a navigator if there is nothing else to be seen. In any case, the concentration of searchlights gives bomber crews all the guidance they need.' Part of the phobia about black-out in both Britain and Germany came out of distrust, a sinister suspicion that some agent was actually signalling to the enemy! In Germany, there were anti-Nazi groups for people to worry about. And so Klara was careful about her black-outs.

The last of her jobs was to see that the overnight bag was replenished with all she would need for a night in the shelter should the alarm go. Always the bag was put in the same place, ready to be grabbed on the way out.

At last the time was her own. She strolled contentedly out into the garden opposite her apartment and looked out over her city. These days she was somehow more conscious of its beauty. When she walked along the streets so utterly familiar in the past, her eyes tended to take in far more, to note the architectural embellishments, the appeal of the ancient squares, the ornamental façades and variety of roof lines. It had once seemed so permanent, so solid. Now she knew how vulnerable and fragile it all was.

It was now dark except for the pallid moon. Without the flashing advertisement signs, without the flickering cinema lights and without the glaring hotel signs, the old city, lit softly by moonlight, acquired a poignant beauty. The twin towers of the cathedral seemed lighter coloured, standing out prominently, and the church of St Maria-in-Capital, the model for a whole series of later Romanesque churches, looked superb.

She sighed and turned back towards her apartment, humming softly to herself the latest popular song, with its comforting ring, 'Every December is always followed by May.' The war would come to an end soon, and Cologne would once more be floodlit in its former magnificence. Never for a moment did she think that soon old Cologne would disappear forever.

In the Lindenthal district of Cologne, an attractive residential area, Hildegard Steinborn[4] was in that particular bloom of beauty that comes to a young woman carrying her first child, unmistakable radiance. And she was very happy. Already she felt the four-month-old baby stirring inside her, and her joy at the prospect was unbounded. Friends and relatives had expressed shock and surprise when she told them of her pregnancy. They said she was silly really to have started a family at this stage of the war. But she paid no attention to their remarks. She was pleased, quietly and warmly contented with being who and what she was on this pleasant evening at the end of May 1942.

She had a well-built, unimpressive-looking house, in the select Immermannstrasse and a hard-working, attentive husband,

Gerhard, who certainly would not be leaving her to fight on any front. He was a few years beyond the age of military service, and furthermore he was in a particularly responsible job: it was his task to be the eyes and ears of Dr Goebbels with regard to air raids. Being a specialist film photographer, he was appointed by the Minister for Propaganda to make a permanent film record of all the bomb damage in the Rhineland. In addition to making these top-secret films he made news films for the German cinema gazette, *Deutscher Wochenschau*.

Consequently during and immediately after heavy air raids he would be out, lugging his heavy camera and tripod over the rubble-strewn streets, to film exactly what the bombers were doing to German sites. It was a tiring, dangerous job, but one that fascinated him – and Hildegard too. She had often gone with him, carrying the black bag of lenses and extra film on her shoulders. Recently though, because of her pregnancy, she had stayed at home during the raids.

'Looking back,' she recalled, forty years later, 'I don't know how we did it. With bombers not far away we'd stagger through a pile of pulverized brick dust and mortar, stumbling over the rubble and the dead, lying in all sorts of horrible postures. Gerhard took his life in his hands – and I did too – many a time. I wouldn't dream of doing it now.'

On that evening in May, Hildegard was sitting in the brightly lit living-room of their house repairing some curtains and talking to Gerhard as he cleaned and prepared his camera and equipment. He never knew for sure where or when he would be needed the next day. He liked to have everything ready for immediate action. Although he was an independent operator, he had to be on the spot and have his film at the Ministry without any delay whatsoever. He took a pride in being always in the midst of the action when it happened.

And so the evening passed pleasantly. Neither of them worried much about air raids, because their house was in the green belt, the outer fringe of Cologne surrounded by a complex of hospitals – the Evangelischer and Hildegardis Hospitals, the St Anna Hospital and many smaller clinics, all of them clearly marked with the sign of the Red Cross. The other buildings apart from private dwellings were churches and schools. No industry, no railway, no military target anywhere near. They had been assured by no less an authority than the Ministry of Information that residential districts such as theirs, especially those close to the hospital complex, would never have to face the horror of air bombardment.

Nevertheless, they had taken all precautions. Though their villa was well-built with massive walls, the cellar had been reinforced with sturdy oak beams, the walls strengthened to make sixteen-inch thick 'fire walls', and connecting doorways had been knocked through the walls of neighbouring cellars on either side. This was now common practice after news came out of one Cologne family who crawled through the rubble of twenty-seven cellars in Kappelmannstrasse to safety when their own house and all the neighbouring ones had been blasted by a 4,000-pound RAF 'Cookie'. In every room of the house and on the stairs were bags of sand, shovels and buckets, ready to deal with incendiary bombs. The attic had been cleared of all the inflammable rubbish that often clutters loft space. It was now bare except, again, for sand, shovel and buckets of water.

If things got very bad, they could always go to the new government-built bunkers of thick steel-meshed reinforced concrete. ' "These bunkers will stand up to anything the RAF can drop," we were told,' recalls Frau Steinborn. And they were right. The bunkers were ugly, some as tall as an apartment building; with a roof ten feet thick laced with steel rods and heavy girders, they defied the might of the RAF and USAAF, and later they would not even give way to the Royal Engineers who tried to demolish them. Now, forty years later, they stand as a reminder of man's ingenuity in the absurdity of war.

But at least the Steinborns, like all other Cologne citizens, were well prepared for total war. Such was not the case in Britain, where the 1914-18 mentality still prevailed. Shelters often consisted merely of a garden dug-out covered with a sheet of corrugated iron, called an Anderson shelter. Other houses might have a reinforced cage about the size of a dining-room table into which the family could crawl. Later, street shelters of brick with a concrete roof appeared but by that time their main use was for courting couples wanting a little dark and privacy.

But on that evening of 30 May 1942 the Steinborns were not thinking much about air raids or shelters, for they had just been reassured on the radio that the 'Tommies' were not getting through any more now that Germany's magnificent new air defence system was fully operational. Perhaps the announcer was right for once.

There had been no real air raids for weeks now, almost two months in fact.

And so the Steinborns went to bed, anticipating another peaceful night's rest.

For fifteen-year-old Willy Niessen, wartime Cologne was exciting.[5]

'It seems an awful thing to say now,' he recalled forty years later, 'but for someone of my age – just too young for the army but old enough for manly things – wartime was a time of release from the confines of school and home, to a much fuller, responsible life. At that time I was actually very keen on collecting "militaria", particularly anything to do with the air war. And for some reason or other I had grown up with a tremendous respect for England. Maybe it was something to do with my history teacher, who had been in the First World War and detested the French as untrustworthy but had a high regard for the fighting qualities of the English soldiers.'

The part of Willy's militaria collection which had grown most in the early years of the war was his collection of leaflets. He had started picking them up when only thirteen but knowing even then the awful risks he was running.

'Anyone who picked up these leaflets was dubbed a defeatist, and anyone who read them or passed them on was liable to be shot. Nobody was allowed to bend down and pick one up. However, young boys can do a lot of things on the sly, and I managed to get a really good collection. The big danger in all such things was from the thousand-headed monster called Gestapo; many people lived in mortal fear of every neighbour and of the house-warden and the block-warden and the SS man at the corner and of anyone who could get you into trouble if they wanted to say something wrong about you.'

On that Saturday evening Willy had passed the time playing cards and 'Halma' with his mother, Frau Walburga, and his five-year-old sister, Leni. In the midst of the game there came a blast of trumpets from the loudspeaker of the radio; everyone immediately stopped speaking and moving as the voice of the radio announcer fervently demanded attention for a special communiqué: 'Attention please. Attention for a special communiqué from the Eastern Front.' The Niessens always listened to these, for Willy's father was out there, last heard of driving a train near Dnieperpetrovsk.

'Our High Command reports from the Eastern Front that, during the last five days of air counter-offensive from Kharkov, our victorious divisions destroyed or captured 1,237 Russian aircraft, 1,435 tanks, against a loss of only 59 aircraft and 31 tanks on the German side. Russian losses in dead, wounded and prisoners are enormous, amounting to no fewer than 29,000 men. It can be safely said that all Russian tank units, including their reserves, in this sector have been wiped out, their air force has been crippled and any attempt at a counter-offensive has been nipped in the bud.'

As the communiqué ended, there came another fanfare of trumpets and the radio burst into the Horst Wessel song. During this, no doubt, in public places, hotel foyers and the like, where these announcements were relayed, right arms would fly upwards in the Hitler salute, towards the Führer's picture, accompanied dutifully by the staccato of three measured cries – *'Sieg-Heil! Sieg-Heil! Sieg-Heil!'* Finally the radio went into *'Deutschland über Alles'*, verse after verse, which Willy carefully turned down in volume until for a moment all was quiet.

Even as a young lad he had learnt that a bombastic announcement of good news usually came just before some calamity. What, he wondered, were they going to be told next?

They put away their games and cleared the table for a light supper of baked potatoes and cheese; at eight o'clock it was time for Leni to go up to bed. As his father always used to do, Willy first went up to his young sister's bedroom to check that she was all right and to leave a glass of water and a small electric torch by her bedside. In those days, fifteen-year-old Willy and his brother were filling the role of 'man about the house' whilst their father was away with the army engineers in Russia. Next, as his father had instructed him, when last on leave, he checked the attic sand bucket, water bucket and shovel. Now he too could go to bed.

'I always used to put my clothes in exactly the same place and folded them the same way so that I could get into them without thinking and in the dark if "Meier's Magic Horn" went. You know, we called the siren that because the fat man, Goering, full of butter and bombast, had boasted earlier in the war that, if Berlin were ever bombed, his name was Meier (a name common among German Jews) – and this, to Goering, was the ultimate insult. After Berlin *was* bombed, people called the air-raid siren "Meier's Horn".'

One thing Willy always did before getting into bed at night was to look down the street to see if the cars were parked outside the small Gestapo unit, because whenever there was a 'yellow warning' the SS cars would be the first away, taking their precious lives into the safety of their bunkers outside the town.

Through the open window he could hear the clattering and rumbling of wagons being shunted along the lines from the Cologne-Nippes railway to the west of the four-storey house in Geldorpstrasse where his family had an apartment. And faintly, too, there was the ever-present hum of machinery that came from the Franz Clouth rubber works. Day and night, non-stop, they turned out cables of all kinds and other material urgently needed for the German war-machine. 'The railway workshops and the rubber works would be attractive targets for bombers,' Willy mused. And the Niessen house lay mid-way between them!

Now, at 10.45 p.m., as Willy gazed through the window he could see everything clearly. There were no cars to be seen in the clear light of the moon. A bomber's moon.

Aenne Blum had also been looking up at the sky with its full moon and patchy clouds.

'There'll be an alarm tonight,' she said to her husband, Peter.[6]

But after a long evening putting up new shelves and cupboards in the house, Peter was too tired for speculation about the possibility of air raids, particularly as there had not been any real raid for about two months and he had not heard anything on the radio to indicate any need for alarm. He felt like an early night. 'No, there'll be nothing tonight,' he said, more out of reassurance to his wife and daughter than from any inner conviction.

He went into the garden to smoke a last cigar and by 10.30 was comfortably tucked up in bed, as he was later to write, 'not knowing what tragedy would occur within two short hours'.

Young Toni Stellmaszyk was feeling a little better after the first bad days of sickness with scarlet fever but he would have felt better if he had not had to face that awful picture which hung on the wall opposite to his bed. It was an official portrait of the Führer, Adolf Hitler.[7] Those touched-up pictures of Hitler with his bulbous nose chiselled to nobler lines and the mean little smirk around his flabby mouth wiped off and the puffy eyes filled with visionary fire, had to be hung in all public places, including hospitals.

The story went round that these pictures easily fell off the walls during air raids and that, 'After the last raid on Cologne, the houses were so badly shaken that the Führer's picture came flying out of the windows for hours afterwards. *Heil Hitler!*' But you had to be careful about who you told stories like that to.

So well known was this 'touched-up' official picture of Hitler's face that people forgot how the real man looked. Vera Veitsch's actress friend was shocked when she saw him at the soirée. Afterwards she said to Vera, 'He had a remarkably fixed, even glassy expression in his eyes, his face looked bloated and puffy, and as he passed from one table to another he seemed to stagger as though he had drunk too much, yet he was supposed never to touch it. Or maybe he really was ill. He looked awful, and I kept wondering to myself how this man could have such a hypnotic effect on the masses.'

Ten-year-old Toni Stellmaszyk need not have worried about facing Hitler's hypnotic stare though. It would not be there for much longer; neither would the wall, or Toni's bed.

That evening Hans Heines got ready reluctantly to go on duty with his anti-aircraft battery behind the Cologne railway repair yard.[8] It was, after all, Saturday evening, and he had planned to go out into the city but had been put on full alert. Someone was sick, he assumed.

When he got to his post, he closed the door and took off his belt and special flak service greatcoat and hung them on a hook on the wall. He sat down on an old chair that someone had 'found' in a nearby bombed ruin. The corporal passed him a mug of hot chocolate. Nodding his thanks, he wrapped his huge, scarred hands round it and sipped slowly. There was plenty of time. There always was. Time to be passed. Hour after hour waiting. Yet always at the ready.

There had been times earlier in the war when they had waited months, even a year, for the opportunity of firing at an enemy bomber, yet all that time they had to behave as if one were expected any moment. And then, when one did arrive, it was sometimes possible to fire at it for only a few seconds; perhaps, if the Luftwaffe fighters were overhead, they were not even allowed to fire at all. And so they had fought a battle with the canker of all armies – monotony. Often they had been stationed at desolate places, miles from any village or town, making their own comforts and entertainment as best they could.

Inevitably, like the British AA Regiment, they had to play second fiddle to the fighters, and they usually had to perform the relatively humdrum job of breaking up large formations of bombers so that fighters could get amongst them. And understandably so, for the direct destruction of a bomber by an ack-ack gun was very difficult – a shell had to burst within fifty feet of the target to be really effective, and for this to happen not only had the gun to be perfectly aimed but the fuse must be accurately set for exactly the right place and moment. Getting the fuse right was a problem for British ack-ack gunners throughout the first five years of the war simply because the Swiss engineers who had made the fuses pre-war had all gone home. It took British engineers years to solve the problem. On the other hand, German anti-aircraft batteries were superbly equipped and organized into one great lethal arc from northern France through Belgium and the Netherlands, trailing eastwards across northern and western Germany to Berlin. Backing up this main defensive zone – the Kammhuber Line, as it was called – there were additional local zones around prime targets – such as Cologne, the Ruhr with its 'Flak Alley' and other major cities.

The German anti-aircraft service was really a force to be reckoned with, in the opinion of 'Bomber' Harris at that time, for although night fighters caused most of the losses suffered by his bomber fleets, the German gunners were certainly taking their toll. They were, with the fighters, determined to crack the morale of Bomber Command by shooting them out of the sky so that losses reached an unsupportable percentage. Their commander, General 'Dolfo' Galland, a fighter ace himself, had put the situation quite simply to his Luftwaffe AA gunners: 'If you can bring the casualty averages up by just a fraction, say $2\frac{1}{2}$ per cent higher, the RAF will have to stop these raids. Or change its tactics.'[9]

Not a lot to ask? Not a lot of margin for Harris to gamble with either, and no one knew better than he what a gamble he had taken on that night, when Galland's men were at the ready and waiting.

Hans Heines' unit was certainly well prepared for the Tommies that Saturday night. Fresh stocks of heavy-calibre shells for the big 8.8 anti-aircraft guns were neatly stacked in the gun pits, and searchlight-unit electricians had made their final checks on the massive power plants to ensure that when the switches were thrown dazzling fingers of light would probe among the clouds for intruders. In their special posts, the steel-helmeted spotters had made their final adjustments to the range-finders' night lenses and were already getting their eyes adjusted to the fading light. They were beginning to note that – as predicted earlier that day by meteorologist Magnus Spence at High Wycombe – the heavy rain clouds that had been hovering earlier were now slowly clearing. From low down in the sky a pale, full moon was rising.

Thus they waited, not yet knowing how thoroughly they were to be tested – and thrown into confusion, for German ack-ack guns were then using short-wave electricity for their prediction, and this was perfectly effective when bombers were spaced a few minutes apart. Then each gun could pick up and concentrate on that one aircraft – as would the night fighters. But with a thousand bombers concentrating over the target in the short time span of ninety minutes, neither guns nor fighters would be able to select a specific target. So how were they ever going to satisfy 'Dolfo' Galland's request to push the bombers' loss rate up another two per cent? Could they be flexible enough to adjust in time to the new situation? Or would there be chaos?

Adjusting to the new situations had become second nature to opera singer Erika Wagner in Cologne.[10] With the outbreak of war, all her contracts had come to an abrupt end. But the monthly payments for her flat and food had not. Living for months on a staple diet of potatoes, tomatoes and cabbage had soon taught her a thing or two about adjusting to changing circumstances. But if there were not to be long-term contracts for opera seasons, she soon found there were opportunities for singers in a different setting altogether, especially if she was prepared to forsake Verdi and Puccini occasionally for something a little more plebeian, such as the repertoires of Sara Leonardo and Lala Anderson.

So Erika Wagner joined the forces entertainment circuit. She was not only well paid but very well entertained too, with meals in military messes, and sent home with little presents of extra rations afterwards. With her special brand of fierce determination, she built up a reputation that served her well, keeping her profitably occupied in all the better units of the district. She seemed also to have a good relationship with senior commanding officers.

So it was not unusual for her to speak directly by phone to unit commanders before setting out for a concert at their barracks, as she did, in fact, that evening. She was about to set off for the performance when, as she was to recall later, 'A strange premonition made me pause in the doorway. Acting purely on impulse, I then went back to the telephone and called the adjutant at the barracks. "I'm just about to set off," I said, "You are expecting me this evening, aren't you?" '

The reply stunned her. 'Oh, I'm glad you called. We have been so busy I forgot to ring you. Do *not* come tonight. Stay at home. We are expecting a raid.' He paused and then added, 'A big raid!'

Not to have to go out was welcome news. She could do with a rest and would enjoy a chat with her father whilst catching up with a few jobs around the house. But later on, as she was undressing for bed, she had once again a strange feeling of unease. How did they know? What made them so sure? The adjutant's final words were still going through her mind as her head touched the pillow: '*A big raid!*'

4. Count-down

'Remember that these crews, shining youth on the threshold of life, lived under circumstances of intolerable strain. They were in fact – and they knew it – faced with the virtual certainty of death, probably in one of its least pleasant forms.'[1]

Marshal of the RAF Sir Arthur Harris

Now the men and the machines were almost ready. The signal sent out by the Commander-in-Chief for maximum effort to be made to muster one thousand bombers had produced magical results. For in mid-May the daily average of aircraft serviceable with crews in Bomber Command was a mere 416. Now, on Saturday 30 May, 1,048 were available and ready.

But even at this late stage the momentum of the effort was still producing results; reserve aircraft and men were still being drawn in from wherever they could be found. Volunteers from staff at station, group and command were crewing up, others were still coming from operational and heavy conversion units – instructors and trainees. More than a few 'reluctant heroes' were brought summarily back from end-of-tour leave, disembarkation leave and even honeymoon leave. Everyone who could be brought in had been – by telephone, by police calling out names in the local pub and by telegram. 'Maximum effort' spared none.

Naturally a telegram in wartime Britain was always bad news – sometimes worse than others. But that urgent message for Yorkshireman Ron Lawson,[2] a rear gunner home on leave in Barnsley from the Middle East where he had done over and above a complete tour of ops was greeted with particular irritation.

'Report immediately to Chipping Warden,' it read.

He went back in an angry mood.

'You're on ops. Crewed up,' he was told.

'Not bloody likely! I'm on embarkation leave.'

'Go and see Squadron Leader Martin then.'

He went.

'You'll fly with me, boy. And that's all there is to it,' he was told. He did not argue. Martin was a forceful character, used to getting his own way. And, in any case, Ron Lawson realized he could not have been in better hands: 'Mickey' Martin, who would later be remembered along with Guy Gibson and Leonard Cheshire as one of the greatest bomber pilots of the war, was not only a skilful and courageous pilot but also a very careful one.

So Ron Lawson really did not mind so much once he was back and knew who he was flying with. But just to reassure himself he took care to put on his lucky trousers – an old pair he had worn right through his previous tour. Lawson was as superstitious as the rest.

Ron was, by this time, the old man of the crew – nudging thirty. He had not really wanted to join the Air Force but the Navy. As it was, being a civil servant in Wakefield and doing a job of 'national importance', a 'reserved occupation', they would not let him join anything. The job he was on though gave him 'the willies', he recalled. 'I was billeting officer at Wakefield, meeting hordes of screaming, shouting kids coming from Hull as evacuees. I put them into local houses and farms. Within days many of the women would be back in the office. "Take 'em back," they said. "They're dirty, flea-ridden, they've messed under the table and are an absolute menace to everyone".'

A few weeks of this and Ron Lawson decided anything would be better than handling arguing kids and women, so he went to see the clerk to the County Council, Sir Charles McGrath, to get permission to join up, which was granted, providing he joined as aircrew. Then Lawson followed the usual trail of training at Padgate, Wilmslow, Manby and then for some obscure reason Blackpool as a sergeant, where nobody knew what to do with him. For a week or two he just strolled along the prom. Eventually Records caught up with him, and after that he never stood still again – Harwell OTU, then Marham and the Middle East.

Now, before even beginning to get the taste of his disembarkation leave and British beer – watery and scarce as it often was then – he was back on his unit waiting for yet another operation to begin.

Newly married, twenty-four-year-old Ernest Wilson was at home in Sheffield when the telegram arrived instructing him to report immediately back to his unit, 21 OTU, at Moreton-in-the-Marsh.[3]

He was just closing the garden gate on his way back when his wife shouted after him, 'Have you got it?' Ernest knew what she meant and he patted his tunic pocket. The lucky rosary and the Miraculous Medallion, blessed (they said) by the Pope, had been sewn into a small silk purse and given to him by his wife's aunt. It was not that he was a Catholic but he had got through one tour of ops safely and he never flew without them. Nor has he ever done so since – even on package-tour holidays.

His pal from Newcastle was leaning out of the carriage window as the train drew into Sheffield, and at Birmingham they met another two of the Moreton instructors. The four of them discussed the recall and could come to only one conclusion about this massive recall. The Second Front was starting!

As soon as they got to 21 OTU at Moreton-in-the-Marsh, they were told to crew up amongst themselves. Wilson and his crew took off then in a battered old Wellington long since relegated to instruction use, to fly with a squadron at Snaith, South Yorkshire. He recalls: 'When we got there, we took the Wellington up for a good air test, and the windows blew in, so they were hurriedly patched up with canvas. The engines were not so clever either, despite being tickled up by the Snaith engineers. And I suppose some of the crews from Moreton "weren't so clever either"; anyone who had done two cross-country flights solo was put straight onto the raid. It was a big enough shock for us as instructors to be put back suddenly onto operations but it was an even bigger shock for the student aircrew. We just wondered what was in store for us.'

Flight Sergeant Craven and his pals too were feeling safe as instructors at 114 OTU Cottesmore, despite the appalling accident rate.[4] (In RAF training accidents 5,327 officers and men were killed and a further 3,113 injured.) Five out of sixteen on the previous course had 'gone for a Burton', making a total of thirty-eight killed in the few months prior to Saturday 30 May 1942. But instructors felt they did not have to face that near-certainty of death over Germany several times a week and so, once posted to an OTU, they naturally felt reasonably safe.

And life at Cottesmore was pleasant. Leave came at regular intervals, and hitch-hiking up the Great North Road to Hartlepool presented no problems. The pleasant Rutland towns of Oakham and Melton Mowbray were close enough to provide relaxing evening entertainment. They could scoff at death even as they drank with the local grave-digger, who vowed he would have them one day. In this fashion the tired and tour-expired aircrew instructors made the best of the stressful task of training raw, ham-handed crews in old Hampdens and Ansons, long past retirement age and lacking in maintenance.

Then came the 'buzz'. A big raid was coming. Everybody was on it. No one seemed to know the target but certainly something big was brewing. When the bomb loads started trundling into the training camp, there was no doubt in anybody's mind. Everybody from the NAAFI girls to the local vicar seemed to know – not surprisingly either, because it is not easy to disguise a lorry load of bombs coming into a non-operational station.

Neither David Craven nor his pal Bill Newman liked the look of things. It was bad enough when they had been on the crack 50 Squadron (with pilots who were later to form the famous Dambusters a year later) but what would it be like with a scratch crew of instructors and half-trained men?

Fortunately David Craven was not the sort of man to ponder unduly on that sort of thing. He had developed a way of coping – to push things right out of his mind. Otherwise he knew he could 'go the same way as those who did think too much – start wearing sandshoes in the mess, twitching his eyes and then be taken quietly away to Matlock' (the RAF psychiatric hospital at Rockside Spa, Matlock, of which we shall hear more later).

There was, however, one thing that he did worry about on that Saturday – the shape of his aircraft in the dark. With twin engines and twin boom flying alongside a triger-happy gunner in a four-engined bomber, the old Hampden could easily be mistaken for a German fighter. And then what would happen?

The 'maximum effort' order brought many more unexpectedly into the raid. For example, at Harwell instructors there had already

registered that empty feeling in the pit of the stomach as they saw
'real live bombs' coming into camp. Orders came for them to form
crews.

Instructor John Price chose the gunners from trainees. One of
these was Sergeant Eric Prince.[5] He did not know what to think,
whether to feel chuffed at being chosen or just shocked, for
although he was now a sergeant wireless operator/air gunner he
had never in the first place applied for aircrew. He had not liked the
idea of being called up into the 'poor bloody infantry' and so had
asked to join the Air Force in something like signals or radio. Before
long he was training at Blackpool as a wireless operator. PT in the
Winter Gardens ballroom, dancing in the Tower at night. Not a
bad life at all. Then, halfway through the course, they were all
called for a medical examination. Once more he was passed as 'fit'
but he found he was not just 'fit' but 'fit for aircrew'. Soon they
were treating him as aircrew, and before many weeks had passed he
was on a gunnery course, quickly followed by another wireless
course. After that he was able to sew on his sergeant's stripes and
was posted to OTU at Harwell.

It was a life of luxury, he found, compared with the
rough-and-ready accommodation on training. Now, in a pre-war
sergeants' mess, which even boasted waitresses in frilly caps and
aprons, he was as happy as Larry. Oxford and Didcot were within
easy hitch-hiking distance, there were ENSA shows in the station
theatre, and evenings of bridge or in the nearby Horse & Jockey.
He was just getting used to this pleasant routine when the shock
came. 'You're on ops tonight.'

John Price, his gunnery instructor, gave him a few last-minute
tips, and off he went to air-test his guns in the old Wellington.[6] He
was to be in the front turret. Even to Eric Prince, novice such as he
was then, the aircraft seemed to be labouring painfully as it
climbed.

But the instructors fared no better. John Price found himself in
an old Whitley, T for Tommy 495K, which had done yeoman
service in 1940-41 but since then had been hacked about on
instruction duties. But that was the way things were when
'Bomber' Harris made the decisions.

Sandy Milne,[7] who had rushed down from Dumfries to North
Wales gunnery school, thought the Wing Commander Flying was
joking when he handed over the old drogue towing Whitley he was
to take to Driffield. 'It's ... er ... serviceable all right ... but don't

take it over the Pennines!' Shortly after take-off he realized the Wing Commander had not been joking. He had to make an emergency landing at Squires Gate, Blackpool, for repairs to the engine. But eventually he nursed the old aircraft to Driffield in time for the raid.

The telegram that brought the newly married Ken Williams[8] hot-foot back from leave in Bradford to 115 Squadron in Marham arrived before the post that Friday morning. By tea-time he was standing amazed at what he saw: 'Grannies' of the Auxiliary Air Transport Service (women who ferried RAF war planes from America to Britain) delivering new aircraft, bombs trundling in by the lorry-load, ground crews frenziedly servicing aircraft – 'action stations' as in a Hollywood film. And with it all was the 'buzz', muttered knowingly round the crews. It was not at all to his liking.

'A big daylight raid – Berlin.'

'We all immediately made our last wills and testaments,' recalls Williams with his wry sense of humour, 'for we didn't care for that long haul at all. No one knew for sure. There was a certain pub in King's Lynn where you could ring and ask for a certain barmaid who usually knew before anyone else where we were going that night but we were all too busy for that. Our Squadron Leader, Trevor Freeman, a marvellous leader, wasn't saying anything. He genuinely knew nothing. So we each got on with our jobs. I inspected the radio and cleaned all the equipment until I was sick of the sight of it. We air-tested our own Wellington and then another someone else was to fly. They hadn't yet returned from leave. What a shock they were going to get when they did get back, bleary-eyed and late, to go straight out on a raid!

'The crews had been regrouped whilst I was on leave. That didn't worry me much, although you do get a feeling about pilots. We had liked young Edwards but Tom Patterson, our new pilot, was well known to us all – navigator Sergeant J. Robson, front gunner Sergeant S. Skinner, rear gunner Sergeant Newbound and myself as wireless-operator/gunner.'

After all the tests were completed, there was nothing left for Williams to do but wait. Fortunately his old school pal Bill Whitehead by a strange coincidence was on the same station, on the sister Squadron 218 Stirling, so they were able to resume their marathon snooker tournament.

*

At about the time Ken Williams was breaking off on the snooker table, young Ken Pexman was filling his time with a casual walk around the hangars at Honington, watching the furious activity going on with a detached kind of interest. He was not involved. Yet.

There were men in overalls for the first time in their lives, men who normally never left the warmth of their offices or stores helping out wherever directed. Some were plastering the leading edges of a Wellington's wings with de-icing paste. Amidst all this hustle he felt out of place. Then, suddenly, he heard his name being called, loudly! He had to go at once to the squadron office. An air gunner had gone sick. Could he take the job? He could – and he did.

Skipper Harry Langton told him where to draw his kit. 'And get yourself some longjohns and all the warm clothing you can lay hands on. It's likely to be "brass monkey" weather tonight – a long, cold night.'

The Wellington in which Pexman was to fly was notorious for being cold – and the coldest part of all was Pexman's seat in the rear gun turret. However, it was a reliable aircraft which had been in service since the beginning of the war, though, modified and improved, it still left much to be desired when compared with the new four-engined Halifaxes and Lancasters now coming off the production line.

Ken Pexman was pleased to be part of the bustle now, not at all put out by the sudden call, and so he drew his kit and then sat down to write a letter to Mabel, his bride of exactly one week.

It was in those last few moments that men suddenly remembered things that just had to be done. Jim Davidson at Croft remembered. 'Whisky!' he said to himself. There was just time. He raced to his room. He was met at the door by a bounding, silly, grinning springer spaniel, beautifully marked in liver and white, 'Whisky'. It threw itself at Jim, barking ecstatically.

No words were needed. It was enough to drag the leather lead off the hook from behind the door. The dog went skidding across the brown linoleum, down the narrow corridor of the hut and, with a further burst of joyful barks, out into the cool late-afternoon air.

Countryman Jim Davidson breathed in deeply. All his life he had liked being out on his own, walking in the fresh air, shooting, fishing, riding his horse and even talking to it as he rode along the Scottish lanes.

This afternoon, though, he was quiet, thinking of the way things had worked out. But for the war he would have been in India, possibly an inspector of police by this time. That had been his intention and he had passed all his exams. Then the war had come and in 1939 he realized that sooner or later he would be called up for military service, so he thought he might as well choose where he went and decided to join the Air Force.

An insistent and excited barking interrupted his thoughts. The dog had got a sniff of fur and was racing after a rabbit, sending a white 'scut' bobbing through the tussocks on the edge of the airfield. Jim looked at his watch. It was time to go back and wait for the call which must come soon, surely.

As he passed the airmen's cookhouse he paused, smiling, to listen to a new rendering of the ditty to a pregnant WAAF with a 'Sleeping Out Pass' which some kitchen hand was bellowing to the tango tune of 'Jealousy':

'Twas all over my SOP
That settled how my fate was to be,
For he was an officer in the RAF
And I was a poor little innocent WAAF.

He gave all his kisses to me,
And now all too late I can see
I'll have to tell mother
There's going to be another,
'Twas all over my SOP.

A WAAF corporal in the station headquarters signals office at RAF Finningley was not feeling at all like singing at that moment for she had just been given a roasting for something that really had little to do with her. Now she was confined to camp for the night instead of going down to the local where she had arranged to meet her friends and, as was her usual practice on a Saturday night, play the piano. It paid for all their drinks.

Now, because of some stupid clot at Command ...!

That afternoon a signal had come. A long one. Too long for Corporal Irene Shaw[9] to bother reading in detail so she just scanned it quickly, deciding its distribution as her eye ran quickly over the first few lines – a copy to the station commander, operations officer, one to her flight officer and one to her file. Despatching that message was like lighting a quick-burning fuse. Within seconds the doors of each of these offices opened onto her own and she faced a barrage of questions.

'Who took the message? Have you left the room? Have you made any telephone calls? Has anyone else been in the room since the message arrived?' Satisfactory answers having been given, the fuse fizzled out into an audible sigh of relief from the ring of senior officers around her. 'Right, Corporal Shaw. You will be confined to camp after duty today. You and everybody else. This is a very important message.'

The twenty-six-year-old corporal had really been looking forward to her Saturday night out and, feeling a bit resentful about having to stay in, felt bold enough to ask, 'Well, if it's so important, why was it sent in plain language?'

'Ah, now you've hit the nail on the head. Someone's for the high jump over this.'

The officers went back to their separate offices, leaving Corporal Shaw desperate to read in detail what was so important about that message. Taking the section copy from the file, she saw that it was addressed to all stations in the group, giving details about the number of aircraft required from each station, bomb loads and all information about the night's raid. Now she could understand why everyone had been so irate, so nervous. A top-secret message sent in plain language over the teleprinter where anyone could read it! No wonder there had been red, spluttering faces, for there at the bottom of the message was the answer to the question people had been asking for the past week: the target was named!

But, thought Irene Shaw, how many other people now knew the target? How serious was this awful security leak? (See p.207, reference 14.)

That signal certainly brought an end to the waiting. Now things could get moving. Everything was ready.

The eager and the not so eager, the reluctant and those raring to go, the veterans and the raw first-timers were now all trooping into the brief rooms on fifty-three airfields. Well and truly had stations responded to the 'maximum effort' call.

The education section hut at RAF Croft, decorated with mildly left-wing posters on current affairs preparing the 'erks' for the coming socialist revolution, was so full that men lolled against the walls; the benches were packed and there was hardly room on the tables for maps and papers. Now the time had come for them all to know what was on.

For many of the aircrew of 78 Squadron it was to be their first operation, and anxiety showed on their faces despite the shield of jocular, animated chatter. The 'veterans' of maybe a dozen operations sat poker-faced. They knew what it was all about, whatever the target. Death. And the terror that turned boys into old men.

Suddenly the babble of voices faded. A senior officer stood up and called them all to attention. Then a murmur of surprise rippled through 78 Squadron. What was the group commander doing there? The atmosphere was electric, charged with suspense and expectation. For Air Vice-Marshal Roderick Carr to come down for a briefing it must be something big. He flapped a hand at them as they rose and stood for a moment facing them in silence. Then, in the time-honoured manner the briefing began: 'Gentlemen, the target for tonight is COLOGNE!' There was a moment of stunned silence as the message sank in, followed by an audible sigh of relief. They had expected worse.

The Air Marshal held up his hand. 'Tonight, gentlemen, though, the raid is no ordinary one. We shall be bombing with one thousand aircraft!'

This time the reaction was instantaneous – the air was filled with incredulous cries of 'Bloody Hell!' and whistles of amazement. Now the worst really was behind them. The waiting was over. Almost.

The Air Marshal went on to explain the importance of the target. Cologne, he said, was a highly industrialized centre ... light and heavy engineering ... factories for guns, tanks, vehicles used on the Russian Front ... an important railway centre ... junctions for troop movements and goods ... marshalling yards ... chemical factories at Ehrenfeld, Kalk and Mulheim lying on the east of the river ... Cologne, the crews were told, was one of the most important of German cities, about as big as Manchester, with a population of 900,000 people. It was important not just because of its munitions factories and military installations but also because it was centre of trade and political activity, so that its destruction would be felt all over Germany. It would strike a major blow against German morale – weaken their will to fight!

The intelligence officer then took over the pointer (a billiard cue). He was a small, thin-faced man of about thirty who looked like a lawyer, and the first thing he did was to lean forward and poke a hole in the air with his forefinger and say: 'One thing we have to make absolutely clear is that Cologne is now one of the most heavily defended of all German cities. So listen carefully.' His voice sounded tight and brittle and strained. 'I know many of you have been there before but what you don't know is that during the last month the German High Command has moved an even greater concentration of anti-aircraft defences into the city approaches.' He paused thoughtfully and then went on: 'You are asking for trouble if you do not stick rigidly to the flight plan. Only in this way can we be sure of saturating the defences enough to cut our losses.' Then he stabbed a finger again at the assembled gathering and said: 'I have one special warning for air gunners. Along the route you are following there will be some of our own night fighters with the intruder force attacking the Luftwaffe bases, so for Christ's sake be extra careful about what you fire at!'

Grimly Jim Davidson told himself, 'If they fire at you, fire back with all you've got.'

About twelve miles to the south of RAF Croft, a similar scene was being enacted in the far more impressive surroundings of RAF Leeming, one of the first stations to be equipped with the new four-engined Halifax bombers. There, in a large brick building close to the guardroom, No. 10 Squadron was being briefed for this special raid.

Already the experienced 'Shiny 10', as it was known, had an impressive list of battle honours to its credit. It had weathered the worst flak barrages ever known, in the 'Battle of the Barges' over the invasion of the Channel ports of Lorient, Le Havre, Antwerp, Cherbourg, Boulogne and Calais. There the German invasion fleet had gathered – ocean-going barges, with 200 hp engines capable of ploughing through seas at 10 knots, and thousands of smaller barges had packed into the ports to be protected by flak guns of every calibre. They could put up a cordon of steel to ensure no bombs fell within miles of the barges. Or so Goering had thought. The 'Shiny 10' had thought otherwise. As the great invasion scare flooded Britain, 10 Squadron swept in low and knocked the barges for six. It had been a hair-raising experience but one which got the 'Shiny 10' 'well blooded' for the new bomber offensive about to begin on this May night.

Sergeant Fred Simpson was sitting with the rest of his crew and their cheery, dedicated skipper, Squadron Leader Tony Ennis, a man who inspired confidence in a short time and who was known to be one of the coolest and most aggressive of bomber pilots.

The briefing followed the same formula as elsewhere, and again the news that a thousand aircraft were attacking the city of Cologne evoked a kind of cheer. But, as one man explained later, with the frankness of forty years hindsight, 'It wasn't so much that we were "chuffed" about killing Germans and knocking hell out of their city that made us cheer but the simple fact that, the more bombers there were in the sky, the better were our chances of surviving. We were not thinking of bringing victory any nearer but of staying alive longer.'

When it came to the intelligence part of the briefing, a small, pink-faced officer jumped up and began talking rapidly. He was obviously worked up about something and had a few strong words to say to everyone – whatever their rank.

'It should not be necessary for me to have to tell you now, at this stage of the war, that everything which is said in this room today is for your ears only.' He paused and his face, ridiculously reminiscent of an angora rabbit, flushed deeper. Then he went on more slowly and deliberately: 'We have all heard about careless talk costing lives, we've all seen the notices, but I think we are all guilty at some time or other of little indiscretions, little slips of the tongue and occasionally flagrant breaches of security. The fact is that far too often every Tom, Dick and Harry civilian for miles around knows what's happening and when. It's just great when the milkman can tell you where your target is and what aircraft are taking part. This time let there be no slip-up.' (See p.207, reference 14.)

He stared at them stonily for a few seconds to let his words sink in. Then he began to emphasize another point: 'The key to success in tonight's raid is simply this: saturation. Tonight's attack will be concentrated into the shortest possible time-spread – ninety minutes!'

Here again there was a murmur of disbelief. The older hands were now clearly disturbed 'What about collisions?' they asked themselves. Almost immediately these experienced crews were beginning to view the whole raid with a perceptible lack of enthusiasm. They had no longer quite the same trust in the 'egg heads', the 'boffins', who worked out these things. When the intelligence officer did mention the risk of collisions and passed it off with the assurance that the chance of collision would be only one in a thousand, there were cries of disbelief and derisive laughter.

'Don't worry. Get right in there and find the target!' said the intelligence officer, slightly patronizingly, which invoked a doleful response from the back: 'As the actress said to the bishop!'

But there was little time to dwell on the collision risk for now the details of the target were being given – and it was rather puzzling for the more thoughtful of the men gathered there. On the enlarged map of the city, the end of the briefing officer's cue was resting on a rectangular gap in the city centre not far from a large cross which was obviously the famous cathedral. 'The central aiming point,' he was saying, 'is right here.' He tapped the square. 'At the Neumarkt. Look carefully. It's just this western side of the river.'

Sure enough, there it was, right in the middle of the shopping and residential area of the old city. Not on the big Ford Motor factory, not on the chief war factories at Kalk and Mulheim to the east, but right in the middle of the city. Why the Neumarkt? The few who asked that question of themselves did not like the answer. The intention was to bomb not solely industry but also civilians. The age of terror bombing was about to begin.

Throughout Bomber Command that afternoon and early evening the briefings again and again emphasized that the vital factor affecting success of the whole operation would be concentration. A heavy concentrated attack would saturate the defences and thus reduce the loss rate, and at the same time overload the fire-fighting services, causing large, uncontrollable areas of fire.

Gradually towards the end of the briefings the information was slanted in such a way as to build up confidence, minimize the hazards involved and have the best possible effect on morale. Losses would be much smaller due to intruder operations. Bostons, Blenheims, Havocs and long-range Hurricanes would be attacking the German Air Force on their own bases, keeping them pinned down or at least fully occupied. This was also greeted with a certain amount of scepticism by the old hands who had learnt the hard way how to interpret euphemistic information.

At the end of the briefing at Croft, Air Vice-Marshal Roderick Carr took the stage again. 'There has never been a raid like this before,' he said solemnly. 'If this raid succeeds, it will cause panic and despondency throughout Germany. It could even finish the war. Good luck to you all. And now I have a final message for you from the Commander-in-Chief himself.'

The Air Marshal moved two or three steps sideways as he drew from his pocket a sheet of paper, unfolded it beneath the naked electric light bulb and began to read:

'From the Commander-in-Chief, Bomber Command, to all aircrew in Operation Millenium. The Force of which you are part tonight is at least twice the size and has more than four times the carrying-capacity of the largest air force ever before concentrated upon one target. You have an opportunity, therefore, to strike a blow at the enemy, which will resound not only throughout Germany but throughout the whole world.

'In your hands lie the means of destroying a major part of the resources by which the enemy's war effort is maintained. It depends, however, upon each individual crew whether full concentration is achieved.

'Press home your attack to your precise objective with the utmost determination and resolution in the foreknowledge that, if you individually succeed, the most shattering and devastating blow will have been delivered against the very vitals of the enemy. Let him have it – right on the chin!'

The solemnity of the occasion was wasted on the greenhorns. The raw crews went off chattering excitedly, asking questions and making corny jokes. It was always the same on the first trip. When they came back it was different. They were silent.

'It was as if they were entering another world. Very soon they became old hands,' said Arthur Briggs.[10] 'After ten operations you were a veteran, and you adopted the only philosophy that kept you going. There was nothing you could do about it. If you were going to buy it, you bought it. It was a lesson in life and death. So you joked your way along.'

After the briefing, there was little men could do but think of what awaited them or else push it out of their minds in whatever way they could.

'It was an awful period,' wrote one of Britain's best-known bomber pilots, Guy Gibson VC of this time of waiting.[11] He had just taken over 106 Squadron at Conningsby and was getting ready to put eleven of the new Lancasters and five Manchesters in the raid. 'I, for my part, hate the feeling of standing around in the crew rooms, waiting to get into the vans that will take you out to the aircraft. It's a horrible business. Your stomach feels as though it wants to hit your backbone. You can't stand still. You laugh at small jokes, loudly and stupidly. You smoke far too many cigarettes, usually only half way through, then throw them away. Sometimes you feel sick and want to go to the lavatory. The smallest incidents annoy you, and you flare up on the slightest provocation. When someone forgets his parachute, you call him names you would never use in the ordinary way. All this because you're frightened, scared stiff. I know – because I've done all those things. I have always felt bad until the door of the aircraft clangs shut: until the wireless operator says "Intercom OK," and the engines burst into life. Then it's all right … Just another job.'

Others felt ill. For example, Eric Clarke felt sick not only at the thought of the raid but at the thought of the feeling of sickness that always came over him in flight. Some trips were worse than others, and he put it down to the smell of the synthetic rubber oxygen-masks that made his stomach turn over no matter what precautions he took beforehand. After a frugal pre-flight meal he went to have a lie down and get some rest.

Some just tried to sleep. There were many who felt like lying down for a rest that evening, particularly those who had been dragged back from leave, having travelled overnight propped up in the corridors of crowded trains with little chance of sleeping. The experienced ones knew the danger of going on a mission in this state. Lack of sleep slowed reactions and made the whole crew more vulnerable to attack from alert night-fighter pilots. A moment of drowsiness, a second's hesitation could make all the difference between living and dying.

And so, feeling dead beat and cursing the clot who put them on the 'Blood List,' they retired to their rooms to grab a half-hour's snooze. They knew it would pay dividends later, especially on the way back, when, with aching fatigue of cramped limbs and sleep fighting to overcome tired brains, they would be forced onto the 'wakey wakey' tablets (of benzedrine and caffeine). Then they would not be able to get to sleep properly when they did get back to bed afterwards.

For some it was all a familiar routine. Going to the pre-flight meal, usually fried bacon, bread, sausage and the traditional egg. There would inevitably be one who would say, pushing his clean plate away and taking a final swig of his tea, 'Well, I've had my egg, so they can scrub the whole damn show as soon as they bloody well like.' And then another would ask the corny question, 'Can I have your egg for breakfast if you don't get back?' And they would all laugh. They always did.

Others kept themselves busy. There would still be time for them to go to their rooms to strip themselves of personal belongings, maybe write a quick letter and make the final routine checks. Fred Simpson would collect his baby's blue bootee; Church of Scotland man David Walker would hang his ivory Buddha around his neck; John McFarlane would stuff his lucky threepenny bit into his pocket and pin his little bead man onto his vest; Ernest Wilson no doubt would pat the purse containing his medallion and rosary; Ken Williams would make sure that the Russian half-kopek coin given to him by an old man for luck when he was but a kid was safely stowed, and Ron Lawson would definitely be getting into his lucky old trousers.

A few, a very few, pondered the whole significance of the terrible business. It was in this curious 'in between' time that the questions would come into David Walker's mind: 'What does God think about all this? Whose side is God on?'

Sitting in the officers' mess with the squadron's Roman Catholic padre on one such evening, David turned to him saying: 'You know, Padre, on our aircraft one of our crew members is a Catholic, and you bless him before we go off on our bombing missions over Germany. Now the same Catholic religion is blessing a German Catholic crew member who comes over and destroys our cities. So the question I ask is: "Whose side is God on?" '

'Well, that's a tough one,' he replied. 'All I know is that, if we let Hitler rule the world, there will be no place in it for you and me, or any other Christian for that matter.'

This did not answer David Walker's question, for he could not help but wonder why the German Catholics and their Church did not withdraw their support from Hitler. He did not get the answer to his questions until after the war. In the meantime he got on with the job.

One or two just simply could not take the strain. They broke down. That evening young Harry Radcliffe, a padre of 25 Squadron, who had recently been a curate at St Olave's in York, was trying to be of service to his station at RAF Linton-on-Ouse, seven miles to the north of his old parish. Apart from weddings, aircrew did not bother padres much, but the latter were always cheerful and available. Somehow it seemed an irrelevance for them to be in uniform, but, like young Harry, they all tried to be helpful. As he was to say later: 'I'm sure the quiet talks I had with young airmen in the mess were more of a help than a formal service would have been. Their secret fears came out. One young navigator, I can still see his earnest young face, confided that his big nightmare was not in being shot and killed but in parachuting down and being seized by an angry mob and hanged. At that time I knew it was not an entirely groundless fear. We had all heard stories of crews that baled out, falling into the clutches of a mob who flung them onto a fire or hanged them from a lamp-post.'*

On the evening of 30 May something happened to Harry Radcliffe during one of those little chats that was to haunt him all his life. He was sitting in his usual armchair in the mess chatting to anyone who came along when the squadron commander arrived looking upset, tapped him on the shoulder and led him to one side. He asked Harry to have a word with one of his pilots who had just decided that he was not going to fly that night or any other night from now on. He had had enough.

'He flatly refuses to fly,' said the squadron commander, and explained to Harry that this young pilot was very near the end of his tour of operations and that it would be a pity for him to have to go through the shame and disgrace of being stripped of rank and brevet and sent off branded with 'Lack of Moral Fibre'. If he could be persuaded to go on this raid, he could be cushioned through the rest of his tour.

Harry did talk to the young man. 'The hand holding the cigarette shook uncontrollably, around his eyes were big black smudges as though he had not been sleeping, and his face was so pale and drawn that I thought he was really ill.

'He was not really fit to fly. Not fit to drive a car. But what you've got to remember is that I was still only a very young curate dressed in RAF uniform with very little experience in life. I had been told that LMF could run right through a squadron if some got off flying without being court-martialled and I did not want the poor lad to suffer that. So I was acting a part, the padre in the film if you like, doing what I was expected to do. And I suppose I must have played the part well.'

Nearly half a century later, the Reverend Harry Radcliffe said sadly: 'I wish to God I had never spoken to him. It was the worst

---

* A number of Germans were tried after the war for having lynched flyers who had parachuted to the ground. See *Rise and Fall of Third Reich*, William Shirer, p. 944.

Left: 'I suppose it is quite clear that the aiming points are to be the built-up areas, not, for instance, the dockyards or aircraft factories.' Extract from Directive to Air Marshal A. T. Harris from Chief of the Air Staff, Marshal of the RAF, Lord Portal (*pictured left*).

Above: 'Bomber' Harris at Bomber Command HQ, High Wycombe, with his Senior Staff Officer, Air Vice Marshal R.H.M.S. Saundby.

Wartime propaganda. In Britain that spring of 1942, there was a smell of defeat in the air: one could tell from the ration books how badly the Battle of the Atlantic was going; the Germans were at the gates of Cairo; the Japanese all over South East Asia; the Russians at the point of collapse. The British public was urged to save food, 'Dig for Victory' and above all to keep cheerful.

✠

YOUR COURAGE
YOUR CHEERFULNESS
YOUR RESOLUTION
WILL BRING
US VICTORY

Below: On 6 March 1945, the German Army General Staff reported to Hitler, 'the ruins of Cologne have been left to the enemy.'

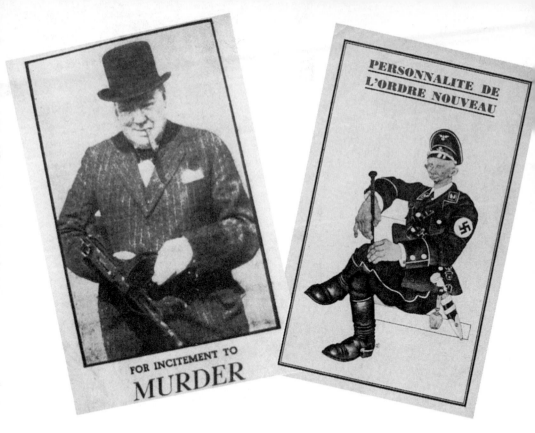

FOR INCITEMENT TO
MURDER

PERSONNALITÉ DE
L'ORDRE NOUVEAU

A gentleman's war. In the early days of the conflict both sides had been content with dropping leaflets on each other. *Above*: A German view of Churchill seen in a leaflet dropped over Britain and a leaflet showing a sinister, black-uniformed figure representing Himmler's SS, the terror of Europe. *Below*: Dropping leaflets.

Lübeck (*right*) and Rostock were bombed by Britain to show what a strong Bomber Command could do. Harris said, 'I wanted my crews to be well-blooded, as they say in fox-hunting, to have a taste of success for a change.' Terror tactics had arrived.

Below: Five York citizens owed their lives to a 'Morrison' air raid shelter in an attack on 29 April – a month to the day before the Cologne raid.

Reichmarschall Herman Göring (*left*) talking to Adolf Galland, General of the German Air Force, Fighters.

Right: Major Prince Sayn Wittgenstein who shot down 83 bombers before being killed himself

Final briefing of German night fighter pilots and (*above*) a German night fighter with radar antennae.

Right: General Kammhuber who took over Germany's night-fighters in July 1940. By 1941 he had a line of radar zones which formed a protective barrier right across the approaches to the Rhineland and Ruhr.

Below: Colonel Streib, Commander of NJG I.

The elite troops of the German anti-aircraft regiments, pictured in 1942 with the 2 cm *vierlingsflak geschutz*, a four-barrelled gun for use against low-level attack.

Left: The 'hole'. The underground Operations Room at HQ Bomber Command.

Stirlings of 149 Squadron, Oakington. 71 Stirlings took part in the Cologne raid.

Bombing up D Dog Oakington, 7 Squadron.

Final instructions.

Ken Williams at 7 a.m. on the morning of the first 1,000 bomber raid, May 1942.

10 Squadron Armourers, RAF Leeming knew well the hazards of being a ground crew. On the extreme left is Corporal Hill who earned a Mention in Despatches for throwing away incendiaries and photo flares which had dropped and ignited beneath a fully loaded bomber. Second from the right, back row, is A/C Alan Waters whose leg was almost cut off by the Air Gunner firing a test burst into the ground.

Crew of 115 Wellington Squadron arrive at dispersal point, Marham.

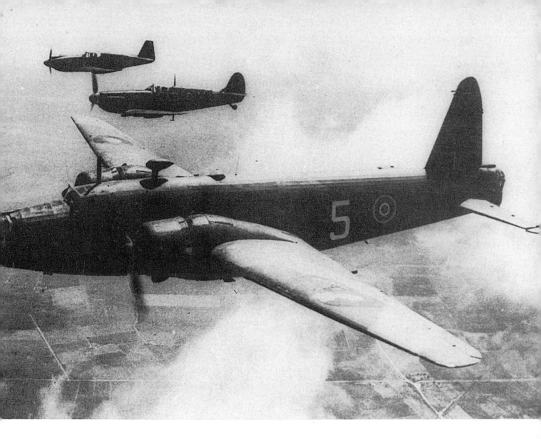

Wellington III, 496 attacked the
target.

Armourers check the bomb–load of
a four–engined Stirling.

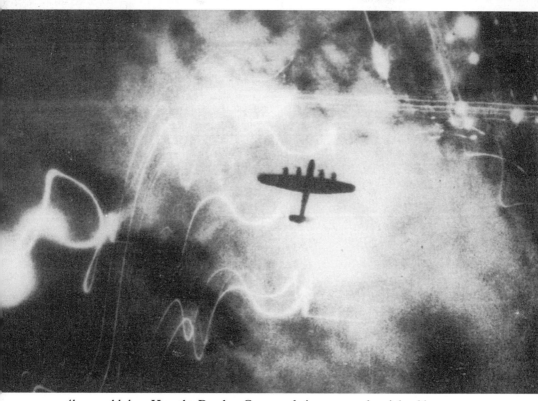

Above and below: How the Bomber Command aircrew saw the night skies over Europe and the doomed city of Cologne.

Below right: Journey's end. Packed bags lie neglected in the dust beside their owners who have need no longer of earthly possessions.

'We shuddered to think of what we were doing to people down below; families and young children like our own.'
David Walker, 44 (Rhod) Squadron.

Eberhard Schhmidt on the Eastern Front in 1942. Eyewitness of how forward German infantry were deprived of Fighter protection and anti-aircraft guns after the Area Bomber Offensive began in 1942.

Right: Willy Niessen, then a fifteen-year-old boy in Cologne, stands in his home street Geldorpstrasse on the morning after the raid. He is on the right of the picture wearing the uniform of the Flieger Hitler-Jugend (Airforce branch of the Hitler Youth).

Mothers rush to the shelter, parking their prams outside. In all 1,486,224 bombs were recorded as falling within the city limits. The population of 800,000 was reduced, by death and flight, to 40,000.

Ken Pexman's wedding, one week before the Cologne raid on which he was killed.

Leslie Manser, VC.

Flt. Lt. 'Sandy' Milne.

Eric Clarke.

Jack Wilson, killed over Hamburg, 1943.

Flt. Lt. David Walker DFC with his wife
Barbara after the investiture at
Buckingham Palace.

Eric Prince.

Jim Davidson's log book.

John Macfarlane with his
faithful old 'Butch' that ran
on petrol or paint stripper.

The Cathedral at Cologne remained structurally intact despite blast damage.
Large stone fragments litter the floor. March 1945.

'There was something awesome about the ruins of Cologne, something the mind was unwilling to grasp,' wrote war correspondent Alan Moorehead. American infantry advance cautiously through the outskirts of the city, past the Opera House (*pictured below*), March 1945.

'My first impression on passing through Cologne was of there being not a single house left. There are plenty of walls, but these walls are a thin mask in front of the damp, hollow, stinking emptiness of gutted interiors.' Stephen Spender in *European Witness*, 1946

Right: As 'Bomber' Harris intensified his campaign, scenes like this became an everyday occurrence in German cities. This old lady leaves her home with a few salvaged belongings on a small barrow.

The Hand of Friendship. An American soldier shares his chocolate ration.

The smell of death. A woman holds a handkerchief to her face as she passes the coffins in the street after a raid in 1942. Stephen Spender commented, 'The great city looks like a corpse and stinks like one also, with all the garbage which has not been cleared away, all the bodies still buried under heaps of stones and iron.'

Refugees flee from the battered city.

RAF aircrews lying dead in a German field. Of approximately 90,000 young men who flew with Bomber Command, 1939–45, 55,573 were killed, 8,403 were seriously wounded and 9,835 became prisoners-of-war.

Rockside RAF Hospital for aircrew suffering from 'anxiety neurosis' or combat fatigue. One of eighteen special hospitals in Britain established to treat this condition. *Above right*: Flt. Sgt. Caudwell (*left*) who worked at the hospital.

American Air Force had problems with anxiety neurosis too. Seen here are 186 USAAF Heavy Bombers, undamaged, but landed in Switzerland when operations were aborted by crews. They were handed back to USAAF after Japan capitulated.

The peaceful graveyard at Harrogate where so many of the young crews of the Royal Canadian Air Force now lie at rest.

1977. Mayor of Cologne, von Jan Brugelmann (*left*), shakes the hand of writer Sqn. Ldr. Eric Taylor, while wartime Chief of German Fighters, General Galland (*inner left*) shakes hands with RAF Sqn. Ldr. Jim Davidson who bombed Cologne in the first Thousand Bomber raid.

thing I ever did in my whole life. It troubles me to this day – for the boy never came back.'

Even those eager to fly and fight did strange things. In the quiet of his room in Alconbury, a keen young pilot, a fun-loving husband and gentle family man, Flight Lieutenant Jack Wilson, did a curious thing. He took off his tie and then removed his identity discs from around his neck. Then he placed them on the bedside locker top. 'They all know me here on this station and I'm coming back anyway, so what's the point of wearing them?' was the way that he explained it to his wife, Christina. Later, when she spoke about this curious behaviour, she recalled: 'He never had any fears about going on operations.'[12]

But did wearing identity discs mean admitting to himself that they might possibly be needed at some time for identification of his own dead body? Was that a thought that he could not harbour in his mind?

Similar feelings were aroused in these young men by a notice in the locker room which said simply: 'Leave your locker keys with the NCO i/c locker room.'

Jack Currie, a Lancaster pilot, remembers a newcomer reading the notice and asking, 'What's the idea of that?'[13]

'In case you don't come back, stupid, so they don't have to break the door down to get at your gear,' he was told.

'Bollocks. I'm coming back. I'll keep the key myself.'

Now all over Bomber Command, aircrews were going through their pre-flight rituals in their own ways. Somewhere at Finningley a pilot would be playing the last chords of the Warsaw Concerto, and there would be many a young man contemplating the smoke curling upwards from his last pipe before he took off.

These ordinary young men, from ordinary homes, with their dolls to decorate the gun turret and clutching their lucky charms, knew what lay ahead all right. A test of courage.

Courage to keep cool on that final straight and level run up to bomb the target, to keep flying through the black night with its ever-present menace of night fighters, to head straight through seemingly impenetrable flak, to carry on when coned by searchlights and to withstand the wearisome never-ending miles back across the bitterly cold North Sea that was always waiting for those who 'ran out of sky'.*

* 14,000 aircrew were rescued after ditching by RAF Air/Sea Rescue launches.

Courage to fight down fear. It was a constant battle, one they did not always win. But in spite of it all, the strain and the horror, they mainly contrived to do all that was expected of them and with a remarkably buoyant spirit.

And so the final preparations were complete. Even the 'Awkward Squad' were ready, talking excitedly together in the corner of the locker room, where crews were now pulling on their Arctic-looking gear, silk socks and woollen stockings, flying-boots lined with lambswool (later the envy of the US aircrew), Mae West and mufflers, with their hands full of charts, papers, headsets, chocolate, packed meals and thermos flasks full of hot tea and coffee – even collecting carrier pigeons.

Dusk had now turned into night.

Crews were mustered. Pilots answering their names whilst struggling into their flying-clothing. Then they were climbing aboard trucks for the ride to the dispersal points where bombers stood waiting like monstrous dinosaurs sniffing the evening air.

At intervals around the peri-track the trucks stopped. Groups of young men got out with parachutes clutched or bobbing from their harness, flying-helmets, leads, straps dangling, and made their ungainly way towards the aircraft. As they scrambled inside, some made their secret pledges to God, others put their trust in a lucky charm. A few prayed.

The fingers on the wall clock in the watchtower approached Zero Hour. The Force was now ready to take off – amazingly enough, forty-eight more than the planned strength of one thousand. Count-down was over. The operation could begin.[14]

5. Every Six Seconds!

'Over Cologne the traffic was something you had to go through to believe.
It literally was like rush hour in a
three-dimensional circus.'
                        Pilot's report to Reuter

At exactly 22.30 hours on the rain-swept airfield of RAF Wyton,
the first huge Stirling bomber took its place at the end of the
mile-long flare-path. Its engines were run up to full boost. Flashes
of red and yellow flames spurted viciously from its exhausts.

Its pilot, Wing-Commander J.C. MacDonald of No. 15
Squadron, his face lit eerily by the luminous clocks on his
instrument panel, peered intently into the murky night waiting for
the green from the controller's Aldis lamp.

Seconds as long as hours passed. Then, away to the front, a green
light flickered.

'You've got your green, Skipper. Take it away, boy!' came from
the bomb-aimer.

Throttle levers were rammed open. Engines roared to full pitch,
a shudder ran through the metal frame of the aircraft, brakes came
off and the great bomber rolled slowly forward, gathering speed
with each second. The screaming engines rose to a pitch where they
seemed to be straining to haul the burdened bombers upwards
from an earth reluctant to leave go.

Then it was up, rising slowly to vanish into the dark night. The
man chosen to be the first over the target was airborne. The first of
a thousand taking part in this momentous raid.

Still in the Fen country of Norfolk, midway between King's Lynn
and Newmarket, at RAF Feltwell, at sunset the lights of two
flare-paths sprang up where formerly there had been only one. At

the end of each was a long queue of bombers – forty-seven Wellingtons all ready for take-off. Among them was Jack Wilson, on his first operation, confident and eager to go. At vantage points along the end of the runways from which the bombers would start was a crowd of anxious and excited onlookers – WAAFs with boyfriends on the raid, ground crews, admin. personnel and anyone not otherwise on duty.

Directing the whole operation was the station commander himself.

What a take-off it was! Suddenly the green lamp winked. Engines roared – two at a time, and off they went at a fantastic rate. One every six seconds. Twenty from 57 Squadron and twenty-three from 75 Squadron plus four from Flying Training Command.

'There were bombers in every quarter of the sky, and above them it seemed were bombers from surrounding airfields; Alconbury, Wyton, Oakington, Mildenhall, Honington, Lakenheath and Marham. The sound of their engines was like a great waterfall. It was frightening enough for us. God knows what it must have been like for those poor devils in Cologne,' said one of those watching them go, former Feltwell postman Peter Greenham.[1]

As each one took off, a senior officer saluted, WAAFs cheered, some cried and there was many a silent prayer offered as they waved goodbye and good luck to their lads. It would be the last that anyone would see of many of them.

With this vanguard of the bomber force now climbing away from the east coast was Harry Langton and his crew from Honington with their new rear gunner, young Ken Pexman. They were the fire-raisers, 'the Guy Fawkes boys' charged with the responsibility of lighting the fires which others could use as a beacon. They were scheduled to be over the target in the first fifteen minutes of the raid.

It was precisely 22.30 when their Wellington rose into a cloudy sky streaked with red, gold and purple. As pilot Harry Langton pushed the nose of his Wellington into a steady climb, the temperature in Ken Pexman's rear turret dropped rapidly but so far there was no problem with icing.[2] The weather seemed to have improved over that part of England. With luck the target might be free of the thunderstorms which had threatened to wash out the whole operation. But it was still touch and go whether the sky would keep clear enough for any fires they started to be seen by the less experienced among the crews following them.

Not far from RAF Honington was one man who was determined to have his share in the action in this raid, the group commander himself, Air Vice-Marshal 'Jackie' Baldwin, a tough fifty-year-old who kept himself fit by exercising racehorses on the heath at Newmarket before breakfast every morning.

Having been involved in the planning discussions for this raid, he saw that it was going to bring an entirely new approach to the whole bomber offensive against Germany, and he wanted to know from first-hand experience what it was really like.[3] He was going to fly that night even though it meant breaking every rule in the book forbidding very senior officers from going on raids themselves. The Chief of the Air Staff thought their expertise was far too valuable to risk in the hostile skies above Germany, but Baldwin on this occasion thought otherwise.

Thus, on that very busy Saturday, having made sure that every available aircraft that could possibly fly would be at the starting-line on the runways of his group at the appropriate time, he made one last telephone call to a station commander discreet enough to keep his mouth shut for a short time, Group Captain 'Square' McKee. He told this cheery, enthusiastic New Zealander that RAF Marham Station should expect a passenger that night. With that done, this determined group commander, who had bombed Cologne from a 'string bag' kite in the First World War, went home to dine with his daughter, Pamela. After coffee the staff car rolled up the drive for him. 'Don't wait up for me,' he called to his daughter. 'I'll see you at breakfast.' And off he went as if going on a routine staff visit.

At RAF Marham, twenty-five miles to the north of Baldwin's residence at Newmarket, the station commander, 'Square' McKee, had interpreted the 'maximum effort' order to mean 'maximum and more'. Thus not only did both squadrons have their full complement of sixteen bombers each ready on the starting line but 218 had nineteen Stirlings there and 115 had eighteen Wellingtons.

It was not done without some minor inconvenience: Ken Williams and Bill Whitehead had to postpone the final frames of their marathon snooker competition, now they were about to clamber aboard their respective bombers – Bill in a Stirling and Ken in his Wellington.

Bill Whitehead faced an obstruction in the dark fuselage on the way down to his rear turret and in his polite Barnsley way requested this bulky figure to move his 'fucking arse'. He received a muttered protestation. Now Bill Whitehead was in no mood to tolerate what he thought to be some unco-operative technician who should long ago have left the aircraft, and he told him to 'go and have a shit'.[4] Thereupon he settled himself in the rear turret and began his pre-flight routine, plugging in his leads and giving the perspex a perfunctory polish to remove condensation, never giving the rapid exchange of words any more thought than why he had missed the pink on that last frame of snooker. He certainly never thought that he had ordered an Air Vice-Marshal to the lavatory!

In his aircraft at Marham, Ken Williams was reporting that all was ready. The extra 'goodies' he had got for the citizens of Cologne were safely stowed and he had gone forward to the take-off position.

Heavily laden with flares to light up the target and incendiaries to set it alight, the Wellington bumped along the perimeter track. Behind it, at spaced intervals, came the dark, savage-looking monsters, rearing up immense and impressive in the gathering darkness. There was a blasting roar as engines opened up, then, as Ken Williams looked out, he saw the green light in the distance flashing. He sat down, tense now, feeling puny and vulnerable as only human flesh can feel in those last few seconds before being airborne. Then suddenly the muscles of his jaw relaxed and tension left him as he saw the airfield falling away behind, the green light blurred now, blinking in the distance.

At RAF Lichfield there was a hitch in the timing when twenty Wellingtons were lined up ready for take-off. One of them would not start. Hurriedly its place was taken by what must have been the oldest aircraft on that raid. It was one of the first six Wellingtons to leave the Vickers factory – and it had no guns!

Cyril Ainley, a flight mechanic airframe who had been confined to camp with everyone else busily involved in preparations, was then standing on a little humped-back bridge over a canal from which to view the take-off.[5] He voiced his thoughts to those standing near him: 'I wonder where they are all going?'

Forty years later he still recalls the surprise he got then: 'Incredibly it was the civilians who told us that the target was Cologne.'

All over eastern England airfields were getting read for the big moment.

Engines thundered and roared into life. One by one the Stirlings, Wellingtons, Hampdens and Whitleys of the fire-raising force raced down the short stretch of concrete and soared into the night sky. There was Bill Whitehead, swinging the guns in his turrets, still unaware of the Air Vice-Marshal sitting further up the fuselage with the navigator; there was Eric Prince with a fine view from the front turret of an old Wellington, wishing that it would eventually climb a bit higher than 4,000 feet but slowly realizing that it would never make it, and John Price,[6] a little happier in the training Whitley that still could manage to lift its bomb load to a respectable 12,000 feet, flying at a modest 120 mph, and David Craven, cruising steadily upwards in a Hampden. Former flying instructor Jack Wilson was revelling in the experience; Micky Martin was taking the bottom out of Ron Lawson's stomach as he confidently swung his Wellington in a steep skywards turn; and there was Ernest Wilson, front gunner in the Wellington with patched-up windows. At Finningley the Awkward Squad were getting airborne to ribald comments that they would be 'lucky to get as far as Bawtry'.[7] But they would, in fact, be lucky, very lucky, and they would get a good deal further. Others did not. Within the first critical forty minutes almost a hundred bombers returned in frustration for faults of one kind or another. The remainder pressed on. There were Canadians, Poles, Rhodesians, New Zealanders and Americans (who had joined the Canadian squadrons – some calling themselves the 'Royal Texan Air Force'), amongst the men of the RAF squadrons, one of whom would later be awarded the Victoria Cross. All climbing upwards, assembling for the great assault ...

What a golden opportunity was offered that evening to the German night fighter force! The sky over the airfields full of heavily laden bombers labouring to gain height. Circling to rendezvous. Sitting ducks. But no fighters came. Hitler had forbidden them!

It was a matter of pure propaganda. The German people, argued

Hitler, wanted to see the 'terror bombers' brought down beside their own shattered homes. Far-away victories over Britain would do nothing to improve their morale. The fighter chief, General Josef Kammhuber, had protested but to no avail.[8] To him the order was an absurdity, especially as at that time nearly seventy per cent of all RAF bombers shot down by the German Air Force were over RAF bases as they took off and landed. That was when they were most vulnerable, as everyone knew.

Imagine then, what a field day a small force of JU88s could have had on this Saturday evening when, by stepping up the night offensive against Germany, the RAF had been forced to adopt a technically complicated take-off and landing system. Was something like this in the mind of the briefing officer, who said that evening: 'This raid, instead of being the costliest in history for the enemy, could be the costliest in history for us.'[9]

It could have been not only the first thousand-bomber raid but the last.

History may well decide that here was the greatest missed opportunity of the whole bomber war. According to one Air Ministry publication, *The Rise and Fall of the German Air Force* the fact that from late 1941 to 1945 the RAF was able to operate undisturbed from its home bases contributed decisively to Germany's final downfall.

Like so many other major tactical mistakes of the war, this one was made by the Supreme Commander of the German Forces himself, Adolf Hitler.

Certainly on a day when, as we have seen, there were so many security leaks about the thousand-bomber raid on Cologne, it seems strange that the German night fighters did not attack the massing bombers now heading across the sea to a point 250 miles distant, through the glaring searchlight belts and the fierce flak barrages that marked the route to Cologne.

A great calm now settled over the airfields of England as the last of the droning motors faded into the distance. Small groups of people began to wend their way back to the various messes; after all, it was Saturday night. Soon, over the radio, Jack Jackson and his band would be thumping out that very popular tune of the time 'Boys and girls all like a Saturday night', and already through the windows of the NAAFI canteen the plaintive voice of 'the Forces Sweetheart', Vera Lynn, could be heard crooning: 'I'll Remember

You'. Vera Lynn certainly did remember and appeared at the Reunion Dinner of Bomber Command with Air Marshal Harris forty years later.

The men now in the sky were 'remembered' especially in the station control rooms, where a staff of operators stood by, straining their ears for the slightest whisper of a voice which might come out of the ether.

The greatest attack yet made in aerial warfare was well under way. Now it was up to the God of War to decide whether the disaster would be experienced by the citizens of Cologne or by the crews.

Soon after take-off low cloud began to hide the landmarks. Eric Price, like many other front gunners that night, had to act as spotter, calling out whenever he got a pin-point on an island off the Dutch coast. Soon though, the unmistakable signs were seen, all-too-familiar ones − the probing searchlights and the firework effects of flak exploding in the night sky.

Pilot Harry Langton lifted his Wellington a little higher. It was an automatic reaction for he knew that height meant safety. But not unreservedly tonight. He remembered well the warning given at briefing: 'Stick to your given height and given speed, or else ...' − and there was no need to spell out the word 'collision'.

Leslie Manser, with the same idea in mind, was not so lucky. His Manchester could not cope with the heavy load of fuel and bombs, though it had climbed reasonably well on the morning's air test. Whenever he tried to push it beyond the 7,000-foot mark, the suspect Vulture engines overheated dangerously. The choice for Manser then was the same as it had been for the pilot of Eric Prince's Wellington from Harwell − push on or turn back. And they both came to the same conclusion − quite rationally too. A calculated risk. Both pilots weighed the situation carefully: it could be safer, for once, down below at 4-7,000 feet than between the 12-20,000-foot levels where the bulk of the force would be flying and attracting the attention of flak and fighters. Manser told his crew that they might get through unnoticed at this relatively low level, but he knew that if they were picked up by a searchlight it would be 'goodnight, nurse', as one air gunner put it. There would be no escape, no room to manoeuvre at that height.

Soon they would know. Ahead on the horizon lay the Dutch

coast and with it, in depth, the ground-control interception zones ready and waiting with fighters and flak.

Below the dim-shaded lights of the Fliergerkorps Air Defence huts on the Dutch coast, the afternoon air of indolence and boredom had been swept aside. Now all was action, concentration, precision and curt instructions.[10]

Along the Dutch and north German coastline the shallow dishes of the long-range Freya radar sensors were turning slowly, edging first a little one way and then the other, searching for the first signs of the incoming bombers. Something was there.

At 23.14 hours the first contact was made. Quickly directions were passed to the pair of short-range Wurzburg radar units. They could now monitor more accurately the height and direction of the intruder. Night fighters were scrambled to orbit high above a beacon. Now, on the ground glass-topped 'Seeburg' table in the T-shaped hut, one Wurzburg plotted the bombers' position and the other that of the attacking fighter's. They were seen by the ground controller as two small circles of light – red for the bomber, blue for the fighter.

Tension mounted as the controller directed his night fighter. The circles of light moved closer. Now the night fighter should be able to see his prey. Now he should be swooping down to make his kill. Now, quickly, before the bomber passed through the Wurzburg box and out of range. Now! What was that fighter pilot doing? The dots were together on the radar screen. Was the pilot blind? In a few seconds the bomber would be through. Out of the zone. Out of plotting range.

The ground controller bit his lip in anger and expectation. Then he smiled and relaxed. The red blot had disappeared. One down. But how many more to go? Would the great defensive system created by General Josef Kammhuber in the years from October 1940 be able to cope with the tightly packed stream of hundreds of bombers now approaching the belt of radar-guided fighter 'boxes' running from Ostende to Denmark?

The system was simple but normally effective. Once the Freya long-range radar had picked up the bombers (often just off the east coast of Britain), the Wurzburg radar took over, precisely plotting height and course. Once this was done, the neighbouring searchlight units waited, watching their screens. Then, suddenly, three beams would pierce the darkness, fasten onto a bomber and show it to the supporting searchlight units. Then they too would latch on. Now, with a master blue light on it and supported by a dozen more beams, the bomber was there for the night fighter to take.

But it was not all that easy. The night fighter pilot had his problems too. First he had to be away from the lights himself, for to be illuminated invited a hostile response from the bomber's Browning machine-guns. Then he had to approach so that he was not blinded. And during these vital moments the bomber pilot was using all his guile and tricks to escape from the cone. He boosted his engines, hoping to burst through the twenty-mile range of the Wurzburg radar and into the protective blackness beyond. But sometimes coned bombers were handed on from one searchlight belt to the next, and they all wrestled with the problem: the bomber jinking and weaving, the searchlight crews anticipating and following – and catching. During all this the night fighter would be attacking until he scored a victory or returned to base empty-handed, leaving the bomber to the flak batteries.

Until early 1942 this system had worked well. It had been improved shortly before the thousand-bomber raid by the introduction of a new 'giant' Wurzburg with a range of fifty miles. Still the plotters got their instructions by phone from the controllers, and they, in turn, directed the fighter pilots. This tended to make the system somewhat ponderous and liable to human error but it was working. And, of course, they were always ready for a raid, rarely taken by surprise not only because of their intelligence reports but also because of their highly efficient radio listening system. Specially trained Luftwaffe operators listened in to RAF wireless operators on sets adjusted to the same wavelengths. When one of these listening sets came to life with a whistling and chirping, it meant that RAF operators of a bomber unit over Britain were testing their sets. The news was promptly handed over to the night fighter units preparing them for action. In his definitive study of the Luftwaffe, German author Cajus Bekker tells how Captain Kuhlmann's radio intercept service would send messages such as: 'About sixteen bombers will take off from Hemswell and about twenty from Waddington.' Thus, even before the bombers were on their way, the German night fighters were aware of their preparations.

What remained to be seen was if they would be able to cope with the mass of bombers coming from Britain. They knew they were coming. The question was now, 'How many?'

Planes were still taking off. But this time it was the heavies, the blasters that would spread the fires.

At RAF Croft Jim Davidson crawled into the cramped quarters of the Halifax rear gun turret and had a recurrence of that sinking feeling before taking off, that lonesome foreboding that made him always want to say, 'Bloody Hell? Is it really me here again?' Alone, isolated from the rest of the crew, listening to the engines slowly revving up and without the support of his friends' backchat, he felt utterly exposed. On his own in a different world.

Now came the most agonizing moment of fear, the dash to the 125 mph 'unstick' speed. They seemed like an eternity to Jim, aware that he was sitting on top of 1,300 pounds of high explosive and 2,000 gallons of high-octane fuel. A faltering engine, a burst tyre, faulty flaps, a pilot error amongst any number of factors could, and often did, bring a spectacular end to all fear. For ever.

This time they were to make it. Harry Woodly swung the aircraft round in a slow climbing sweep in the direction of Flamborough Head. Soon they were sailing securely over the North Sea in the cold moonlit night. Far, far below a friendly light was winking 'goodbye' from the last dark headland. Somewhere down there, thought Jim, there were warm farmhouses whilst we ... He jerked his mind back to the job in hand and blew into the mike. 'Skipper? OK to test my guns?' And putting on a strong Yankee accent, 'Just to make sure I have lead poisoning at my finger-tips.'

'OK, Jim. Go ahead, boy,' replied Harry.

There was the metallic crash of the bolts sliding home as he cocked the guns. Now he felt fine. He was doing something. He depressed the guns towards the white-capped waves dimly seen far below and pressed the firing button. The guns chattered and the staccato explosions shook the aircraft, startling the crew. Long red tracers arched downwards and outwards into the night.

'OK, Skip. Guns OK.'

'Good lad, Jim,' came Harry Woodly's voice.

Now Jim Davidson felt much better. It was just another raid. They were on the way. OK. No stoppages with the guns. No problems to solve. He hated wrestling with the guns in the dark. It brought on a sweat despite the cold, and then later it was even colder with a damp vest. For the next few hours, here was his perch. Here he would sit swinging the turret from side to side, each movement slow and deliberate, marking a passage of time. Nearer to the end of this raid. Nearer to the end of the tour. But first there was the long haul across the North Sea. It always surprised him how long it took.

Not far behind Jim was Rusty Hudson in his Halifax from Linton-on-Ouse. The take-off had been perfect and merited the grin he always gave to Flight Engineer John Smith. It was all part of the ritual – good take-off – grin – a good omen. If it ever went otherwise, Rusty was sure he would be for the 'chop.' It was his 'lucky charm' thing.

As he looked into the darkness over the plain of York, he too saw himself rushing through the moonlit night away from a place where people sat in comparative comfort and security and talked and read of the war. His war. He slid back the window a little, and the roar of the engines and the outer rush of the slipstream intensified. Soon they would be hurtling towards that long-dreaded coastline where already hundreds of eyes were looking for him on a screen. The thought brought a new feeling of excitement. It was a kind of game they were playing. Gambling with lives – their own, the German fighter pilots and those of the citizens on whom the bombs would fall. A game in which technical skill and luck were combined. Right! He must play it well. Watch, think, keep alert.

A call came from the wireless operator. 'I can see ships on the sea ahead. Could be flak.'

An explosion cut into their voices. It was flak! A flak ship sent up a long, slow plume of tracers, a panoply of red and orange bursting around them. Rusty felt a growing tightness in his stomach – the old familiar mixture of fear and excitement. He knew what lay ahead and he knew that each time he forced himself through that difficult barrier it took a little more of his dwindling stock of courage.

Guns now winked viciously from the moonlit earth, and all he could see in the sky ahead were more and more of those deadly spiky explosions.

Cologne was still a long way off . . .

David Walker, signals leader in a Lancaster of the 44th Rhodesian

Squadron at Waddington, was well on with his role in the game.[11] He too saw it all that way. As he looked at newspaper photographs of devastated German cities, he would think and sometimes say: 'My goodness! Did I have a hand in that?' But at the same time, though the evidence was before his eyes in the photograph, it still was not real, because he never saw the blood and the bodies in the places he bombed and he was not directly conscious of what he was doing. He was only aware of the aircraft rocking under flak, of bullets ripping through the fuselage. It was something else. His part of the game was up here – at least for the moment. Later it would be different. And he never thought he would lose.

Flying at 20,000 feet, his crew had checked the engines, fuel, radio, navigation and guns. Now they were ready to enter enemy territory. So far all was surprisingly quiet. They were having a peaceful, even a pleasant flight across a moonlit sea. No flak, no fighters. Nothing. Below, in the bomb bay, was an 8,000-pound bomb, almost as long as the aircraft itself, riding snugly in its cradle. Enough explosive to demolish an entire factory or several blocks of streets. They would go in and drop it and that would be that. David Walker never for one moment thought that he would not be back for breakfast.

The navigator called out: 'Approaching Dutch coast now.'

David Walker stood up and took his position in the look-out post in the top of the fuselage. The pilot began to bank, first one way and then the other, to give David a wider field of view.

Suddenly, ahead, searchlights sprang up and clutched an aircraft. As it dived and turned, another beam picked it up, and then another clamped on it. It was fascinating to watch. But that was not what he was there for. He turned his gaze away to concentrate on the search for fighters. Already in the distance he had seen a string of fighter flares go down. The game was really on now. He would have to watch carefully and be ready to call out instructions to pilot and gunners without hesitation.

The crews from Leeming were having a quiet trip out.

Fred Simpson, in this his first long trip, thought he was favoured. Nothing to worry about. It helped a lot to have Tony Ennis as pilot. There was something definitely reassuring about the way he sat, bolt upright at the controls, hand on the throttle, eyes on the gauges, looking for all the world like a hero in one of those flying films where the pilot always gets through the stormy night with the mail.

Already the peaceful moonlit flight across the sea had added to Fred's feeling of security, and from his post in the astrodome he could see nothing to arouse alarm. Nothing but shadows here and there and the stars. They seemed that night to be twinkling and throbbing more vibrantly than ever before. 'What a wonderful world,' he thought. Orion was there, majestic and brilliant with belt and sword. He thought back to the nights when he and Dot had stood close together picking out the Plough and the two stars pointing to the North Star and to the constellation they had grown to call their own – Orion.

It was at this particular stage of the operation, after take-off and before the appearance of enemy fighters or flak, that many aircrew felt a sense of detachment, almost a sense of calm which made them feel that they were soaring serenely high above everything. Above all fear and worry, high above the clouds. It was a dangerous state to be in for they had had a tiring day 'standing to', being briefed, air-testing the aircraft, and then, just as the normal working man would be going home to put his feet up for the evening, they were about to meet the enemy. At such a time they would be going through a routine that could easily become automatic and without much conscious thought. A good skipper kept them on their toes. And there were few better skippers than Tony Ennis. He frequently came through on the intercom, checking and reassuring the crew.

Fred Simpson needed no reassuring. He was thinking what a pleasant trip it was. Nothing to worry about. Piece of the proverbial cake. Which was just as well, for he was going to need all his nerve before this night was finished.

The crew had quickly become a team. It was the first time they had flown together. And it would be the last.

Fred's pal from Leeming, in a 10 Squadron Halifax, was also feeling quite happy about the way the trip was going. He was even enjoying the flight for once – except for one thing: someone, unmistakably, was farting. Continuously. The navigator was the prime suspect. He had had a heavy session in the Willow Tree the previous night, getting over the loss of a friend. It was well known to the old hands that, unless you took care what you ate and drank, you could have a most uncomfortable trip. As the air became thinner with the increased altitude, the intestinal gases expanded painfully and had to be vented. And someone was doing just that – farting constantly.

To this odour frequently found in operational bombers, there was often to be added a far more penetrating one – vomit. This was John MacFarlane's speciality. No matter what 'cure' he tried, he would be found puking into a paper bag at some stage of the flight. The old remedies of dried bread and apple had not worked with him. And he dare not go to the doc, even off the record over a pint in a pub. You could never be sure that it would not lead to a carpeting before the commanding officer being accused of malingering or worse still of 'going LMF', 'Lack of Moral Fibre'.

Medical officers had been briefed even in the early days of the Advanced Air Striking Force in France to watch out for such symptoms and for what was called 'change of demeanour'.[12] In those days it had become something of a standing joke in the mess when, if one of them was a bit touchy after a heavy day in the air, someone would call out: 'Steady, lads. Doc is watching us for a change of demeanour'. But now it was no longer a joke. Everyone would think twice about going 'sick'. And so John MacFarlane and his crew just had to put up with it.

Today, though, he had not been sick. There had been no cork-screwing, no weaving, no diving. Not yet. It had been a smooth, level flight over the sea and coastline. In fact, the trip could not have started better, although MacFarlane did have one early shock. As he looked out of the astrodome the hairs pricked on the back of his head and neck, for there, just alongside almost, was a monster with four red-ringed eyes. He looked again. It was all right. Not an hallucination, not delirium tremens yet, merely the four bright red circles of the exhaust shrouds of another Halifax drawing alongside, too closely. It slid across their bows, and the slipstream made them lurch and buck. After that they had a quiet trip until in the distance John MacFarlane saw the searchlights on the coast, scissoring.

Soon they would be getting the controller's undivided attention.

Wireless operator Eric Clarke suffered terribly from air-sickness too but, for the same reason as John MacFarlane, never said anything to the medical officer.[13] After his nine-hour trip to Munich, however, he was so ill when the aircraft landed back at base that he had to be taken to sick quarters, where he was kept for five days. During this time the MO would come in every day and was surprisingly chatty, ranging over a wide spectrum of topics. Eventually the bed stopped heaving like a boat, and Eric Clarke was able to go back to his own room. It was only then that he realized what had been happening on the medical officer's visits. He was being assessed psychologically to see if he really was sick or just being a candidate for an LMF stamp.

However, on this particular trip he was feeling quite all right. No queasiness at all. In the distance he could see the searchlights scissoring across the sky trying to pick out one from the mass of them now well on the way to Cologne.

First over the target were Wing Commander Macdonald and Squadron Leader Gilmour of 15 Squadron, who had been airborne from Wyton at 22.30. Now, at 00.45 hours on the Sunday morning, seven minutes before the scheduled time, the two Stirlings began their run up towards the aiming point right in the centre of that ancient city, the Neumarkt.

These two experienced bomber pilots, specially chosen for the marking task, were surprised how quiet it was, how relatively ineffective was the anti-aircraft fire. They had all the time they needed to look down on the broad ringroads circling the city, the Hohenzollernring and the Militärischeringstrasse; the tramlines shining, the beautiful cathedral standing there proudly, the network of narrow streets in the old part of the city leading down to the silvery river, the little houses, the shops, the churches and the railway lines looping right round the city – all so clearly seen in the bright moonlight.

These two officers must have felt, more than any others did that night, how unreal it all seemed now. A few short hours ago it was a mere spot on a map in the briefing room. Now it was real – and yet not real. More of a fantasy. There was something eerie about this still city which had now gone to ground. Waiting. The nearness and clarity of the scene below and the desultory reaction of the defences at this moment gave time for thought. Below were families, tired fathers, harassed mothers, naughty children – so near and yet so far – now all sleep, dreaming perhaps, completely unaware of how dramatically many of their lives would be transformed this night. At any moment now a thumb would flex, a button be depressed and the old city would begin to disappear for ever.

The wires on the bombsights crossed. 'Bombs gone!' Sticks of incendiaries showered onto the Neumarkt, followed by small 30-pound bombs. Combined they made the beginnings of a funeral pyre for others to spread.

As the Stirlings veered away towards the turning-point at Euskirchen, Harry Langton's plane was approaching the target. He turned his Wellington gently onto its new and final course. He checked his height. The wide curve of the Rhine lay beneath them. 'Now she's all yours, bomb-aimer,' he said. His voice deliberately controlled, his eyes fixed on his instruments, his concentration on keeping a level course.

Cologne's defences had now sprung into action. Around them other aircraft of this fire-raising force were under heavy attack. Cones of searchlights held a Stirling on Harry's starboard side. Shellbursts studded the sky around it. All this he could see in his peripheral vision, never once taking his eyes off his controls, determined to give the bomb-aimer the best possible chance for an accurate fix. One good run in, no stooging around for a second chance. In this kind of Piccadilly traffic it was 'just not on'.

'Steady. Steady ... quite steady.' A fraction too much lift on the nose of the aircraft now and bomb-aimer 'Tiny' Welsh would lose the target altogether from his sight. Seconds passed. Interminably the run-up continued. 'Left ... left a bit. Hold it.' The dark, narrow streets crept along the sword edge of the bombsight. The flames from the few scattered fires merged with the moonlight to illuminate the target closely. There it was. The Neumarkt!

Violently the nose of the Wellington jumped upwards. 'Bombs gone!' shouted the bomb-aimer. 'That's it. Now let's get back!'

Harry Langton pulled the bomb-door lever and felt the change of trim as the doors shut out the air flow. Below, the first of the fires erupted into a fountain of sparks as blasts from the small high-explosive bombs hurled burning debris high into the air, scattered it over roofs of damaged buildings in the neighbourhood. Now Harry Langton turned onto a south-westerly course.

Over Euskirchen he banked and headed for home. At that moment the plane was caught in the brilliant glare of a searchlight beam. Others clustered round it in seconds. Langton reacted reflexively, turned sharply to port and dropped the Wellington's nose to get more air speed as quickly as possible. He watched the indicator creep slowly round the dial until it registered 270 miles an hour. Then he lifted the nose and opened up the engines, to shoot out of the beam into the blacker void beyond. The searchlights continued to swing near, probing, but they lost him. Gradually Harry Langton lost some height and settled into a steady speed for the long flight home, leaving behind an ever-increasing glow in the southern sky. He released his breath into a slow sigh of relief. But prematurely ...

Now the action over Cologne was hotting up. Bombers converged from all points of the compass – they approached the target from north to south and from south to north, from east to west and from west to east. It was a traffic nightmare as they criss-crossed, making a mockery of the briefing instructions for all aircraft to approach the target from the one direction. Every crew member had to be on the look-out – not so much for fighters but to warn their pilot whenever another bomber got too close.

Ken Williams was looking out from his Wellington onto a fantastic scene. Coming into the city shortly after Macdonald and Gilmour, they caught the brunt of the flak; already the coastal guns had torn holes in one wing and taken a chunk out of one propellor. But that was nothing compared with the reception they got over Cologne.

Shells burst beneath and around them, hurling fragments that rattled against the bomber like the sound of a snare drum. They were buffeted upwards and thrown vertically downwards like dropping in a liftshaft. They lurched through rainbow showers of exploding flak and falling flares.

Then, worst of all, about 200 yards ahead and slightly above them on the same course, Williams saw a dark shape. At that moment a shell exploded alongside it. A bright flash of white, yellow and orange flames lit up the whole sky to reveal a bomber disintegrating, showering wreckage. It fell in all directions, spinning, wings aflame. Parts of the fuselage and engines hurtled down, missing the Wellington by inches.

Still rocking in the slipstream of yet another bomber, they made their own run-up to the target. It was a straight in-and-out job too. Anything more would have been inviting disaster. In any case the lucky half-kopek was already working overtime.

Below, the city was now well shaken. Incendiaries cascaded downwards, splashing brilliant white as they hit the ground and turning red as the timber caught fire. Now, as they banked carefully away from the city centre, Williams had his own special contribution to make. His family had suffered from the Baedeker raid in York and he felt, just for the devil of it all, like sending a little extra as a 'tit for tat'. First went the whistling beer bottles, making their own peculiar penetrating whine, then the special 'shriekers' provided by his pal the organ-maker and, as one last gesture for all the 'shit' that had been thrown at them during the last few minutes, he emptied over the city the whole stinking contents of the Elsan toilet.

Forty years later he recalled: 'You did daft things like that sometimes just to keep yourself going. It was better than getting the twitch.'

History records that the German 'pre-alarm' to herald the change in air warfare sounded at exactly 23.45 hours on that Saturday.[14] But Cologne's sleepy citizens were slow to stir themselves. There had been over a hundred raids since the beginning of the war and, like those who had suffered bombing in Britain, they were inclined to wait and see before they bothered to get down to the shelters. The sky was clear, there was a bright moon, but no sound of aircraft. They were reluctant to leave their warm beds for the safety of the shelters.

For Klara Zarges it all started when the door burst open with her father rushing in. He stood at the bottom of the stairs shouting: '*Los! Los! Klara, come quickly. There's thousands of them up there. It's raining fire bombs.*' Together they rushed into the reinforced cellar, pushing and half carrying the perambulator with a thick, heavy blanket folded over the top. Once inside they felt safer but by no means secure against the mounting savagery of the bombardment that could be heard and partly seen through the iron grill of the cellar window.

Never before had bombs fallen in Cologne-Klettenberg like this. Now the cellar of Hirschenbergstrasse was full, and the bombs seemed to be directed right at them, falling immediately around the building. The strengthened parts of the cellar had looked safe enough when they put in the four stout posts to support the roof but now ...? Now the real test was coming. There had never been a raid like this before, and few of them felt safe. The whole ground was shaking as if in an earthquake. They sat and listened and suffered the twin ills that afflict all who find themselves under attack: the knot of fear in the stomach and the desperate desire to know what is really going on. The worry began to nag at their minds. What was happening to their house during all this bombardment? Was it on fire?

One of Frau Zarges' neighbours could stand the suspense no longer. 'I must go and see that my house is all right,' he cried as he struggled past the packed men, women and children huddled together in the reinforced part of the cellar. He had just reached the outer door when there was a thundering bang right overhead. An air mine. A tremendous rush of air ripped the cellar door right off its hinges and flung it amongst the cowering group nearby. It was followed by a billowing cloud of dust and black smoke carrying with it jagged fragments of wood, pulverized brick and concrete. The whole of the outer cellar floor was covered as if by a truck-load of demolition debris tipped over it. And beneath it all lay the man who had worried about his house.

Children began to howl. They could not breath in the air so thick with powdered cement and dirt.

Outside, the fire-engines could be heard racing through the streets, their sirens wailing. Now the sharp, clear bark of the 88mm anti-aircraft guns added their contribution to the crump of bombs and the never-ending rumble of falling masonry. Somewhere outside someone was screaming like an animal caught in a trap.

Cologne's nightmare had begun.

6. Lake of Fire

'In darkness, and with dangers compass'd round.'
John Milton

Harry Woodly saw it first as he crossed the Dutch coast: a crimson red glow. The dark dome of the sky was shot with blood, like nothing he had ever seen before on all his raids. 'It must be a decoy,' he thought. 'Pyrotechnics creating the effect of fire.' He checked his course and stayed with it. The red glow stayed. Dead ahead. Strange. A decoy usually took them off course.

Then, gradually, realization of what that awesome sight really was came as a tremendous shock. It was a city on fire. Cologne was ablaze from end to end. Fires were feeding upon other fires in the very heart of the city. And all over the smaller darker patches there could be seen the white glare of incendiaries bursting.

Harry was still marvelling at the astonishing spectacle, doing a gentle weave at 14,000 feet, when his mind was jolted back to the immediate situation by a shout from the tail gunner, Jim Davidson, and the rattle of machine-guns which reverberated throughout the aircraft.

'Fighter attacking. Right. Now!' Automatically Woodly put the aircraft into the practised drill: a tight diving turn towards the fighter, cutting down the target size and aiming-time for the fighter. It was the beginning of a running fight. The Junkers 88 pilot was a hot one. He lifted one wing, did a stall turn and somehow managed to get into a position to attack from the port beam. 'Yes, this man is really good,' thought Woodly. He pulled the control column hard back into his stomach. Just in time. Two ropes of red tracer shot right under the port wing. Woodly held onto the column, hard back until he felt the aircraft about to stall. Then just at the precise moment he pushed the nose down and opened the throttles. But the Junkers' pilot was not to be denied. He came in again, diving from above the tail, ignoring the tracers whizzing at him from Davidson's guns, his plane shuddering under the recoil from the cannon. Yet again the Halifax corkscrewed downwards. The black shape of the Junkers flashed by. And then it was gone.

'Jesus, Jesus,' breathed Davidson heavily, 'that was too damned close!'

Now Woodly was getting back some altitude. He called for a course and began again his steady weave towards the stricken city ahead. Checking his crew, one by one. No one hurt. No damage. Yet.

Now the fire was nearer. Wisps of thick smoke began to blur the pilot's vision. There was only one thing he could do, but it involved breaking from the flight plan. He would have to climb above the pall of smoke drifting away from Cologne. He climbed to 17,000 feet. He steadied the bomber on course. Now for the run in.

'All yours, bomb-aimer.'

Shellbursts were getting unpleasantly close. The aircraft shuddered in the blasts of near misses now. Jagged lumps of flak ripped holes in his wings and fuselage. There was a vicious flash and a roar in front. Bomb doors were open. No point in looking for the aiming-point now in that conflagration. But the bomb-aimer had selected a patch still untouched by fire. Calmly he gave course corrections. Now all else was blotted out from the minds of both the pilot and the man with his eye in the sight. Immediately below the twin towers of the cathedral passed, and then the silvery river flashing with reds and yellows and white of bursting incendiaries. Steadily they went. The whole of the cockpit lit up. A thumb felt for the button. A hand contracted into a fist. Bombs fell away in quick succession, and a pattern of flashes below sparked off further flares which soon brought with them belchings of thick black smoke of burning rubber.

Harry Woodly opened the engines to full throttle and made a descending turn to port (instead of the planned route to Euskirchen), rapidly losing height and gaining speed to set a fast course home. As they left the ancient city of Cologne, pursued by bursting shells, an excited Scottish voice came over the intercom: 'Jesus! Jesus! Jesus! What a fire!'

Twenty-one-year-old Eric Prince, in the front turret of the old

Wellington and on his first operation, had never imagined anything could be as horrific as the sight below him now. In what to him had seemed an eternity as they had edged their way between questing searchlights from the coast, he had seen the 'hellish red glow' in the sky ahead grow bigger and bigger. Now the inferno that had painted the night sky raged beneath the very perspex of his turret.

It was unnerving, he felt isolated, unsure of the combat procedures – as anyone still in training would – wondering about his rawness and any shortcomings that might still have to be rectified in his unfinished training. Could he play his part in what everyone had stressed was essentially a team effort? Never before had he set eyes on the men he was flying with. How good were they in their jobs? The pilot and rear gunner especially. What were they doing here now?

What would happen if ... he pushed away thoughts of an all-obliterating flak burst and looked down purposefully now at the fire-swept city and the silvery Rhine, so easily identified through wisps of scattered cloud.

Suddenly, as if appearing from nowhere, there loomed a huge four-engined bomber. Heading right for them! He shouted ... someone else was calling out ... then he was hurled violently forward as the Wellington's nose dipped and the pilot trod hard on the starboard rudder. The black shape slid right above them, leaving the Wellington shaking and rattling in the turbulent wake of its slipstream, its crew trembling in relief.

This, most definitely, thought Eric Prince, was not a time to linger over the target, now engulfed in lakes of fire.

There was one man who wanted to linger. It was for that very thing that he had risked the Commander-in-Chief's wrath. Air Vice-marshal Jackie Baldwin was circling the city for what seemed an age but was in fact just enough time to give him first-hand experience of what a thousand-bomber raid involved as far as concentration over the target was concerned. It was knowledge which helped to save lives later on in the bomber offensive. As Air Vice-Marshal 'Pathfinder' Bennett was later to point out: 'One must remember that practically no senior officers of the Royal Air Force had any appreciable first-hand operational experience in the current war, and they were therefore at a grave disadvantage in any tactical planning. This, I would emphasize, was not generally their own fault and should not in any way be held against them. It should however be held against the Prime Minister, the Cabinet and the Air Council that it was their policy to prohibit operational flying by senior officers over enemy territory. It cost us thousands of lives and many failures, and was, in my view, the most deplorable of all mistakes which we made during the war.'

The objective report which Baldwin wrote immediately after the raid gave a vivid and dispassionate picture of what it was really like. After the first wave of bombers had dropped their loads,

'Suddenly, thirty or forty miles from Cologne, I saw the ground and then the flak. It grew clearer and clearer until, near the city, visibility was perfect. First I saw a lake, gleaming in the moonlight, then I could see fires beginning to glow, and then searchlights which wavered and flak coming up in a haphazard manner.

The sky was full of aircraft all heading for Cologne. I made out Wellingtons, Hampdens, a Whitley and other Stirlings. We sheered off the city for a moment, whilst the captain decided what would be the best way into the target. It was then that I caught sight of the twin towers of Cologne Cathedral, silhouetted against the light of three huge fires that looked as though they were streaming from open blast furnaces. We went in to bomb, having for company a Wellington to starboard and another Stirling to port. Coming out we circled the flak barrage, and it was eight minutes after bombing that we set course for home. Looking back, the fires seemed like rising suns, and this effect became more pronounced as we drew further away. Then, with searchlights rising from the fires, it seemed that we were leaving behind us a huge representation of the Japanese banner. Within nine minutes of the coast, we circled to take a last look. The fires then resembled distant volcanoes.'[1]

Now at least one senior officer knew exactly what such an operation involved. For Baldwin, who had taken no small risk in defying the Commander-in-Chief's explicit ban on senior officers flying on operations, the experience told him far more than any combat report could. Aircrew admired him for it. Even at that time of the war there were murmurs of discontent about 'chairborne commanders' sending men out on extremely doubtful and hazardous missions. As one historian was later to write: 'The gulf between the realities in the sky and the rural routine of headquarters was too great for most of the staff to bridge. High Wycombe was fatally isolated both from the front and from sharp critical debate on policy. Now, at last here was one commander at

least who was prepared to bridge that gulf, he had seen for himself
how a city could be set afire.'[2]

One of the bombers following Baldwin's Stirling was Micky
Martin's Wellington, from which Ron Lawson had a perfect view
of the inferno. 'The anti-aircraft batteries must have run out of
ammunition or the gunner's gone completely "bomb happy"
because when we got over the target there was hardly anything
coming up at us. Even the searchlights seemed to be manned by
loonies waving them about aimlessly,' he was later to recall.[3]

They came in low, at 4,000 feet. 'You could see people running
in the streets. Everything stood out clearly, as if you were seeing it
on stage, brightly lit.'

Even the hard Aussie Micky Martin was so awed by the
devastation and Hell-fire below that he was almost mesmerized by
it and swung his bomber over the city three times looking for a
suitable target. Finally he selected a point where railway lines
converged. Obviously a main line station. The bomb load fell on
the already shattered station. Never had he seen anything remotely
like it before. It moved someone to say over the intercom: 'More of
this bloody lot the better. It'll soon settle their hash once and for
all.'

That was one way of looking at it. Others felt differently. Ernest
Wilson felt the city was just lying there completely at the bombers'
mercy when they arrived in the old Wellington from Snaith. 'They
seemed to have just left the searchlights pointing straight up and
others appeared just to be wafting about as if in a breeze. I felt sorry
for everybody below.' He did not have much time to think about
the unfortunate German citizens for suddenly they were all shaken
rigid by a close encounter with a Stirling that zoomed right across
and over them, dropping bombs as it passed. Too near a miss to
leave anyone room for thoughts of what was going on below. Only
some idiot of a backroom boy would ever calculate the risk of
collision in such a raid to be as low as 'one in a thousand'.

Now the heavies were coming in. The blasters. They would
spread the conflagration.

In one of these was David Walker, and he did have time to think.
He had seen the crimson red glow of blazing Cologne a good
seventy miles from the city, and the nearer he approached the
inferno beneath the flak-torn skies, the more misgivings he had.
Not about himself or the crew but for the citizens of Cologne. He

felt a chill in his heart at what he and his companions were about to do. How could it possibly be justified? How could they subject all these people to what must be a Hell on Earth? But this was no way for him to think. He forcibly switched his mind onto more belligerent thoughts. This war was not of his making. It was a job that had to be done. He remembered the talk he had had with the station padre, he thought of the tyranny of the Nazis, the concentration camps. Here was an evil that had to be removed, a cancer that threatened civilization. And just as in cutting out malignant cells some good tissues had to be sacrificed, so innocent people would have to die before this scourge could be removed once and for all.

The chill of remorse did not last long (though it was to come back later). He fixed his eyes now on the fires raging below, and he felt strangely elated. Here at last was the first big bomber battle. And for the first time the bombers were winning.

Ten thousand feet below now, Cologne appeared through the smoke haze. 'We searched for an area that was not already burning for it seemed that Cologne then was ablaze from end to end. We had been briefed that the main post office was the aiming point. "There are ammunition factories across the street," we were told. Many of us, however, believed that we were bombing the civilian population because we knew that in most cities the main post office is not surrounded by factories.

'The tension grew as the pilot opened the bomb-bay doors. The noise of the aircraft intensified. This was our most vulnerable moment. Our bomb, which seemed nearly as long as the four-engined aircraft itself, was now exposed. Coloured tracer bullets arched through the sky. If anything hit that bomb, we were finished!

'The bomb-aimer now took control of the aircraft. Pointing his sights towards the target area, he gave the pilot his instructions: Left ... left ... right ... right ... left a little ... hold it ... steady ... on target. Bomb away! The plane shuddered, and I heard the "whoosh" as the four-ton bomb fell away from the aircraft. An endless minute went by as we waited until the photoflash illuminated the area we had bombed. Once the damage had been photographed, we set off for home.

'As we banked and turned steeply away, I could see the shocking sight of a city burning from end to end. Dense smoke could be seen drifting away leaving a brilliantly illuminated plan below. My immediate reaction was a mixture of sadness, fear and guilt. And into my mind flashed a comparison between the holocaust below and the preaching of the pastor at home. I thought about the men, women and children who had lost their lives. Why am I taking part in the slaughter of thousands of innocent people in this huge city?'

And then, from his long-standing religious background, there came another disturbing question: 'What does God think about such dreadful work?'

God's 'agents' kept quiet. Very quiet. Except for one or two brave men who thought not of their careers, such as Bishop George Bell of Chichester. When he protested vehemently in the House of Lords and in the Press, he was made to feel almost like a traitor. He agreed that when military objectives were bombed it was inevitable that civilians would be killed. But, he declared, that there was absolutely no justification for the deliberate bombing of civilians – the 'Terror Bombing' as the Nazi Propaganda Minister called it. 'Dehousing [as Government advisers euphemistically called area bombing] is barbaric,' he said. It probably cost him the archbishopric of Canterbury.

And what about the other Churchmen? They followed the lead of men like the newly appointed Archbishop of York who had devised a formula of conscience-easing words. Dr Garbett is reported to have said: 'Frequently a choice has to be made of the lesser of two evils, and it is a lesser evil to bomb a war-loving Germany than to sacrifice the lives of our fellow countrymen who long for peace, and to delay delivering many now held in slavery.'[4]

The Bishop of London, Dr Fisher, went even further in giving his 'blessing' on the raid. Addressing the London Diocesan Conference a week later, he said he had no doubts whatever 'on the military necessity and value of the raids. Canterbury and Cologne had each in its own country a special place in religious life. Cologne, though, as a centre of war industries, had military significance and its destruction was legitimate and a legitimate cause for satisfaction.'[5]

Pleas on moral grounds for restricting the bomber offensive fell on deaf ears. Bishop Bell never got a frank answer to his questions. Harris later said the Government should have had the guts to come out into the open and put their point of view on record.[6] Instead, Secretary of State for Air Sinclair confined his replies to vague statements such as: 'Bomber Command is the only force upon which we can call in this year, 1942, to strike deadly blows at the heart of Germany.'

As for the Roman Catholic Church in Britain, what was the response of the Cardinal Archbishop of Westminster to the bombing of the most Catholic city in Germany? We do not know. He remained discreetly silent.

In the end it was left to men like David Walker to make peace with their own consciences in whatever way they could. In his case comfort was to come much later and not without cost.

A young man who had grave doubts in a rather different way, Rusty Hudson, settled himself further into his seat as he approached the target area. He braced himself against the fear which threatened to break the barrier of his control ever more menacingly with each operation. It was then, at the very moment he began his run up to the aiming-point, that a curious comforting thought entered his head. 'Anyway, if it happens, I shall leave something of myself behind. A child.'

In the short period of time between briefing and take-off he had broken all the rules of the game and slipped out of camp to telephone Jackie. Then it was that she told him that she thought she was pregnant. There had been no recriminations. No questions. She had asked nothing.

A loud crash near his head jerked him back to the present. For a moment he was blind. Another crash and a horrifying glare of light sailed slowly down as something huge blossomed into a brilliant white sheet of light. Some other poor sod had bought it. And they would tell him it was a 'scarecrow' when he got back.*

Now Stephen Grange's voice was coming through the intercom giving precise directions in his calm Kentish accent, guiding the bomber onto the target. Below him the shellbursts were rising closer and closer. The Halifax wallowed but kept on course. Then a mighty fist hit the front of the bomber, lifting it high into the air. Bomb-aimer Grange lay motionless in a tangle of perspex and aluminium. Navigator John Smith struggled forward in the now pitching aircraft. He put an arm under Grange's shoulder and turned him over. The front of his chest had been torn away, leaving a pulpy mass exposed. On his face was the sardonic grin of a dead man. A wave of nausea came over the young navigator, and then an

---

* Intelligence officers on debriefing told returning aircrew that these brilliant white flashes were not aircraft exploding but shells (scarecrows) fired by anti-aircraft guns to frighten pilots. The German Luftwaffe denied using these. However, many aircrew still believe these were shells of that type fired.

intense feeling of anger gripped him. He took hold of the bomb-aimer's right fist, prised open the fingers and thumb and pressed the bomb switch, shouting: 'Take that, you bastards!'

There was no need to tell Rusty Hudson. 'I know ...' he said before Smith could say more than a couple of words. His face was beaded with sweat as he fought the controls. Every so often the aircraft shook like a small ship struck by a gigantic wave, and the flak rapped at the thin metal skin like pebbles thrown up with the spray. 'Give me a course for base,' he called. Already he was feeling the odds against getting there were far too heavy. His arms felt feeble and shaky, and he wondered if he was really fit enough to do the job. Then, from out of the black night, came a new resolve. He would have to get back. By God, he would!

Another pilot having difficulties was Leslie Manser. He was not worried about his own capabilities but those of his aircraft. It really was not fit for a raid like this.

It had been a long and anxious flight. Once again the RAF's most disappointing aircraft had failed to live up to its specifications. (The Manchester was a dismal failure. Of 209 built, sixty-five per cent were lost. It was phased out of service in June 1942.) The Twin Vulture engines constantly threatened to overheat, and never once was there enough thrust to lift the bomber away from the dangerously low 7,000 feet that made it a sitting duck for the German anti-aircraft gunners.

Manser would have been fully justified in turning back at any point of the operation but once the decision to carry on had been made he never wavered in his resolution. His Squadron, No. 50, 'Bull's Eye', had a well-earned reputation for hitting the target, and Leslie Manser was not the sort of man to give in easily.

As he approached the ravaged city, the Manchester was caught in a cone of searchlight beams, and almost immediately the anti-aircraft shells began to rip through the bomber from below, rupturing hydraulic lines and tearing holes in the wings. Typically Manser held his aircraft on course until bomb-aimer Barnes released the bombs. By this time it must have seemed as though all the flak batteries in the Cologne area were concentrating on this one lame duck. A storm of shrapnel now punctured the fuselage from end to end. The force of exploding shells lifted the heavy aircraft bodily and threw it about the sky. Now all Manser's skill came into the conflict as he took violent evasive action to get away from the searchlights and flak. The once sluggish Manchester was now rocketing about in a way that would have given its designers heart failure had they been watching. But it was to no avail. No matter what manoeuvre Manser employed, the searchlights stuck to him and the shells continued to pound the bomber to pieces. In desperation, he pushed the aircraft into a dangerous dive to less than a thousand feet. Shells burst closer. One tore a huge piece out of the fuselage near the tail and hit the rear gunner. A second later another burst under the port engine, which gushed forth a trail of flame spreading right across the wing.

At any moment now the main petrol tank in that wing would surely explode. This was the moment when the young skipper had to make the vital decision to abandon the aircraft or try to keep it on course long enough to give anyone who parachuted a fair chance of avoiding capture. It was a heavy responsibility for such a young man to carry – not only the aircraft but the lives of his crew were in his hands. An icy gale roared down the fuselage, bringing with it thick smoke. The whole aircraft was now shaking and quivering. Manser's hands tightened on the control column. He had made up his mind. Calmly he gave instructions to his second pilot, Baveystock, to feather the engine and use the extinguisher. There was a chance, and every chance had to be taken before giving the order which seemed inevitable – to jump and get away from it before it went up with half its load of petrol.

Miraculously, though, the flames died. The aircraft was still flying, the shells were further away. There was still hope after all.

Now, for a brief spell over the blazing city, the bombers seemed to be having it all their own way: little flak came up, no fighters were seen.

Sandy Milne in his obsolete Whitley had all the time he wanted to pick his own target in that conflagration below, a black patch not yet burning. Wireless-operator Bob Vollum in a Hampden from Warrington thought his lucky steel mirror was working overtime so free from flak were they, and Bill Higgs coming in at 17,000 feet in the Halifax from Linton could not believe his eyes or his ears. 'Inside the aircraft it was light enough to read, the fires were so bright, but there were very few guns firing and I saw only three stationary searchlights. It was, for me, a magnificent sight, for, being a Londoner who had suffered in the Blitz and seen my girlfriend's house bombed in '41, I felt that now we were really getting our own back.'

What had happened to the defences of Cologne? Had the intruder force from RAF Fighter Command neutralized the German night fighter system? They had not. In trying to attack the German night fighter airfields with inadequate numbers and with inadequate navigation aids, the RAF fighters achieved little more than a temporary inconvenience. It was the sheer concentration of bombers which threw the German defences into disarray. The system designed for the interception of bombers passing singly through the ground-control interception zones manned by one fighter simply could not cope with a massive number.

But if the fighters were in disarray, why was the anti-aircraft fire so sporadic? There was a period when confusion seemed to reign. Searchlights went out and flak stopped. Then up stabbed the searchlights again as if lighting the stage for the fighters to come in. The flak remained silent but no fighters appeared to pick off the bombers over the aiming-point.

Orders seemed to go awry. Whilst flak batteries obeyed a cease-fire, the fighters did not get orders to engage over the target area. Perhaps they were busy in other zones or refuelling.

Another explanation given is that the flak batteries ran out of ammunition and could not get more supplies easily because of the blockage of roads by debris.

Whatever the reason for these temporary lulls, it was a lesson that was quickly learnt and a fault that never happened again. Josef Kammhuber, Chief of XII Air Corps and General of Night Fighters, immediately set about reorganizing the system. He created more night fighter groups and brought in new methods of ground control.

But to the crews of some of the Halifaxes and Lancasters attacking Cologne early that Sunday morning it certainly looked as though the defences were stupefied.

John MacFarlane was moved to feel pity for the defenceless citizens: 'I had never been on an easier target. We just floated in and made no pretence at navigation. We picked our target carefully, dropped our bombs and had time to look down at Bomber Command's handiwork. It was an awesome sight. We could see the river clearly running through a mass of fires. Every street was etched in fire. It stretched right across the city. The light from them was so bright I could see other bombers coming in to bomb. It was appalling, a really sickening sight which left me stunned.'

He found words coming unbidden from his lips: 'My God! I feel sorry for all the women and kids down there.'

But he was jolted back to the reality of his job by the coarse voice of the Australian skipper beside him: 'Well, mate, if you feel that way, you can bloody well jump out and join 'em!'

A remarkable feature of this raid which aircrew talked about afterwards was that their experiences and reactions over the city varied so greatly. As we have just seen, some crews sailed serenely through to the target and back, unscathed, whilst others – even those in the same wave – were ferociously engaged by flak and fighters. A matter of minutes could make all the difference.

And so, whilst John MacFarlane was pitying the poor citizens of Cologne, his pal Fred Simpson was about to be savagely mauled.

His pilot, Tony Ennis, was right on course, flying at 14,000 feet, approaching the orange-red glow in a clear sky. And as Fred looked around he could see no other dark shapes, no cloud, nothing. They were on their own. Twenty-five minutes from the target.

Suddenly he jumped, as if given a jolt in the back, for a dazzling beam shot straight at them. Another scissored probingly across. They knew what they were after. And what they had found. A single aircraft! At last, after being overwhelmed, the defences had rallied. Four more beams pierced the sky. Inside the Halifax now it was brighter than day.

Ennis pushed hard on the right rudder pedal, swung the control to the left and studied for a moment. And so it went on for what seemed an age, weaving, diving and doing everything possible to get out of those lights. No guns fired.

Ennis held on to his course. Straight ahead. No need to panic. Push on. Now the beams were coming back, drawing nearer, converging. 'The gunners must see us now,' thought Fred Simpson, heart pounding. A cry came through the intercom: 'Damn!' It was Ennis. 'Hold on!' He jinked the aircraft and began to weave. Then a glare of light with an orange centre hit him full in the face, destroying his night vision. Another beam, seemingly blue, fastened on to them. But still no guns.

On the ground the German gunners were patient. Plotting the course. Correcting. Waiting for Ennis to fly straight and level again.

But Ennis was waiting for no one now. Twenty-five minutes of this game was enough for anyone. He spoke to the bomb-aimer, then held the aircraft steady for a few seconds, and the bomb-aimer jabbed the button. The bombs had gone.

Ennis tried a short dive to starboard and pulled up level. Again the beams latched on, filling the cabin and fuselage with such an intensity of light that they all felt completely exposed.

'It was like being in a vast arena of light as though you were in the centre of a great circus with all the world watching,' recalled Flight Engineer Fred Simpson. 'Wait for it,' he said to himself. 'Now it will come. Any moment now.'

It did. Three massive shocks rocked them at once. Even brighter glares split the sky like lightning all around. Something hot and painful knocked rear gunner Bertram Groves off his balance. He tried pushing himself up but his arms seemed helpless. All was black. Slowly he lifted an arm to his eyes. Somewhere near there he felt a pulpy mass. Then, from one eye he could see lights, feel pain, and then a power within him made him get to his guns, squint down the sights directly into the brilliant searchlight itself and begin firing. And he kept at it. The turret reeked with cordite, as all around now heavy shells exploded, lumps of shrapnel gashed the shuddering, plunging aircraft. The perspex next to his knee burst and vanished. A terrible pain shot up his leg, and somehow he could not breath properly.

Up front a near miss burst just below the pilot, and a cannonade like a roll of kettle drums swept right along the fuselage to end with another terrifying bang that pushed the heaving bomber into a sideways tilt. The port outer motor was hit and stopped.

'Wing hit!' Ennis called. 'Diving now.'

Fred Simpson, now in the nose, held the guns at arms length, firing directly at the searchlights. As the air speed built up, faster and faster, the slipstream surged against the fuselage like surf on a beach. Flak battered against the sides and belly of the plane. Never had Ennis, or any of them, dived like this before. They had all heard tales of wings folding under the strain. Now they were well beyond the safety mark of 340 mph. The airframe shuddered, creaked and groaned as if wanting to twist. Down from 10,000 to fifty feet they went. From his place in the nose, Fred could see exactly where they were going – into the centre of three gaping holes of the electricity cooling towers!

It was then that he felt sure that 'this was it'. He had often wondered how it would be for him. A numbness flooded his body and mind during the next few seconds, waiting for the impact.

Above him, Ennis was back on the controls. He felt the Halifax responding, lifting itself out, curving upwards as the mounting 'G' force rammed him hard down in his seat, pulling the flesh from his jowls, tugging at his eyeballs until his vision blurred. But not for long. Now the Halifax was out, flying level, just over the roof-tops. Fred Simpson scrambled back to the seat by the pilot and collapsed into it.

No one spoke. Not even the loquacious Aussie, Ben Gibbons. All Fred could do was think, 'My God! We're going to make it!'

He sat in the utter immobility of relief and exhaustion. Then, impulsively, he stretched out a free hand and patted his pilot's shoulder. There were no words to say just how he felt anyway. Later he was glad that he had then made that simple gesture of admiration, thanks and affection, for, as events were to prove, of young Tony Ennis's life there was little left.

Sitting upright again in his seat, the skipper spoke. His clear voice and strong intonation captured the attention of all the crew. 'Give me a course back. We're on our way home.'

Then he called the crew members one by one. From rear-gunner Groves there was no reply. Ennis nodded to Fred Simpson and pointed backwards. When Fred got back to the turret, he found the door jammed. He wrestled and tugged. It opened to reveal Groves lying crumpled against the perspex, his face drawn together in an intensity of pain. Carefully, from that cramped space, Fred Simpson eased the badly injured Sergeant Groves backwards into the fuselage. Helped by the wireless operator – another Simpson, a pilot officer – Fred unzipped the sleeve of Groves' Irvin jacket; he got one hand inside and put the tip of his knife into the sweater and shirtsleeve, then, with a deft sawing movement, slit the wool and cotton until the forearm was bare. He unclipped the canvas first-aid pack and took out one of the morphine hypodermic tubes. Partly by touch and partly by sight in the pale gloom, Fred Simpson nipped a roll of warm forearm flesh, pressed the needle into it firmly and squeezed until the tube was empty.

Gently they turned Bertram Groves to one side and took a closer look at the ugly wound by his right eye and the torn, blood-soaked leg of this flying-suit. Together, one slitting the material, the other slipping in the thick emergency dressing over the wound, they made him as comfortable as possible. It was going to be a long trip home but the eyes of Bertram Groves were now closed and his breathing was slow and regular, like the now heavy rhythmic thrum of the engines. He was now way out beyond the bomber, beyond feeling and pain.

'We'll soon be home now, lad,' said Fred as he wedged a parachute alongside Groves' head before stumbling back up to the fuselage to take his seat again alongside Ennis. From there he looked out across the sky to England, and then, as the aircraft banked, he took one long last look at the fires and flashes lighting the pall of smoke above Cologne. The heavies were now going in thick and fast, dropping their 4,000-pounders that would hurl burning buildings all over the place, starting fresh fires. And to him then came a realization of the madness in which they were all caught. And he felt stunned. Only one fearful thought was in his mind: 'What must it be like down there?'

MacFarlane had said it already: it was Hell down there. The raid had now reached a crescendo. In the midst of the chaos and conflagration an air-raid warden in Cologne-Mulheim rushed down the street shouting frenetic commands for everyone to leave the cellars and get to the bunkers. The biggest bomb ever had fallen and not yet exploded!

People surged forward into the brightly lit street. Women carried half-asleep children, lolling limply in their arms; old people stumbled with their blankets and bags. All moved purposefully, quickly, and no one spoke. All had the blank look of fear upon their faces. And just as suddenly as they had appeared, the street was empty again.

The sky was dotted with lights of all kinds, flares, exploding shells, burning aircraft and a continuous eruption of sparks floating upwards from hundreds of fires all over the city. And through all this display of fireworks the long, bright beams of the searchlights probed. 'It was a terrifying sight but there was a *Götterdämmerung* grandeur about it all,' recalled one lady.

The anti-aircraft batteries in north-east Cologne were firing as rapidly as they could as Willy Niessen looked through the mesh of his cellar window. Now above the sound of the guns came another sound that he had never heard before in any raid. The tremendous roar of hundreds of aircraft. It seemed to him that the sky was full of them. As he looked round the cellar, he saw that there was one thought in everyone's mind as they sat close together: Would they – could they – ever survive such a raid?

A stick of high-explosive bombs whistled down at the other side of the road. Involuntarily Willy Niessen ducked from the grill and crouched on the floor, with his mother clutching his shoulder and at the same time huddling protectively over his little sister, Leni. The falling bombs sounded to him like a squadron of Stukas diving onto their targets. What was worse, it seemed as though they were diving down upon him personally, singling him out for destruction. Bombs of all shapes and sizes fell around their house, incendiaries came cascading down, hissing and sputtering before bursting into an incandescent whiteness which either turned yellow as it caught inflammable material or guttered out into nothing.

And through it all could be heard the sweating, skin-crawling sound of someone crying out in extreme pain as the concussion and splash of sparks from incendiary bombs bounced off the road opposite onto a living body. As he watched, the flames from the roof began to eat downwards. Suddenly Willy Niessen had an alarming thought: if incendiaries had landed on the roof of the house opposite, they would have fallen on his own too. He raced upstairs with a neighbour, burst into the attic and found two incendiary bombs blazing fiercely on the wooden floor. Shielding their eyes, the two youths dashed nearer to the spitting flames and with one quick scoop of a shovel had one and then the other of the bombs flung out of the window. Then, panting for breath, they stood for a moment looking out at the sight before them. To the south the whole city was engulfed in smoke and fire. Again the thought came into his mind: 'O God, let us survive!'

Through the open window drifted the brutal smell of smoke and the powdered rubble of dissolved houses now lying in unrecognizable heaps lower down the street.

But they quickly cut short their sightseeing when yet another unfamiliar sound came from overhead – the menacing roar of low-flying bombers. They came at roof-top height, zooming low over Geldorpstrasse in Cologne-Nippes.

Further down the road two soldiers and a nun worked side by side in demented frenzy, throwing bricks, heaving great lumps of concrete with far beyond their normal strength. A woman who worked in a nearby bar joined them, hurling the debris further back until at last they freed a woman clutching tightly to her side a flaxen-haired girl of five or six. Their faces were smeared with blood and dirt, their eyes watering to wash out the grit, but they were alive. People round about were now hurrying out of damaged cellars into bunkers in nearby streets. Messengers, some of them far too young for the job, were struggling through the chaos of tangled telephone wires and ruptured emergency firehoses.

All over the city, thousands of men, women and even children, in and out of the Defence Services, were rising to the occasion with a steadfastness of nerve and resolution rarely seen. In this, their 107th raid of the war, they were learning that it was possible to withstand and survive bombing on this unprecedented scale.

'Most of us got the wind up at first but we were all unwilling to show just how frightened we were. You looked around and saw the rest doing their job. You couldn't let them down, you just had to get on with it. You began to make feeble jokes to each other and gradually you got accustomed to it ... The fires had a stunning effect. Wherever the eye could see, vast sheets of flame and a terrific roar – it was so bright you could have read a newspaper,' said one former fireman. 'The heat of the fire scorched the skin, dried out your eyes and you felt you were making no impression at all on the fires. Whole blocks of riverside warehouses were ablaze, and it seemed futile for black dots of firemen directing pathetic jets of water at the wall of flames.'

Firemen from neighbouring towns were now coming fast into the city to help deal with the spreading conflagrations. Reaching the fires with the fire-engine became increasingly difficult, for roads were pitted with craters and strewn with dead and debris. After the Franz Clouth rubberworks received a direct hit and then the railway works at Cologne-Nippes, fires sprang up all round the area. Black clouds of asphyxiating smoke kept firemen at a distance from some of them. Rats in hundreds ran out of gutted warehouses.

At one time it looked, to young Willy Niessen, as though his own house could not possibly escape being set on fire, as the breeze carried great showers of sparks and embers onto nearby rooftops. 'It was an unforgettable sight. The glare was like daylight, and the streets were filled with driving galaxies of sparks. You could not distinguish known buildings through the great clouds of smoke, except when sudden spurts of yellow flame lit up a recognizable feature.'[7]

By this time the fire brigades were at full strength, with many painful and strenuous hold-ups as they searched for water. There were remarkable escapes of firemen and civilians trapped by encircling flames and managing to find a safe passage in the nick of time. The story is told of one man who swung hand over hand on a tramway cable across the road from the top window of one building to the corresponding window of the one across the road. A family in Cologne-Duetz found themselves crawling unhurt up the rubble of an enormous crater without any idea at all of how they got there! Their last recollections were of leaving their vanished home to go to a bunker.

Some were not so lucky. A Cologne fireman still has nightmares of that fearful night as clearly as if it were yesterday. On his way from one fire he saw a small crew directing water against a blazing factory.

'It must have been paint or glue or something like inflammable treacle that was pouring like volcanic lava down the front of the building. White hot! Suddenly the whole front of the building billowed outwards like a sail in a high wind and came crashing down on the crew below. One moment they were there, and the next all there was to be seen was a huge smouldering heap of glue and rubble. All we could do was stare transfixed, open-mouthed at the loop of hosepipe leading from it.'

The breakages in the mains water supply caused tremendous problems: special lines were laid from the Rhine, and extra pumping equipment was brought in, but many of these extra lines from the river were soon crushed beneath falls of brickwork from the blazing buildings. Others were laid.

To this backcloth of Dante's Inferno jagged lumps of metal and masonry hurtled into living bodies. Casualties were more gruesome than the mind can imagine. Men and women with bodies ripped open still managed to talk. Friends and relatives became at a stroke no more than a piece of twitching, pulsating flesh, too revolting even to be pitied. 'Young lads in their teens working in rescue teams saw death more horrific than we were later to see on the battlefield of Falaise,' said one ex-soldier. (The battlefield of Falaise was so strewn with German dead that Eisenhower was later to write: 'It was literally possible to walk for hundreds of yards at a time, stepping on nothing but dead and decaying flesh.') 'Mutilated torsos, heads wrenched off bodies, torn-off arms and legs. We just had to shut off our minds to handle the broken bodies that were likely to live. Bits of humanity, that's all the others were.'

Young girls who had volunteered for the Auxiliary War Service, working in transport services in hospitals, matured into women overnight helping with casualties. But dozens did not survive. Their burnt and twisted bodies were later laid out in lines for relatives to identify and carry away to private graves if they wished, before the rest went for mass burial outside the city.

A warden remembers tripping over a boot which still had a foot in it and part of a leg, but nothing else of a body nearby. An accountant found a woman lying with her brains spilt over the pavement and bent to pick her up with hands bleeding from broken glass, to carry her to the decency of cover behind a garden wall. A brewery worker passing some stables that had been hit saw a tangled mass of mutilated men and horses heaving about on the ground. The screams of the animals mingled with cries and wails of men. Horses stampeded, galloping madly out of the inferno with tails on fire.

Scenes like these and far worse were all too common. They were among the realities of the night, realities which we cannot ignore.

In every street and in every shelter there was a story worth telling, a little drama of pathos or gallantry played out under the cover of the great impersonal drama of blast and fire.

Everyone now in Cologne was finding a new and bitter meaning in Propaganda Minister Dr Goebbels' words: 'We're all in the front line now.'

7. The Way Out

'And I will show you fear in a handful of
dust.'

The Waste Land, T.S. Eliot

The opera singer who entertained front-line troops, Erika Wagner,
had been warned by the garrison commander that it was going to
be a 'big raid' but, like most of Cologne's citizens that night, she
was just a little blasé and was rather slow off the mark in going to
the air-raid shelter. Instead of heeding the radio warnings and siren,
she followed her usual practice of waiting for her pet dog to howl
before stirring herself. Consequently she was only just arriving at
the shelter when there was a sound like an express train whistle that
became a wailing, rushing, rustling roar ending with an
ear-splitting explosion. It lifted her off her feet and flung her down
just inside the thick concrete walls of the bunker doorway. There
she lay for a few moments unable to breathe, her chest muscles in
an agonizing contraction. But she was safe. For the moment.

Then came more bombs bringing with them the harsh jingle of
flying glass hitting the walls as blasts took the windows out of
houses further down Brusselstrasse.

In the shelter, a feeling of absolute terror gripped everyone. The
bright sky seemed full of bombers. The throb of their engines. The
explosion of bombs and the sharper crack of the 88mm guns
encircling the city shook the very ground on which they stood. But
even with such terror there is a limit to what the mind will take,
and gradually there was a relaxation: fear gave way to an exhausted
calm, and a kind of fatalism expressed in the attitude that, if your
name was on the bomb, there was nothing you could do about it,
so you might just as well accept whatever was in store for you.

Nevertheless, this calm was still punctuated by moments of sheer
terror. Erika Wagner remembers one in particular. A whistle grew

131

louder and louder until it was an ear-piercing shriek culminating in a vicious tongue of flame which leapt right inside the shelter itself, catching everyone in a photographic instance cringing against the wall. When the dust had settled, they heard a less frightening and more familiar noise – the clatter of incendiaries on rooftops. Frau Wagner crawled to a grill, looked through it and uttered a cry: 'I must get out. My house! A phosphorous bomb!'

Without pausing to think, she clambered over legs and bags, children and boxes, frantic in her haste to save her house. She raced up to the attic, saw an incendiary bomb blazing with a terrible brightness and flung sand over it with a fury that cannot be described. Finally she dowsed the smouldering floorboards with water, all the time giving mental thanks to the soldiers who had come round to every house that month providing this firefighting equipment – long-handled shovel and buckets filled with sand and water.

Breathless, and somewhat relieved, she dashed back to the safety of the shelter. This time she stayed nearer to the door in case she had to get out quickly again.

Toni Stellmaszyk was less fortunate. He could not get out. He was buried.[1]

Twelve-year-old Toni had been taken to hospital with scarlet fever. He was lying in bed that evening when he was hurriedly bustled down into the cellar along with thirty other patients who were fit enough to move. *Everyone* knew that this was going to be 'one Hell of a raid', it seemed.

They were just settling down to sleep after a very late supper when there was 'a noise so loud and surging as if all the stormy seas of Christendom had met with all the waterfalls and winds in the world'. An almighty crashing sound broke out above the heads of the quivering patients. The ceiling shivered, flaked, sagged, but held. With a bellowing of bricks and mortar, the hospital was collapsing, burying them alive. The noise was more terrifying. The lights went out. It was pitch dark. They lay, hardly daring to move, wondering what might, at any moment, come crashing down on them.

Toni remembers feeling numb and that somehow he had to go on breathing, despite the clammy, dusty air that filled the cellar. No one cried out in pain. No one so far was even touched. The cellar roof had held. But they were buried under the rubble of a four-storey hospital. All they could do now was wait. They had no food, no water, no light, no extra clothes, no shovels, nothing to help them make their way out.

Doctor Berta Weigan-Fellinger had only just got to bed when the warbling note of the siren sent its mournful cry over the city. 'That must be our regular visitor,' she had said to herself and she lay there for a while wondering whether or not to bother getting up this time. After all, there had not been much to worry about during the last five weeks. But just as she was considering curling up in the warm cocoon of blankets there was a tearing, ripping, whistling sound. She pressed her hands over her ears but the detonation deafened her. The windows rattled so much she felt they would fly in on top of her at any moment. She leapt to her feet and ran out of her room shouting: 'Ottfried! Herbert! Fritz-Ludwig! Maria-Elisabeth! Get up. Get down to the cellar. At once!'

Great flashes of light struck the window in rapid succession. She grabbed warm clothes and shouted as never before: 'Quick! Quick! To the cellar!' Clearly this was no ordinary raid.

'The sky throbbed with bombers. Explosions shook the houses and the earth with a terrifying crunch. The men were not so brave as the women. 'They were too excited,' recalls Dr Berta today.

Another tremendous explosion rocked the walls. Smoke and flames belched through the cellar hatchway and leapt right across the cellar from wall to wall.

'The gas pipes have burst,' shouted Lieutenant Sobeck. 'We're going to be roasted alive!'

Outside bombs were still crashing down all around the house; incendiaries were clattering on the tiles and into the streets. They could not get out, yet if they stayed where they were they would be suffocated or grilled to a cinder.

'Let me out! Let me out!' shouted the young army officer. 'I'd rather die on the battlefront than in this Hell of a cellar.'

But now the first force of the fractured gas pipes had subsided and the flames were confined to only one side of the cellar. It was still safer below ground than outside in the street, amongst flying bricks and blazing timber. Dr Berta and a neighbour grappled with young Sobeck, restraining him by sheer force from rushing out of the smoky cellar into the holocaust outside.

It was then that a new voice, small and high pitched, could be heard. 'We must pray, we must pray,' pleaded five-year-old

Ottfried, who had never liked saying his prayers before.

A bright orange glow from across the street shone through the cellar hatchway and threw everything into strong relief. From almost behind the house, it seemed, an 88mm was slamming away. More bombs fell nearby and there was a gigantic eruption which threw a basketful of flaming golden oranges in the sky. And further back still, in that early morning sky now, a balloon of fire enclosed in its own shroud of black smoke fell earthwards, leaving a comet-like trail of golden streaks behind.

There was no end to the stream of bombers. One after another they came – every six seconds for what seemed hours of non-stop Hell. As fire and devastation spread among the commercial and residential buildings in the city centre, one basement shelter after another became untenable. Hundreds of people had to be moved through a ring of fire to safer refuges. They walked quietly, without sign of panic, behind the rescue teams who fearlessly exposed themselves to risks like this throughout the night. As the bombs rained down, destroying communications, orderly action became increasingly difficult. Firefighters and civil defence workers had to improvise and did marvels to minimize the casualties. But not without cost. Their casualty figures were three times greater than those of other citizens of Cologne that night.

Fireman Walther Seidel cannot forget to this day the smell of burnt flesh and blazing hair as he ran into an old people's hostel where screaming old ladies with clothes and hair on fire were tottering about trying to find a way out. 'I took hold of them, pushing, shouting and heaving them towards the doorway whilst walls were crashing down in other rooms, and blasts of hot air tore out windowframes and doors. In the street incendiary bombs were spurting white flame and setting fire to the tar on the road. Mothers with children rushed blindly by the fire bombs. Some blazing wood fell by one little girl and set her dress alight. An old man flung himself on top of her, using his coat and hands to dowse the flames which had shot straight up to her hair. I somehow herded the old ladies towards a small green patch near a square – a cemetery – where they all flopped down on their faces. Quivering with fear.'

The Cologne civil defence services were most efficient, Dr Berta recalls today. 'No branch of these services was found wanting, and they coped in a way which exceeded all expectations. Everyone rose to the occasion. It brought out the best in people. Quickly they earned the heartfelt thanks, trust and respect of those they served.'

There were some incidents which perhaps seem funny today, though they were frightening then – like the time Theo Stratmann dropped his box.[2] Theo was a ten-year-old boy who slept in a wicker chair under a thick blanket upstairs. Whenever the air-raid alarm sounded, he would be carried downstairs to the sitting-room, and his father would then stand in the doorway of their house in Papgeienstrasse looking upwards at the sky as if to judge the intensity of the raid and deciding whether or not to go to the shelter ten minutes away at the Herz Jesu Church or to the concrete bunker in Berlinerstrasse fifteen minutes walk from the house. This standing in the doorway was a practice his wife deplored, but Theo's father, a tramdriver on the O for Opladen route, was not cured of the habit until a few weeks before the thousand-bomber raid when a bomb crashed into a house a block away and blew both Herr Stratmann and the door right into his own sitting-room. Thereafter it was a policy of straight into the shelter with no hanging about.

With that lesson in mind on the evening of 30 May, the Stratmann family made haste in heading for the cellar of the Herz Jesu Church. And, as usual, Theo had to have a toy or two to help pass the long night. This time he was hugging tightly to his chest a new Meccano construction kit. Already the anti-aircraft guns were crackling away in rapid fire, and the searchlights illuminated the moonlit streets so that it was almost like daylight. It was whilst Theo was gazing in wonder at the firework display above his head that he dropped his much-prized box, scattering the pieces all over the street. Despite all the urging of his mother and father and the swish of incendiaries falling nearby, he refused to go on to the shelter until he had recovered all the pieces of his kit. There was nothing his parents could do in the face of such an adamant attitude but to get down on their hands and knees to search for and pick up the missing pieces. They made a peculiar sight apparently praying in the middle of the street!

Once they were in the cellar of the Herz Jesu Church, the bombs seemed to creep closer and closer. The ground trembled and plaster flew off the walls.

Young Karl Schmidt hated cellars. He would never go in them during a raid for he feared being buried alive. Fortunately he and his young wife lived on the outskirts of Cologne in Aachenstrasse close to the wooded green belt beyond the military ring road.

When a raid looked like being a long and heavy one, he would run out of the built-up area into the woods. He remembered that night vividly:

'I grabbed Gabby's hand, our coats and emergency case, and ran as fast as I've ever run. Panting, sweating, and staggering, we reached the small track leading into the woods but something terrible had happened there. Clothing, pieces of luggage, bundles of rags littered the path. I stepped on one bundle. It was soft and shapeless and gave under my foot. It was part of a body. I fell over a shattered tree and then stopped. In the pale light of the moon and fires that filtered through the trees, I could see in a small clearing an awful sight. Ghastly. The place was strewn with bodies – glimmering where the strange light caught the whiteness of their skin. There were children lying higgledy-piggledy across each other, large corpses flung about in grotesque positions, some limbless, one near me had no head. My wife's hand slipped from mine as she slumped in a faint to the soft earth. I felt empty and sick. I too sank down with my back against a tree stump, cradling my wife. All those people with the same idea, thinking they were safe and now lying cold and wet amongst the rotting leaves.

'Above and around us was a terrible roaring and crashing – engines, guns, bright flashes and blasts that shook the ground. Bombs were dropping everywhere. I thought we too would soon be dead, as dead as those already lying there.

'We began to pray.'

One man certainly had his prayers answered that night. Klaus Furtwängler was running to shelter when a bomb fell so close to him that it lifted him right into the air. 'My head was jerked back so that it almost broke my neck. There was a noise that I just can't describe. A terrifying roar that came with a tremendous rush of air. I seemed to be on the ground and rolling along like a ball in a gale. I couldn't get air into my lungs. I was gasping, choking, until suddenly I felt the air going in again together with clouds of gritty dust.'

Hildegard Steinborn had a somewhat similar experience when she was going down to the cellar in her house in Lindenthal.[3]

'I can still clearly remember the feeling. I was about halfway down the cellar steps when I felt a ghostly hand which lifted me right into the air and deposited me heavily onto the middle of the cellar floor. It was the vacuum of the bomb which had landed right across the street from our house in Bachemerstrasse. We were all huddled tightly together, for the bombs were falling now on each side of our house and the guns were banging away as if they were outside. It was such a terrible noise that we soon lost all sense of time. It seemed to be going on for ever. Chalk flew off the cellar walls making us all look pale as death, and then suddenly there was the most terrifying noise right above us of cracking and bursting wood. We were sure the house had come down on top of us but it was the white varnished wall of wood that separated the staircase from the cellar. It had splintered into fragments and fallen down the cellar steps! With noises like that, your imagination makes everything terrible. Then the emergency lighting failed. It was worse still in the dark as we lay and crouched on the floor. It was fearful!'

Hildegard Steinborn, though, saw some people who seemed to have no fear at all.

'The nuns in Cologne hospital were absolutely fearless. They never stopped looking after the sick, the injured and the dying throughout the raid. Even in the most terrifying moments of the bombardment these nuns could be seen in their long, wide skirts, starched linen head-dress and traditional dark gown floating from one part of the hospital to another, strangely calm in their compassion, hovering around the badly wounded patients. It was unrealistic, unbelievable.

'Eventually the noise grew less and there were no more bombs and so we began to venture forth from the cellars and bunkers. Around us in the Lindenthal streets were sounds of timber burning amidst the rubble that once had been the beautiful houses of our neighbours. And yet there was with the people who stood in the streets at first an elation, a kind of wild joy – we had survived! But our elation was short lived. Once again came the ominous throb of approaching bombers. Back to the cellars we dashed. Just in time. This time Lindenthal itself seemed to be singled out for special attention by the attackers.

'Now, after we hurriedly dashed back into the cellar, we found ourselves bathed in sweat, but not just from our exertion but from fear. On top of all the other noise of exploding bombs and antiaircraft fire, we could now hear the crackling of fierce fires as neighbouring houses began to blaze.

'Even this extra ration of fear did not quench entirely the typical Cologne humour. It was a graveyard type of humour but nevertheless rallied our spirits.

'Towards morning troops came round with hand sirens to sound the "All Clear". We clambered out of our cellar and found our house still standing but without windows and with the frames blown inwards. Upstairs there were four incendiary bombs still flaring but we were in time to fling them out of the windows into the garden.'

Houses in the neighbouring streets were now burning fiercely. Bachemerstrasse had had several high explosive bombs and many incendiaries. People were beginning to gather in front of their homes, unable to grasp what had happened. They had lost everything. Many of them had taken refuge in the hundred-person bunker of the Winterbrauerei and were dazed, standing like cattle at a slaughterhouse, wondering which way to turn. A steady trickle of people now came from the centre of Cologne on foot with a few possessions on their backs in bags. ' "The whole of the city centre is a mass of ruins" they told us,' said Frau Steinborn, 'nothing but a mass of rubble.'

Indeed, it could well have been, for the view from the suburbs gave the impression that there was one huge smouldering fire with a macabre mushroom of smoke belching upwards.

It was into this holocaust that Hildegard's husband now drove with his film-company manager, who already that evening had narrowly escaped death when his truck received a 'near miss' from a high-explosive bomb. They had come to make a film record of the damage done to the ancient city. It was not until later that afternoon that Hildegard Steinborn saw her husband again. His face was white, covered in dust and haggard with stress. He slumped into a chair as soon as he entered the house. And he wept bitterly. He cried for all the human tragedy that he had so methodically put on the celluloid film.[4]

Certainly, this time, the RAF had left the people of Cologne is no doubt of the horrors to come. They had been left dazed and bewildered. But they were not broken in spirit.

The mood of Cologne's citizens was summed up that morning by Frau Steinborn in a way which exposed the fallacy in Harris's belief that he could win the war by sapping morale. She said, 'Never before that night had I known such terror but I know one thing now. I shall never be afraid again.'

Strange irony: morale had strengthened.

Everyone knew the meaning of fear now, civilian and serviceman.

Each individual felt it in different ways. Australian navigator Don Charlwood said at the time: 'I think we all – or nearly all – have this inordinate fear of death. I keep telling myself that this last step is probably like all other steps we have taken – hardest in the imagining. But over the target it doesn't work. I stand petrified waiting for disintegration.' Fighter pilots and bomber crews on all sides had to learn how to cope with this fear. They knew it well. They lived with it. They fought with it.

Gunther Hartmann, an experienced German night fighter pilot of II/NJGI based at St Trond, was no exception. On this particular evening he was orbiting Geilenkirchen and Eindhoven, about fifty miles to the east and north of Cologne – well away from the so-called 'magic fireworks' of the Luftwaffe's anti-aircraft units ringing the city. He was waiting and watching for the returning bombers.

At 0131 hours he called on his radio to base: 'I am in contact with enemy raider and attacking.'

Against the distant glow of Cologne he could see the dark shape of a four-engined bomber approaching slowly, steadily and alone. Well above, in his Me110, he adjusted his oxygen mask, a nervous habit of his, and began to position himself, circling, losing height until he was about 440 yards behind and above the bomber. It seemed to be flying awkwardly.

So far the bomber appeared unaware of the fighter. Perhaps, thought Hartmann, they were pulling out cigarettes and lighting up as the German Intelligence said RAF crews were known to do after the target had been left well behind. It continued jerkily on its course, the perspex glinting in the moonlight.

Hartmann made up his mind. He put the fighter into a steep dive and came hurtling in for the kill. His airframe shuddered as his guns opened up at little more than 55 yards from the bomber. It was a perfect surprise. Cannon shells punched great holes in the centre of the bomber's fuselage. For a brief moment the rear gunner returned the fire, and then the turret disintegrated under salvoes from the cannon. The flames from the fighter's guns flashed a luminous purple in the pale moonlight, and their reflections cast a strange light on the perspex of his windscreen.

Hartmann pulled out sharply into a steep turn, trying to absorb some speed in doing so. For a moment or two nothing seemed to happen. There was no further response from the bomber's gun turrets. It flew on. Then, suddenly, the port engine burst into flames. It burnt fiercely, lighting up the rest of the aircraft, illuminating its RAF roundels and identification letter clearly in the night sky.

Beneath the bomber there was now a low bank of cumulus. Emboldened by the lack of answering fire, Hartmann came up behind the bomber to within twenty-seven yards, firing his cannon as he came. An explosion spewed flame from somewhere in the bomber's inner-port engine nacelle. Suddenly, yet quite slowly, the huge aircraft started to roll onto its wingtip, like a schoolboy's paper aeroplane in a lazy graceful glide enacted in a strangely protracted motion. Flames and more flames broke out from the length of the fuselage, turning the cloudbank below a bright orange colour, as if someone had opened a gigantic furnace door, giving the scene a bizarre kind of beauty.

It was at that moment, as Hartmann gazed in wonder at what was happening, that there was a gargantuan explosion. The whole black dome of the sky burst into a photoflash of brilliance, and the heavens reverberated about it. In seconds the big bomber dissolved into a white-hot cloud of fire, turning night into day.

For a few moment Hartmann was entranced, unable to react as he flew through an eruption of incandescent metal which screamed past the fuselage. Trails of white smoke spiralled behind the debris, and then nothing more could be seen except for a fading orange light coming from the middle of the cloud below. The horror of what had just happened made a deep impression on Hartmann. War was assuming some hideous aspects. He flew on, hands shaking, knees trembling, a feeling of revulsion floating around his empty insides. He turned, Zombie-like, to base and ten minutes later taxied in to file his combat report.

Since he was credited with another combat victory, his mechanics were delighted, but young Hartmann, entering the ninth to his score in the logbook, did not feel the same sort of elation. He could not help thinking about those other young men who had just perished – and others like them still to come, men who shared in common with himself the great adventure of flying, separated now only by the barrier of war. They too thought it only happened to others. Now ... When would his turn come?

For want of something to occupy his mind whilst the fighter was being refuelled and re-armed, he walked across to the dining-room and ordered a 'farmhouse breakfast' of scrambled egg with bits of chopped bacon mixed in liberally. But when it came, the food seemed quite tasteless. And for the first time in his Air Force career he was uneasy about taking off again. There was a peculiar sinking feeling in his gut. Was it fear? He pondered the question, chewing on a tough piece of bacon. No! He was not nervous. No shakes. No tics. But there was something, a kind of disinclination and indifference. A questioning.

From the operation room came the order. The aircraft was ready. Take off immediately. Orders would follow.

Slowly, his mind elsewhere, he pulled on his fur boots, flying-suit and lifejacket, stuffed a thick first-aid pack into the capacious knee pocket and walked across to the aircraft.

The chief engineer reported the fighter checked and serviceable. He helped to fasten Hartmann's safety harness. Then he passed him the ground telephone extension. Final instructions were given: 'Follow course three-six-zero.'

At 02.20 hours Lieutenant Gunther Hartmann was climbing rapidly to 1,500 feet. It was cold. Breath froze on his oxygen mask in front of his mouth and nose. Frequently he slapped his hands, first one, then the other, onto his thighs to keep the circulation moving and some semblance of feeling in his hands.

Now the fighters were gathering again to pick off the bombers split from the main stream on the return flight.

For the bomber crews it was always worse to be attacked at this stage of the operation. They were not keyed up to it in the same way as on the outward journey. They had bombed the target, done the job. Now all they wanted was to get home. Attacks were all the more unexpected, and the responses were those of tired men.

Harry Langton and his crew were certainly cold and tired. But Harry had learnt from the lessons of the last three years that, though his head drummed for sleep, this was no time for relaxing. By a variety of ways he kept himself as alert as possible without having to resort to the 'wakey-wakey' pills. Somewhere along the route home he knew the crunch would come, and he was not going to be caught off balance.

Sure enough, it came. With a tremendous crack to the left of the port engine, the Wellington skewed violently and took a downward, sideways slip. Down 600 feet it plunged before Langton regained control. He looked out anxiously and saw the port engine on fire. As he watched, it shuddered to a dead stop. The aircraft lurched again. Harry Langton righted it. Now, flying on one engine, could the crippled aircraft be nursed back to base? To Honington – no. But to Manston? Maybe.

Over the intercom came confused cries after the anti-aircraft shells had stopped battering them. No one was seriously hurt but young Ken Pexman was having a real baptism of fire on his first trip as rear gunner of a bomber.

Now they were losing height. Rapidly. They would never make Manston or anywhere near.

Langton peered down at the Dutch countryside, grey and misty in the pale of dawn. Was there anywhere he could land? There. Ahead was a field dotted with pools and coarse grass. They were dropping very fast now. The Wellington no longer responded to the controls. Trees loomed, branches tore at the fabric fuselage, grasped it firmly and yanked the whole aircraft to a sudden stop.

Langton shot head first like a bullet through the open hatch. Bomb-aimer 'Tiny' Welsh fell from the aircraft as it broke open. Two other crew members somehow slithered through a gap in the fractured fuselage to land almost unhurt on the soft, wet marshland, where they lay momentarily stunned, unable to believe they had escaped. Slowly they gathered themselves and gazed around, hoping to see something of Langton and Pexman. Langton was nowhere to be seen. Welsh walked round to the tail end of the turret. There he found Ken Pexman, half in and half out of the turret. Dead. Or so it seemed at the time.

German troops arrived before they had time to find out more.

They found Langton lying with serious head wounds. He was taken to a German military hospital. Two or three days later, when he was conscious enough to ask questions, he learnt from the medical officer about Pexman. He had just died. 'We brought him into the hospital here with you three days ago. He never regained consciousness.'

It would have been his twenty-second birthday.

Not far from the spot where Langton crashed was another aircraft in difficulties – Leslie Manser's Manchester.

After one of the Vulture engines had caught fire and stopped, Manser managed to regain some height. But now the one remaining engine was faltering badly. Manser knew they would never make it back to the nearest RAF base, Manston, but he did think they might be able to cross the coast and ditch in the sea, there to be picked up by an RAF Air/Sea Rescue launch.

In an effort to maintain the height needed for this plan, the second pilot, Baveystock, was pushing everything he could lay hold of down the flare-chute to lighten the load – guns, oxygen bottles, anything and everything. But to little avail. They were still losing height. Rapidly.

'Prepare to abandon aircraft,' called Manser. Without further warning the aircraft fell, frighteningly.

What happened next is difficult to tell for everything happened so swiftly. Three sergeants jumped first; the remaining two officers tried to get Manser to leave the controls and jump with them; Manser refused. At the last moment the officers jumped. Manser had known that to leave go of the controls for a fraction of a second would mean the aircraft rolling into an earthward plunge, making it impossible for anyone to reach the escape hatch.

Now, on his own, Manser tried to land the bomber in a ploughed field. For a moment it looked as though he had made it but then the nose went down into the soft earth, and the aircraft exploded into flames. Even then he was not to be beaten. He struggled through the wreckage, his flying-suit ablaze. A farmer, who had run out of his house on hearing the roaring engine, pulled him free. He dragged him to a tree, dowsed the flames and propped him up against the trunk. The fire had brought German troops running to the scene searching for survivors but two of the crew were crouched in a hayloft, another hid amongst the bushes. Manser was easily seen in the light from the burning aircraft but even before the troops got near he was beyond their reach, dead.

In giving his crew the best possible chance of escape, Flying Officer Manser had sacrificed his own life.[5] Through his gallantry four men lived. All next day they lay hidden, and then, after dark, wireless-operator Norman Horsley knocked on the door of the Dutch farmhouse. The farmer was helpful; risking his life, he put them in touch with the 'Comet' escape line. Thus, through the fearless ingenuity of a beautiful and tough twenty-five-year-old Belgian girl, Andrée de Jongh, three of these men escaped through France and via the Pyrenees to Gibraltar, flying back from there to Britain.

A few weeks before the Cologne raid, Andrée, with three of her friends, had called at the British Consulate office in Bilbao, northern Spain, and explained that they had set up a chain of 'safe' houses between Brussels and the western Pyrenees which would form the basis of an escape route for shot-down airmen. Fortunately the

British Consul there had faith in her. He provided financial assistance, and soon valuable RAF aircrew were being returned to Britain and operational duty within a matter of weeks. The promptest despatch was of all seven of an RAF bomber shot down near the Dutch-Belgian border, returned in one week.

So, some weeks after crashing in Holland that Sunday morning of 31 May, Manser's crew were back in Britain telling the Air Ministry the full story of their part in Operation Millennium and of their pilot's valour. Six months later Buckingham Palace announced that the King had awarded his highest decoration, the Victoria Cross, posthumously to the brave young man who had wanted to join the Army but had been rejected, tried to join the Royal Navy and been rejected and finally been accepted by the RAF; Leslie Thomas Manser.

Bravery of a different kind was being displayed by another pilot, Rusty Hudson, who had been going out night after night, sortie after sortie, without complaint, and going to great lengths to conceal his true state of mind from his crew, his squadron commander and his medical officer. He was an intelligent man who had quickly seen that the odds against survival were slim and that each trip brought him closer to death.

But now, on this return trip, his spirit was bolstered by sheer determination to get back. This one time, and then ... And then ...? He pushed all thoughts of the future out of his mind. Get back first. Concentrate. Desynchronize. Weave and evade. Keep alert.

A new strength was flooding through him with the decision he knew he had now made. He knew, without having put it into words, what he was going to do if he got back. Correction, he told himself, emphasizing the word, *when* I get back.

A shellburst rocked the bomber. He remembered the words of his flying instructor: 'If you can see the black puffs of heavy flak exploding, they're pretty near. If you can smell the cordite, sickly and acrid, you can bet the burst has hit the aircraft. If she shudders and you see the flames just before you see and smell the puffs, the next bursts are highly likely to be mortal.' He began to corkscrew, knowing that softly and silently already four or five high-explosive shells were climbing up the night sky towards him.

He switched on the intercom. Another point he remembered now about a skipper's job: 'Your life depends on the skill of other people. Crews that don't work well together have "CHOP" written in capital letters all over them. You've got to be on your toes the whole time. Particularly the rear gunner.'

He checked the crew, one by one. With the rear gunner, Geoff Thomas, a cheery Welshman, he spent more time. He knew from what Geoff had said on other occasions that often he got a feeling of complete detachment, seeing nothing at all of his own aircraft unless he turned sideways in his turret. Rusty had tried sitting there and did not like that feeling of being suspended in space, in itself a bit terrifying. After this he always made a point of trying to bring Geoff Thomas mentally back into the crew through the intercom. Feeling remote and alone, a tail gunner could become pre-occupied with his own solitary thoughts and forget to keep a sharp look-out. On this trip everyone was going to keep their eyes skinned.

Now they were flying high above a bank of cloud lit from below by searchlights which gave it a kind of opaque glow. Rusty deliberately dropped to just above it so that he could quickly take cover if attacked by a fighter. He was flying like a master now. Never had he felt quite so confident.

'A "Brocks benefit" ahead, Skipper,'* The wireless operator had seen it too. A flak barrage. 'Look at it. Roman candles and Catherine wheels.'

Strange, it was on this particular flight that Hudson kept bringing back the words of his flying instructor, almost as if he was making super-human efforts to be infallible. 'Don't worry too much about flak if it does hit the Halifax before you can get away. They're marvellously built. Can stand a lot of punishment and still come up – or stay up – for more.' But Hudson was taking no chances at all. Not tonight. He turned to make a gentle right-hand circuit to avoid the 'fireworks' altogether. Now he was feeling chilled and wanted to ease the cramp in his legs.

Then everything happened at once. A terrific barrage came up. In rapid succession, three flak bursts right under the tail each time.

'For Christ's sake, weave!' shouted Geoff Thomas.

A vicious crack hit the starboard side; shrapnel ripped through the fuselage, cutting into cables and equipment. There was a rush of air. A great gap had been torn in the fuselage.

'You're losing the starboard outer,' called the flight engineer. The propeller came to a stop and stood silhouetted against the hazy

---

* Brocks – firework manufacturers of Huddersfield.

glow of the cloud screen. They must have been hit in the tail unit also, thought Hudson, for he now had difficulty with the controls. Somehow he managed to turn further east away from the worst of the flak, and for a brief moment they had time to take stock: one engine gone, one turret out of action, radar gear smashed, tail unit damaged – and what else?

Losing height rapidly, they reached the Dutch border at about 7,000 feet. At 5,000 things looked very black. The altimeter crept lower and lower, but when, with sinking heart, Hudson was just about to give the order to abandon aircraft, he became aware that the wavering needle showed a slower rate of descent. At 2,000 feet it held. Steady. They stood a chance after all.

In utter silence now and fingers crossed, the crew counted the minutes. Below them now glided the silvery North Sea. Would the Halifax live up to its reputation? Would the pilot's nerve hold? Or would they have to face the ice-cold water thirty miles off the Dutch coast?

The wireless operator now began sending a message, reporting their plight to base and to the emergency landing airfield at Manston. Tensely they waited, willing the Halifax to stay up, hoping for that extra bit of luck that would make all the difference between survival and death. The big bomber pounded on.

First came the coast. They got fastened down. A marker beacon flashed. Then came the lights of Manston. Hudson and his flight engineer went through the landing routine. 'Flaps.' The airspeed indicator dropped to 150 mph. The engines whined. The undercarriage still would not come down. Must be badly damaged. 'Belly landing,' growled Rusty. Then the engines began to cough and splutter. One cut out altogether. Another followed suit. The battered nose of the Halifax now pointed at the ground. The tail would not come down! The aircraft hit the runway with a screeching, rending noise. There was a dreadful racket of tearing metal, a banging and crashing. Wings were torn, petrol tanks ruptured, spewing petrol on the hot engines. Then there was a flash and the whole bundle of metal burst into flames.

The fire tender raced up, with the 'blood wagon' in close attendance. Miraculously, Rusty Hudson came staggering towards it. He had been catapulted out and almost scalped by the canopy. Across his forehead was an ugly gash where the white bone showed through. And then the rest of the remaining crew gathered. They were all carted off to sick quarters and kept in overnight. They lay, recovering, in adjacent beds. Later, Geoff Thomas was reading in the *Daily Mirror*, about 'Jane's' exploits and glanced at his horoscope.

'Hey! Listen to this, lads! "Scorpio: a very busy week on the work scene. Careful not to take on too much and make a point of relaxing at the week-end. Travel aspects not good. Avoid making long journeys." '

'You can say that again, boyo,' said fellow Welshman John Smith.

Rusty Hudson, though, said nothing. He had already decided against any further travel.

The last of the heavies were now well on their way home. And with a mass fleet returning, every airfield controller in east and southern England faced a formidable problem. Confusion could quickly bring disasters.

Fortunately the sky was still fairly clear of cloud, but not all aircraft could get back to their own bases. Damage, fuel shortage, and navigational errors caused pilots to seek permission to land at the nearest airfield sighted. Controllers with anxious crews flying round their flare-paths like moths round a lamp had to decide upon priority, giving it to those in most trouble.

Ennis, with his crippled Halifax from the north Yorkshire base at Leeming knew he would never make it. And, furthermore, he had a badly wounded gunner aboard. How much blood had he lost, or was still losing?

They had been in the air for nearly six hours now. Perishingly cold. The cold drew the warmth out of their very bones, numbed the extremities – fingers and toes. Fred Simpson sat with his head pulled down into his shoulders, trying to ease the tension in his neck muscles, peering into the darkness ahead. Once or twice his namesake, Flying Officer Simpson, the wireless-operator, came up to stand beside him. They did not speak, but each sensed the other's unease. With the outer-port motor stopped and still the possibility of fighters ...

They stared ahead, waiting for the sight of that lovely Manston beacon. They all saw it together. No mistake. The marker beacon of the English coast.

Other planes were in the circuit, flying now on navigation lights. Ennis switched on his, a safeguard against collision. The radio channel was open. Great though Ennis's anxiety was because of the wounded Groves, and intense as the strain had been in coaxing the damaged Halifax back, he did not immediately seek priority.

Then came the controller's calm voice: 'Is anybody in trouble?'

Ennis broke in: 'G George here. I've a badly wounded man aboard.'

'Come in then, G George,' the controller answered. 'Ambulance and doctors standing by.'

Carefully Ennis turned into a long, low approach. Pitch fully fine, nose as high as he dared. He touched the ground, the nose dipped dangerously. Brake off, brake on-off a little more. Concrete rasped under the wheels. The big aircraft slowed gradually. Fred Simpson felt the pressure of the brakes ease and unbuckled his straps. He was in, back from Cologne. Back from his first big operation.

The Halifax turned from the runway, following the red light of a guiding vehicle to a point where the ambulance was waiting. Steps were run up under the door, and the medical officer went straight up followed by the stretcher-bearers. Quickly the MO felt for Groves' pulse.

'Get him away quickly. He's lost a lot of blood. Every minute will count.' Gently Groves was lifted out and the ambulance sped away.

Ennis and his crew got a lift back to debriefing. A very young intelligence officer was there with his pad. But it was Ennis who spoke first. 'Make it short, old chap, will you? These lads are hungry, and they're still a long way from home.'

'Right,' said the young man, smoothing his papers. 'Anything special to report?'

'Nothing special. We've had a bit of trouble. The old Halifax got bent a bit. Rear gunner gone to hospital. Otherwise ...'

The long night of vigil at the fifty-three Bomber Command airfields was now coming to an end. The darkest hour before dawn blackness was giving way to the first light. No moon now. No stars.

At RAF Waddington, the fitters of both A and B watches had been waiting, crowded into the smoke-laden air of the dispersal huts. Sitting it out, drinking hot cocoa, making toast by pressing bread against the sides of the hot stove, eating it with great hunks of 'bungy' Cheddar cheese.

Amongst them was Norman Worthington.[6] Too many cigarettes, the stuffy air and lack of sleep had left him with a dull headache. He remembers it all so well.

'We sat there, dozing in damp greatcoats, talking about nights in the village's Horse & Jockey until out of the mush and atmospherics of the radio a WAAF's voice came: "OK Q Queenie. You may land," and "Hello F for Freddie, you are diverted." Knowing looks were exchanged. Someone in trouble needing plenty of runway. "Ok R Robert, you are clear to land. You may pancake."

'Bang on! That's mine. Come on, Jock, I say to the air frame fitter. We're on. Out we got into unfriendly night, cold and blustery (temporarily blind until our eyes get used to the dark). Now the aircraft are stacked up, waiting their turn to land. We stand expectantly on the approach between the airfield and the hardstanding, a torch in either hand. Here he comes. This one looks like R Robert by the way he's heading. Roaring engines, landing lights on, looking like a huge porpoise emerging from a circus pool. Touch signals. Rev the outer port. OK, come on, come on, round from port a bit more. Come on. OK, that's fine. Crossed torches. Switch off.

'The four engines splutter and with a spasmodic "kick back" the airscrews finally stop. Suddenly everything seems ultra quiet. Chocks under the wheels, then a torchlight inspection of the under surface for the bright, jagged holes of shrapnel damage, the sound and smell of dripping petrol, the stomach-turning sight of a "hung up" bomb. God! Half the rudder's hanging off.'

'Now, standing in a group on the tarmac, the stubble-chinned crew, silent, cigarettes already lit, wait for transport to take them for debriefing. The usual banter begins eventually: "Hey," calls the pilot, "anyone want a spam sandwich?" He fishes in the depths of the green canvas bag aircrew carry. "Here, I was bloody sure Jerry was going to get them tonight.'

'A truck arrives. They scramble over the tailboard and off they go for debriefing. We go up the metal ladder into the warm interior of the fuselage, like a long green tunnel, the reek of sweaty bodies and new plastic and the peculiar smell of warm radio equipment. The creaking and cracking sounds of the fuselage contracting, the fluorescent faces of the instrument panel dials shining, watching you in the darkness. The "gone away" feeling like a railway station after the last train has left. It's OK tonight. Nothing else. No greasy blood to be wiped off the floor and walls.

'We finish our jobs and walk back at daybreak. A solitary bird begins to chirrup, and the others join in as the eastern sky filters in the light of the morning sun.'

By dawn, in the operations rooms at RAF Croft, the progress of the raid had been closely monitored and recorded in silence. Time passed in the dry whir of the extractor fan on the wall and in the far-off bark of a dog uneasy in its room, alone. There was no chatter; shaded lights played onto large boards. Smartly dressed, tight-shirted airwomen, with hair drawn back into Grecian pleats or rolled neatly off the collar in regulation length, had chalked numbers of the aircraft that had taken off onto the board and their expected time of return. Now they would soon know.

A tired-eyed WAAF corporal brought in a mug of tea, deep brown in colour, to the duty operations officer. 'That's real sergeant major's tea, as my father used to call it, sir. You can stand your spoon up in it.'

More people were now drifting into the control room, yet it was still quiet, everyone inert. A middle-aged officer with a lined face sat with a headset in front of a large wooden-framed speaker. Suddenly the peace of the room was pierced by a voice which came patchily out of the heavens. The listener responded in flat, calm tones which belied his inner feelings. He nodded to a watchful airwoman crossing the room. He then gave one word of command: 'Land.'

Outside now, men and women sprang from nowhere and began to peer into the dawn. A cry was heard. And there at the end of the airfield came the wings of a roaring great bird, gliding down like some magnificent eagle coming home to roost; it came in a long, graceful slant to the concrete eyrie, then moved away to its own nest in a clearing of the bushes just off the circuit.

Irregularly now they came back, singly, each landing in its own distinctive way. The count was taken. One still out.

The maintenance crews were now clambering into the bombers, some were being briefed by taut-faced skippers on faults that had developed during the trip. They had to be rectified right away. Tomorrow there could be another operation.

A different body of men now made their way across the tarmac from those who had moved excitedly out for the raid earlier last night. Tension was released, their postures slumped, they were physically tired and mentally exhausted. But no bed for them yet.

Jim Davidson filed into the operations block behind his pilot, Harry Woodly, and with the rest of the crew tailing after him. There a smartly dressed intelligence officer interrogated them. Carefully he listened to their story of the raid. He interrupted with questions. Had they seen a Halifax go down in flames? Were any parachutes seen? What was the enemy interference like? Sometimes one of the crew would add an extra piece of information, but generally they left the answers for the skipper, Harry Woodly, to voice. Most of the time they sat sprawling on the hard wooden chairs round the table, sipping a mug of tea laced with rum. Some drank cocoa. In the warm room they had stripped off their heavy flying-clothing. Gradually the sheet of paper in front of the debriefing officer was covered with notes.

At last, after a final question or two, they were released and went off for breakfast of bacon and eggs or sausage and mash. They were ready for it. One by one they finished their meal and drifted off to their quarters, some to sleep and some to their usual nightmare.

'Operation Millennium' was now a one-line entry in their logbooks. Later that day it would be a two-column entry in the daily newspaper, and the day after that it would be buried under the news of the latest setback in the Battle of the Atlantic. But for the citizens of Cologne ...

8. Aftermath

'So shaken as we are ...'
Shakespeare, *Henry IV*, Part 1

Now there was silence. A moment before, the last powerful crump of high-explosive bombs had been followed by a sharp and clear bark of an 88mm gun hurling its final defiance. Faintly, in the distance, the deep rumble of engines which had been the background to the barrage for the last ninety minutes faded into nothingness. All noise died away, leaving in its wake an uncanny quiet.

Gradually upon this calm came the crunch and crackle of feet treading a carpet of broken glass as the dazed population of Cologne emerged from shelters and cellars to gaze with horror on a scene of desolation. Their faces wore the dead mask of awe and indecision as they looked about, wondering what to do, where to go, and hoping that someone would tell them. After a few minutes though, people began to move purposefully. They set off to find their homes, stepping over tangled fire hoses, walking across streets strewn with all kinds of debris and dead. All over the city scores of thousands were rubbing their smoky eyes, picking their way among the stony rubbish of the streets and rising to the occasion with an impressive steadiness of nerve.

Frau Zarges scrambled unsteadily to her feet and began to move slowly and reluctantly as though coming out of a dream. Only one man seemed to be missing from their small shelter, the neighbour who had gone out quite early in the raid to see if his house was all right.

'We all walked out right over him, without seeing him! We found our way out onto the street. I turned and looked at our shattered home. The front had been taken clean away from the centre of the building. The roof had gone, leaving only a few strips of wooden rafters, and about the shell were heaps of bricks and mortar, beams, doors, railings. Yet the strange thing was that, although there was not a sign of any glass in the house windows for as far as the eye could see, the glass in the street lamps was still intact.'

Scenes of desolation were being surveyed by families all over Cologne. From all the wide variety of emotions and experiences now remembered, two things stand out as being universally true: everyone was dirty, and everyone was kind.

'Never before had the citizens of Cologne shown such spontaneous and heartfelt friendliness. The formal reserve between neighbours, between the distressed and their helpers, between strangers, broke down completely – every hospitality and generous impulse was given free expression without shyness and accepted without embarrassment. And the interesting thing about it all was that, through the common denominator of suffering, a curious mutual compassion began to develop between the young British lads in the bombers – some we had seen shot down – and the bombed-out civilians,' recalls Frau Steinborn.

Tracing the casualties became the priority now. Many people were trapped between walls and floors of the upstairs rooms which had collapsed into the cellars. Doctors administered morphia to those in agony beneath blocks of masonry. Finding missing members of families was a never-ending anxiety. How many were in the cellar? Where was the caretaker? How many human beings were lying under that formidable heap of brick and timber? Fires too were still creeping forward onto these piles of debris. How many people, still conscious, were being roasted alive? These were grim and testing questions to be answered in that dawn.

Searches went on for hours until the relatives and neighbours were assured past all reasonable doubt that every stone had been turned in the hunt for a loved one. There in Cologne a new craft was born, the technique of burrowing for bodies among the ruins of homes. Some houses collapsed into complete disintegration, forming a solid pile of rubble, whilst others collapsed on one side first so that walls and floors at one side held firm as the others swung downwards, forming a V beneath which people managed to survive. Ingenious ways were used to prop up debris as it was moved to make a tunnel through which a rescue man could wriggle towards the inside of a wrecked house. Teams worked with the delicate touch of a surgeon and bomb-disposal expert, easing a brick here, a piece of timber there, out of the way, without disturbing by a hair's breadth another block of timber which might bring tons of rubble down upon him.

There were terrible hazards to be faced by these rescue workers apart from the obvious one of being buried alive. In basements there was often the threat of boiling water gushing from central heating systems, or a torrent of water drowning them from broken mains. Gas leaked from fractured pipes and made enclosed space an immediately fatal trap. Ever present too was the risk of an explosion as sparks ignited this concentration of household gas.

They were a dedicated breed. For hour after hour they worked that day. Every now and again, as they struggled forward, the leader would call for silence and they would strain their ears for voices, a muffled cry, even the noise of breathing.

So it was at the hospital where Toni Stellmaszyk lay buried for two days. For them all, time had passed slowly. Breathing was difficult. Gradually, though, in the middle of the second day, Toni and his twenty-nine fellow imprisoned patients became aware that somewhere in that black emptiness above there were living people working to get them out. And slowly hope began to stir in the breasts of those who had given themselves up for lost. At last the rescuers came to the cellar and signs of life.

'You push and pull, heave and strain for hours. You lose all sense of time. It seems endless. From time to time you are aware of figures around you, a soldier swearing savagely in a quiet monotone, a builder working doggedly, his face pouring sweat, and then at last you're through and, as when a prospector sees the first glint of gold, the pace quickens. Figures are eased out, a child is passed back carefully, reverently. And then you have a gap big enough to get everyone else out.'

And so it went on throughout that day and into the next. It was evident that the citizens of Cologne had learned the art of survival from their previous 106 raids, for the organization worked remarkably smoothly. And on Monday morning everyone took pride in turning up for work, through neither buses nor trams were running. Though often it meant walking miles, the shopgirls, warehousemen, accountants, secretaries, teachers, waitresses and the rest somehow got to work. Losing their homes did not deter them. Even family bereavement often did not. In fact, many took refuge in the routine, for it helped them face their loss more easily.

They needed the support of something fixed and enduring, the comradeship of their fellow workers, and in the re-establishment of their normal daily tasks they found that stability and gripped it hard.

Like the Londoners who had suffered similar catastrophes two years earlier the civilian population of Cologne found no more need for hate and recrimination against the enemy than did the ordinary soldier in the field. Outbursts of hate against the distant enemy were said to be rare. People got on with their jobs, white-faced and heavy eyed but not dispirited.

'It helped to know that the relief organization was efficient,' said Dr Berta Weigand-Fellinger. 'We also, being Catholics of Cologne-Deutz, went together to the chapel of our hospital (our church had been destroyed) and sang our special hymns. And now today I cannot hear their words without tears coming into my eyes.'

Some people discovered means of finding solace other than going to church. They drank coffee and told stories about their remarkable escapes. Such vivid accounts were legion.

A man blown up by the blast from a bomb said, 'I went up like a ballet dancer. Then somebody turned the wind off and I came down like a brick.'

A woman telephonist off duty had a father who died from a heart attack by her side in the kitchen of her house. Being unable to help him any more, she then volunteered for duty. When the telephones were cut, she helped to man a fire pump. When she returned home, her house had been burnt out and her father's corpse with it.

One fireman told how, when men got wet through, they would go up the ladder near the fire, where the heat was greatest, and in two or three minutes be dry again.

Theo Stratmann remembers returning home from the shelter to find the windows all blown out and the pea soup from the previous evening's meal all over the wallpaper. He could still laugh: 'Our main thought that day was — "We have survived". Tired-eyed parents carrying children in their arms could still make jokes.'

So much for Lord Cherwell's and Churchill's belief that people prized their possessions more than their relatives and friends, that 'dehousing' would demoralize them!

No doubt, talking about their experiences helped. Everyone did it. And it got the shock out of their systems. They were, that day, unsubdued. There was a new neighbourhood spirit that grew that morning. People refused to let the bombers drive them away from their homes. As Frau Steinborn was to say forty years later:

'Somehow each one of us developed a new resolution. We had survived the most frightening experience of our lives and felt we could never fear anything worse. A new strength developed from this feeling. But we were wrong. There was worse to follow. Much worse in the horrendous bombing of October 1944 when corpses littered the streets and thousands more were made homeless in one night. But on that first morning after the raid we were determined not to be beaten from our homes.'

The damage was enormous. More than 13,000 'residential units' were completely destroyed, making 45,132 people homeless; 1,500 commercial and industrial buildings were obliterated and 630 badly damaged. There was extensive damage to gas, electricity, water and telephone systems. The death toll, though, was surprisingly light for the size of the raid. American reports put it as high as 20,000 but in fact it was 469, with 5,027 injured.

In spite of all this morale was remarkably firm. However, as a safeguard against panic, everyone leaving the city to stay with friends or relatives in other parts of the country had to sign a declaration saying: 'I am aware that one individual alone can form no comprehensive idea of the events in Cologne. One usually exaggerates one's own experiences, and the judgement of those who have been bombed is impaired. I am therefore aware that reports of individual suffering can only do harm, and I will keep silence. I know what the consequences of breaking this undertaking will be.'

The consequence was death. All letters going out from Cologne were held up for two weeks, and even after that they were censored. Himmler was taking no chances on morale.

But, looking back, eye-witnesses today say that Cologne citizens were not in a mood of despair. And, if it was true of an army, as Napoleon is reported to have said, that it marches on its belly, it was certainly true of Cologne. No one went hungry. Immediately after the raid volunteer mobile canteens were soon set up in the worst areas, where improvised hot meals were served to the shocked and homeless. Though gas and electricity were not immediately available, military-type kitchens were set up in the rubble-strewn streets.

As the city smouldered that Sunday morning beneath a canopy

of smoke which rose to 16,000 feet, Willy Niessen heard once again that dreaded sound of the air-raid alarm. Before going down into the shelter he saw, way up in the sky, the vapour trails of three silver aircraft. Mosquitos. The flak shells were bursting ineffectually beneath them. A few bombs dropped. The aircraft circled and left.

What was happening? A minute after the first dots had appeared, the sky above Cologne was filled with them, evenly distributed and fluttering down, in rhythmic swinging movements from side to side. Leaflets! To pick up leaflets and read them was forbidden by law but fifteen-year-old Willy Niessen picked one up and kept it. The message was: '*Die Offensive der* Royal Air Force *in ihrer neuen Form hat begonnen!*' 'The RAF's offensive in its new form has begun!'

The following day at Hitler's 'Situation Conference', Luftwaffe Chief Herman Goering tried to minimize the effect of the raid. He was not present himself but had General Jeschonnek read out the official Luftwaffe report. His hand were shaking as he stood up to read the 'sitrep' paper.

'According to preliminary reports,' said the general, 'We estimate that 200 enemy aircraft have penetrated our defences. The damage is heavy ... we are still waiting for final estimates.'

It was at this point that Hitler exploded. He ranted and he raved. He pounded the table with his fist and poured scorn on the evasive report. 'You are still waiting for final estimates?' he cried. 'And the Luftwaffe thinks there were only 200 aircraft? The Luftwaffe has probably been asleep last night ... but I have not been asleep. I stay awake when one of my cities is under fire. And I thank the Almighty that I can rely on my Gauleiter, even if the Luftwaffe deceives me. Let me tell you what Gauleiter Grobe has to say. Listen, listen, I ask you to listen carefully. There were a thousand or more English aircraft ... do you hear? A thousand, twelve hundred ... maybe more!'[1]

Later, when Goering arrived at the meeting, stretching out his hand to Hitler in greeting, Hitler ignored him. Deliberately, rudely and pointedly, in front of junior officers, he put the fat *Reichsmarschall* firmly in his place. A stammering, bewildered Goering, swaying between panic and protestation that he had wanted to increase the fighter defences, was left like someone lost. Hitler would not listen. He said again and again that he was not interested in defence. He wanted revenge. His only reply to

Cologne was to send out an inadequate bomber force against the ancient British cathedral city of Canterbury the following night. (As an attempt to boost German morale, it was a complete failure. Only ninety bombers reached the target. But they did score direct hits on the cathedral.)

The reaction of German Propaganda Minister Goebbels was a little more perceptive than Hitler's.[2] 'This raid', he told his cohorts at the morning's ministerial conference, 'is a showpiece for the benefit of the Russians. A British visiting card for the benefit of Molotov when Churchill is negotiating with the Russians over the future conduct of the war.' The best way to deal with this situation, he believed, was to tell the public clearly and accurately just how many aircraft took part and the extent of the damage inflicted. Consequently the next day a communiqué came from the Führer's headquarters that was remarkable for its accuracy and objective tone. It read:

'British bombers carried out a terror raid on the inner city of Cologne. Great damage was done as a result of the severity of the attack with high-explosive and incendiary bombs which caused large fires. Particularly badly damaged were the residential districts, public buildings, among them being three churches and two hospitals. In this attack, which was directed specifically against the civil population, the British Air Force suffered severe losses. Night fighters and flak shot down thirty-six of the attacking bombers and another one in the coastal area.'

Field-marshal Erhard Milch, Inspector General of the Luftwaffe, was not so complacent, nor was he convinced about what constituted 'severe losses'. From his official position (a strange appointment for a half Jew to hold in Nazi Germany), he furiously upbraided Jeschonnek and criticized Goering and Hitler for letting the Luftwaffe's fighter and anti-aircraft defences become so weak that a massive fleet of bombers could reach and bomb Germany's fourth largest city. He told Jeschonnek to do something about it for he was convinced that Cologne was 'the writing on the wall' in letters of fire and blood, and warned that if the Reich did not arm itself with fighter aircraft for defence now, and in ever-increasing numbers, its cities would be obliterated as Cologne had been by the RAF at night and what was left standing would be flattened by the Americans in daylight.

But if Milch was fearfully pessimistic, the young Minister for

Armament Production, Albert Speer, was far from it: 'The RAF will not be able to sustain a series of raids of this size,' he declared.[3]

Hitler must have agreed with Speer, for in a radio broadcast of 3 June he threw down the gauntlet to Harris and Churchill, ending the speech with the challenging words: 'Churchill is invited to continue his raids on the largest scale within his power. Time will show who can go to the greater length in that type of warfare which he has initiated.'

This was precisely what Churchill had in mind. But the outcome was certainly not predictable. It could be that Speer would be proved right and the RAF be incapable of sustaining such raids. On the other hand, it could be that Milch's fears would be realized and that German cities would be devastated one by one. Or, ironically, in a way, both could be right. Only time, as Hitler said, would show. Quite how soon, he did not realize.

In London, Churchill was jubilant. The report on the raid was better than he had expected. He was prepared for losses of up to a hundred aircraft. But to lose only forty!* That was a prodigious achievement. After years of disappointments and defeats, here, at last, was a victory. Here was a way forward. He could smell it, sense it, almost taste it – the nectar of success.

Immediately he sent a signal to 'Bomber' Harris: 'I congratulate the whole of Bomber Command upon the remarkable feat of organization which enabled you to despatch over a thousand bombers to the Cologne area on one night without confusion to concentrate their action over the target in so short a time as one hour and a half. This proof of the growing power of the British bomber force is also the herald of what Germany will receive city by city from now on.'[4]

It was for this that Harris had made his desperate gamble that damp grey morning of Saturday 30 May 1942. Now he knew that the expansion of Bomber Command was assured.

Another bomber chief also in London at that time was equally delighted. Lieutenant-General 'Hap' Arnold, commanding the US Air Force, was thrilled with the massive bomber raid. He thought it a wonderful exhibition and declared to pressmen that he looked forward to the time when it would be possible to make raids like

---

* In addition, three intruder sorties failed to return and 113 aircraft suffered damage to a greater or lesser extent.

Daily Mail

LATE WAR NEWS SPECIAL

No 14,380   ONE PENNY   •   FOR KING AND EMPIRE   MONDAY, JUNE 1 1942

They Flew Just ONE of the THOUSAND

THE men you see here are the crew of "H for Harry"—just one of the thousand bombers that Britain sent over the Cologne area. Colin Bednall, the Daily Mail Air Correspondent, who was with some of these men before the raid, tells below of the change that has come over them since the war began. The schoolboy light-heartedness, he says, has vanished from their messes. Now they are all-absorbed in their task; they talk only of the job they do. Bombs and bombing, and all the technique that goes with it, absorb them day and night. Here there is terrific concentration on the task in hand—and here lies the greatest menace that Hitler's brutalities have conjured up to avenge the savagery of his armed forces on land, on sea, and in the air. Their work is only begun.

ROMMEL FACES CRISIS IN DESERT BATTLE

Whole Africa Corps in British Tank Ring

From ALEXANDER CLIFFORD, Daily Mail Special Correspondent
Outside Tobruk, Sunday.

ROMMEL to-night is fighting for life. The whole of his Africa Corps, armoured forces, and mechanised infantry, reinforced by the Italian Ariete Division, are battering against the British tank wall pinning them down between our main Gazala-Bir Hacheim defence line and the Acroma-Knightsbridge line.

The great tank battle, now in its fifth day, is still raging in the Knightsbridge area, but to-day it has taken a pronounced drift south-west—back towards Rommel's starting-point.

The battle is at its climax. The issue should be known in two days from now. Fighting of such intensity in such terrific heat cannot continue indefinitely. Men and machines are bound to give way.

The new drift of the battle suggests that Rommel may attempt to save himself by blasting his way westwards through the vast minefields of the British defence line

He has been thrown back from El Adem in the east and thrown back from the coast. All reports indicate that his Africa Corps has taken a severe knock

2,000 TONS OF BOMBS IN 90 MINUTES

Cologne: The Full Story

By COLIN BEDNALL, Daily Mail Air Correspondent

COLOGNE, third city in Hitler's Reich, still smoked and smouldered last night from the greatest single bombardment that has ever been launched—from the land, from the sea or from the air. Something like 2,000 tons of high explosive showered on the city in the ninety minutes that it took our forces—"considerably more than 1,000 bombers"—to make the raid.

The first purpose of the attacking swarms was, in the official phrase, "to saturate the defences"

That was done—by the loads unleashed from our gigantic Lancasters, Halifaxes, Stirlings, and Manchesters, as well as from several other types of lighter bombers.

Official accounts tell a graphic story of the havoc wrought and of the scale of the attack. I can add to that account from my own experience, for I was fortunate in spending my week-end at one of the key bomber groups engaged

Our bombers arrived over Cologne as fast and as promptly as they had taken off from all over England. Vistule 140 miles away—to guide the incoming bombers all the way from the Dutch coast

In the words of one Halifax pilot, "It was almost too gigantic to be real"

He added "But it was real enough when we got there. Below us in every part of the city buildings were ablaze

"Here and there you could see their outlines but mostly it was just one big stretch of fire. It was strange to see the flames reflected on our aircraft.

"It looked at times as if we were on fire ourselves with a red glow dancing up and down the wings.

An air bomber lying in the nose of another Halifax said there were aircraft everywhere—"The sky over Cologne was as busy as Piccadilly-circus. I could identify every type of bomber in our force by the light of the moon and the fires.

COLOGNE 'A CITY OF MISERY'

Police Take Over German A R P

It was announced from Berlin last night that the German A R P service has now been placed under the uniformed police (says Reuter). They will be known as the A R P Police. The announcement says: The obvious inference is a breakdown of A R P services in Cologne.

'Phantom' Raid the Day Before

OBJECTIVES bombed by the RAF during its colossal onslaught on the Ruhr and the Rhine were, in effect, attacked twice

The first "attack" took place in daylight hours before any of our planes left the ground

Food Riot in Paris: 20 Shot in Prague

UNREST continues to foment in German-occupied Europe. News was flashed to London last night of rioting in Paris and of Prague firing squads working for the first time on Sunday since Czecho-Slovakia became a German protectorate

PARIS

TWO policemen were killed and a number wounded in Paris's first serious food riot yesterday.

PRAGUE

TWENTY more Czechs were executed yesterday following the German reprisal action of Heydrich bringing the total to 82.

BBC to Cologne: 'We Harden Our Hearts'

Daily Mail Radio Station

WE are not exulting over Cologne, but when we remember Warsaw, Rotterdam, Coventry, and Belgrade, then we harden our hearts." This was the message broadcast last night by "Man in the Street" in the BBC news broadcast last night by "Man in the Street" in the BBC news

He Went to See for Himself

DUMMY FIRES

The dummy fires which the Germans had built to act as bomb counters around Cologne were diverted into an ordinary bomb store, which was the target

Decision on Coal Soon

Daily Mail Political Correspondent

A plan for the reorganisation of the coal industry must wait until the Government has decided far-reaching

State Takes Over Pit

By Daily Mail Reporter

Germans Mine Bridges

S.E. TOWN RAIDED

High explosive and incendiary bombs were dropped on a town in south-east England early to-day. Casualties are feared

SHIP TORPEDOED

From Daily Mail Correspondent Washington, Sunday.—The Navy Department announces that a Norwegian merchantman has been torpedoed in the Gulf of Mexico.

Begin your Coupon Planning with K's

'Best News Ever'—U.S.

Woman Found Shot

General Dobbie

All Quiet on the Eastern Front

MAP shows some of the area bombed by the R.A.F. and the distance planes had to travel to reach their targets in Cologne

K SHOES

The fewer the coupons the more important becomes your choice of shoes. You don't know how long they may have to last you, so go all out for quality and insist on K Plus Fitting shoes. Then you will be sure of long wear, good style and real comfort. Ask your K shoe agent to show you the latest K models—still smart and well cut, still in pleasing variety.

that every night until the enemy could no longer survive. Then he added a few words that would ring all too true in but a few months:* 'Our enemies have demonstrated that they are willing to take their losses; we must be willing to take our losses too!'5

Back on their bases that same Sunday morning, 31 May, the men who should be taking those losses were now getting up and walking bleary-eyed into their respective messes for a late breakfast, noting without comment the empty places, saying to themselves, 'Don't think about it. Eat your egg. Think about something else. A pint tonight? Would there be a stand-down? What now? Where do we go from here?'

By half past nine that morning, 'Bomber'Harris had already answered all those questions. At the end of 'Morning Prayers' at High Wycombe, all was ready, subject to weather. Stage 2 of his 'Thousand Plan' could go ahead.

Consequently on the same fifty-three Bomber Command stations the same tannoy message crackled through just before noon. All aircrew were to stay on camp. Stomachs churned. This time the 'Bloody Hells' were louder and more vehement. And once again there was the waiting.

Then, at teatime that Sunday, on the same stations as before, the same men, not quite so many of them, not quite so breezy this time, trooped into the briefing rooms. Once again there was a special message from the Commander-in-Chief, one that would lift their morale, make them feel good. Or at least that's what they had thought at High Wycombe headquarters as they strolled home for their pre-Sunday-lunch drinks. On the operational stations the portentous message was received with what has sometimes been described as 'a subdued raspberry'.

It read: 'By your skill, determination and courage in last night's operation you have undoubtedly struck the enemy a stunning blow. All and more that was expected of you you have achieved. I now ask you for one additional effort tonight against an even more vital objective before the "Thousand Plan" force disperses and while the weather yet holds. You all know the value of a left and right and I am confident that you will bring it off.'

But it still all depended on the weather.

Time dragged. In the Bomber Command Headquarters, Harris

---

* In two daylight raids on Schweinfurt, USAAF lost ninety-six B17 bombers with 950 trained crewmen.

was waiting for one last weather forecast. Would the clouds clear enough for a raid on Hamburg? They would not. At 1830 hours he made a decision. Operations cancelled for the night.

But he had not given up hope for the following night. And so, once again, on 1 June, 6,000 aircrew were standing by waiting for briefing. Again thick cloud dashed Harris's hopes of obliterating Hamburg in the way he thought he had obliterated Cologne. He could not resist sending this force somewhere though, so he risked it on Essen, but conditions were poor.

Crews got ready and took off on time. The target was difficult enough to find in good weather for an industrial haze nearly always seemed to hide it. On this night, with adverse cloud conditions, it was almost impossible to locate Essen. The raid was a dismal failure. Of the 956 bombers that took off, 767 claimed to have bombed in or near the town. But none of the night photographs showed the target, and only eight out of the seventy-three photographs were within five miles of it. Photographic reconnaissance over the next few days confirmed that little damage had been done to the town, and none to the Krupps works.[6]

After this the 6,000 aircrew of the Thousand Plan force learned the answer to the question 'Where do we go from here?' They went back to their bases. Back to the old routine. Disbanded.

But not for long. Harris wanted one more chance. So did Churchill, for Stalin had just accused Britain of cowardice because of its refusal to open a second front against Germany. He had asked for a Western Offensive that would draw forty German divisions off the Eastern Front. 'You will find that Germans are not supermen if you have the courage to fight as the Russians have,' sneered Stalin.[7]

Stung by this accusation, Churchill was pleased when Harris came along with the project to continue the Thousand Plan raids on a basis of one every full moon. Here, thought Churchill, was an opportunity to show that Britain was not just sitting back letting other people do the fighting for them, as the *New York Times* had recently jibed.[8] Obviously Molotov would not be impressed – he thought little of the photographs of wrecked German cities which Harris sent to him monthly – but the US President might be. Enthusiastically, Churchill wrote to Roosevelt, presenting the plan in glowing terms: 'I am now sure it is most important to keep this bombing up during the summer, blasting Hitler from behind whilst he is grappling with the bear.'

The first target was to be Bremen. The date – 25 June. The result – as disappointing as Essen. Although subsequent photo-reconnaissance showed damage to parts of the town, the most important target, the docks, escaped undamaged. Once again a gamble on the weather had not come off. Forty-nine bombers, crewed by about 250 men, failed to return. Many of these this time were student OTU crews who had found the conditions too difficult.

The Thousand Plan was abandoned. Churchill's 'Arabian Nights', as he had called them, were forgotten. Speer, it seemed, had been right in his forecast.

Dropping the plan did not mean an easier time for Bomber Command though. On the contrary, Harris still felt he could win the war by battering the German cities, sapping the Germans' morale and their resolution to carry on fighting. And so, in one form or another, the bombing went on, week after week, month after month for three long and bitter years after that first thousand-bomber raid on Cologne. The crews incurred casualties which became heavier and heavier as the months went by; they reached a peak in 1943, during the five-month Battle of the Ruhr, when 718 bombers were lost.[9]

Mainly responsible for these losses were Speer and Milch, who, after the shock of that first thousand-bomber raid, had greatly expanded German fighter production so that the strength of the Luftwaffe night fighter force on the Western Front had risen from 180 in May 1942 to 682 in October 1943. Absolute priority had been given to the defence of the Fatherland from the Allied bombers. Even the hard-pressed German infantry fighting against the odds on the Russian Front were deprived of adequate fighting cover.

Against such a force of new fighters, the losses of Bomber Command became insupportable. And during this time the crews were fighting a continuous battle not only with the official enemy Germany, but with the hidden one: fear.

Today, accustomed to a long period of peace and with our greater insight into 'psychiatry', we can readily admit to being frightened, even to being a coward. But then, in wartime Britain, the stigma of being called a coward – 'being scared witless', as they sometimes put it – assumed far greater importance. As one former gunner said: 'Heroes became scum overnight.' So, however hard it might be for us to understand the situation today, the young men in 1942 were under a triple strain: the strain of combat, the strain of fear, and the strain induced by not being able to talk about it.

Exactly how many men actually went down under the strain is still a closely guarded secret. Some received enlightened and humane treatment but others were harshly dealt with by courts martial for 'Lack of Moral Fibre'. One station commander who rose to high rank in the post-war years is reported to have said: 'I made certain that every case before me was punished by court martial and, where applicable, by an exemplary prison sentence, whatever the psychiatrists were saying.'[10]

Prime Minister Churchill had no time for psychiatrists either. He tried to keep them away from the scene. Disparagingly he wrote in 1942, after the Cologne raid, 'I am sure it would be sensible to restrict as much as possible the work of these gentlemen. The tightest hand should be kept over them.'[11]

Somehow, though, they had to keep aircrew flying. A pilot's training was long and expensive; navigators, bomb-aimers, wireless-operators and gunners were difficult to replace. And, as group commanders were quick to point out, if there were to be an easy and honourable way out of operational flying, 'LMF' could rampage through squadrons like weeds in a wet summer.

To check any tendency towards 'opting out' – putting in a request to be taken off operational flying – firm action had to be taken. But it did not prevent the problem's arising.

What happened to affect the nerves, morale and confidence of aircrew could easily be seen, according to medical aviation specialist Dr Roland Winfield DFC, AFC.[12] It had happened to him, for he was a pilot with ninety-eight operations against the enemy to his credit as well as being a doctor. He explained that when newly trained aircrew joined a squadron they were pleasurably excited that the irksome restrictions of training were over and that at last they were going to be employed on the task for which they had been trained – a task which was not without its glamour. When they discovered that this job had a high occupational death rate, they armed themselves with the faith of 'Well, of course, it can happen to other people but it won't ever happen to me.' It took only three or four operations for that illusion to be replaced by the knowledge that it could and probably would.

As Dr Winfield said, 'On the whole, the greater a man's

intelligence and the more lively his imagination, the earlier in his operational tour did he become aware of the hard and inescapable fact that to continue operating against the enemy meant that he had to live his life in the continuous immediate prospect of violent death. Therefore, if he was to continue to operate, he had to come to terms with himself.'

Dr Winfield could remember very well when he discovered that he was not invulnerable. 'My bubble labelled "It can't happen to me" burst during my third or fourth flight from Oakington, and there then followed a period of about four months during which I can honestly say that I never knew a single moment's peace of mind.'

It was during this period of a tour that affected aircrew began to have 'the shakes' and nightmares. A Texan sheriff, 'Tex' Mitchell, who went on to win a DFM as a sergeant-gunner before being killed on the Ruhr later in 1942, suffered terribly from nightmares during the weeks following the discovery that 'Ops were more than likely to end in the "big chop" sooner or later.' He would wake up in the night shouting, 'There's a tracer, red with blood, spurting through the floor.' And his tough Australian pal Chris Martin, sleeping in the same hut, would also wake up with his pyjamas soaked in sweat after similar nightmares.[13]

The only way they could come to terms with the situation was to give up hope of living and think only that death was nothing compared to the vital necessity of combating the scourge of National Socialism. They accepted the philosophy that the cause for which they were fighting was far more important than the preservation of their own lives. As Ronald Winfield eventually did, they had learned to face and accept the fact that they were under sentence of death. 'It was this,' wrote Winfield, 'that gave me peace with myself.'

But not everyone could find peace in this way.

The problem became increasingly grave to group commanders and came to a head when a secret medical document landed on the desk of the Air Member for Personnel shortly before the first thousand-bomber raid.[14] Its author was a medical officer from an operational station who for two years had studied the reaction of aircrew to operations and how some inevitably broke down before the tour of operations was completed.

Officially aircrew had to complete thirty operations on the first tour and twenty on the second. In between there would be a six-month period of instructional duties. It did not take long, as we have seen, for these men to discover that few would even reach the average number that were completed – fourteen operations. The average life of the bomber itself was only forty hours.

The effect of all this on crews was set out by the medical officer reporting on his two years study. In periods of time as:

1. First six months keen on flying and 'raring' to go.
2. Next three to six months 'willing but not volunteering'.
3. After nine to twelve months to end of tour, unwilling but will not say so, until taken off or breaks down.

The long and detailed report concluded with words which were both signifcant and alarming: 'Aircrew are placed in a psychologically impossible position and ... every pilot without exception will, in the end, develop an anxiety neurosis. It is inexorable and inevitable.'

That was not the only report. There were many others. The medical officer from RAF Driffield, for example, reported immediately after the thousand-bomber raid that four aircrew members reported sick the next day 'with anxiety symptoms and psychological headaches'.

Another doctor wrote: 'I have seen one patient who shook like a leaf for thirty minutes before take-off. The thirty-trip rule fails to take into considerations the prolonged nervous tension involved in briefings and later cancellations.[15] This was indeed a valid point. As many crews who went on the Cologne raid were later to say, anticipation could be worse than the trip itself. One of these men, Ernie Cummings, who completed a total of sixty-eight raids but was briefed for a further fifty, recalls well the additional stress all this caused.[16] Forty years later, as Chairman of the Bomber Command Association, he said, 'What the planners forgot was that it was not just the hours you spent flying that mattered – you were too busy then anyway to think – but the hours spent waiting for raids which were later scrubbed. I know it certainly upset me.'

Group commanders wrote to the Air Ministry for advice on where to put those men who had refused to fly. One penned a strong memo, not mincing his words: 'In the best interests of squadrons they should be posted at once, for fear of contaminating others.'

A meeting was called. The Air Member for Personnel,

Commander-in-Chief Bomber Command, all his group commanders and the Director of Medical Services debated the issue. What was to be done? Medical opinion favoured a humane approach, saying that much could be done by the station commander and the medical officer working together to tide a man over a difficult phase. But in the end the commanders came down unanimously for one course of action: a firm line. 'A court martial where an individual refuses to fly has a salutory effect. If there were to be a medical element in the case, then this would be investigated at the trial.'

A typical case is recorded of Flight Sergeant 'B' who went to see his squadron commander with a request to be withdrawn from operational duties. He said he saw no future in flying, and his written application ended with the words: 'I would rather be doing ground duties in complete confidence than flying in mortal fear.' 'B' was charged under Section 9 of the Air Force Act, court martialled and reduced to the rank of aircraftsman. But that was not the end of his humiliation. There was yet another ignominious ritual: a formal degradation in front of the whole station. All ranks were paraded, by squadrons and flights, and inspected in the usual way by the station commander; then the drama of the day began. Lancaster pilot Squadron Leader Jack Currie described a similar scene at his station at Wickenby when two gunners refused to fly.

'When we resumed close order the miscreants were marched onto the parade ground from the left flank and stationed between their escorts front and centre. In a formal toneless voice the adjutant read out the charges against them, followed by the findings of the court.

The ensign stirred limply on the staff. At the rear of 3 Squadron there was a quickly stilled disturbance as a fainting aircraftsman was led away. As silence fell again, the station comander marched to one of the offenders and, with sure quick movements, ripped the chevrons from each sleeve and the brevet from the breast. The gunner was a tall aquiline fellow who might have stepped from Longfellow's *Hiawatha*. He stood erect and motionless, staring straight ahead. The grey-blue sleeve showed darker where the tapes had been. The other gunner stood with shoulders bowed, and would not raise his eyes. He flinched at the station commander's touch. It was a dreadful moment.'[17]

At the time it might have been hard for everyone to feel sympathy for such men but, as one aviation specialist at the time was later to write, 'Now that one can take a more detached view of their conduct, I feel ashamed to have questioned their courage.'[18] Another former pilot said recently: 'There's a certain amount of stuff in a man and when it's gone it's gone. And when you know it's gone, it's better for everyone to pack up.'[19]

This pilot did exactly that. He was demoted, disgraced, but he survived. And he did not suffer – as so many still do – from anxiety and nervous breakdowns. He runs his own business and is not dependent on charity from organizations appealing for donations under headlines: 'NOWADAYS THIS SQUADRON LEADER CRIES.'

Naturally, cases varied from one individual to the next, from those whose nerve went early to those brave men who had almost completed their tour and then found that their stock of courage just ran out. It is very hard for us today to visualize the type of courage needed by Bomber Command crews then but the reader will get a very good idea from the vivid account written by a twenty-seven-year-old pilot who had suffered terribly from two crashes. The medical officer treating him at the time asked the pilot to write down his own detailed report, reproduced here as Appendix C, and from this the reader will be able to form his own opinion about the hazards and manner of death faced nightly by these brave young men.

Medical officers could help considerably. They watched carefully for tell-tale signs. One told of a flying officer who never smoked and only drank a sherry in the mess before dinner (because he had been told on his officer training course that this was the 'form'). After his twenty-first raid he began to smoke and drink by the pint like most other crew members. No longer did he relax in an armchair reading a novel but skimmed through magazines as if unable to concentrate – or as if he knew he would never get to the end of a novel anyway. Often he would sit well away from the others, a pint in his hand, yawning, an unopened paper on his lap. At mealtimes he would be one of the first at the table but after the first mouthful his hunger seemed to disappear and he would push his plate fractionally away and place his knife and fork neatly to one side. Finished. To an outsider he would appear to be a quiet young man; to the alert medical officer he was a candidate for a breakdown.

For such men, well on in their tour, who had got beyond the point of coping, there was sometimes an alternative to court martial. One of the best kept secrets of the Second World War was the establishment of psychiatric hospitals in remote parts of Britain for the treatment of men who showed signs of combat fatigue. In the end there were eighteen special hospitals for the treatment of disturbed neurosis, five centres for mild neurosis, four psychiatric centres and thirteen NYDN ('Not Yet Diagnosed Neurosis') centres. Once a station medical officer reported that he thought a man would respond to treatment and fly again, he would refer him to a neuropsychiatric specialist.

Sergeant 'K', a wireless operator/air gunner, was in this category. Within days he was off the station and escorted to Matlock, a quiet country town tucked away in the Derbyshire hills, where, on a craggy peak in a Dracula-like eyrie, was the RAF hospital housed in the old Victorian Spa of Rockside. In 1942 this hospital treated 859 patients, $2\frac{1}{2}$ times more than in the previous year. At Rockside the patient was given a room to share with a sergeant pilot; there were two narrow iron beds alongside heavy fitted wardrobes (which are still there). Medication began immediately. The whole treatment seemed to be based on rest, complete rest, allowing the body and mind to heal naturally together. Sedation helped. Arthur Wilson, then head chef at Rockside, now remembers how they all seemed to spend most of the first two or three weeks asleep.[20] And former WAAF Sergeant Price was still moved emotionally when she described forty years later the pitiful state some of these patients were in.

'Many of them had a facial tic; they were nervous and hesitant when they talked even about ordinary things. One minute they would be acting quite normally and the next they would be jumping about starting an argument about nothing at all.'[21]

Flight Sergeant Caudwell, one of the staff at Matlock, who had a particular gift with difficult patients, would often invite them to his house, to put them more at ease in homely surroundings, helped by his eleven-year-old daughter, Jean. She was well briefed not to stare but to accept them as they were. 'They seemed more relaxed with me and sometimes I'd have my friends there as well. But you could never be sure what would happen next. I remember, for example, how one of them dropped a fork at the tea table and then burst into tears because he could not pick it up,' said Jean, who now works in Rockside herself on the staff of the Higher Education College there.[22]

Another patient,[23] who was later to spend many years in and out of mental hospitals recalls how: 'Once these aircrew NCOs* were well on their way to recovery, their social rehabilitation began; they would walk down the steep hill into Matlock in their "hospital blues" – a bright blue flannel jacket, white shirt, red tie. The RAF were making sure there would be no desertions. No one would get far in that outfit without being noticed.

'Many would play golf, croquet, bowls, tennis or billiards at any time of the day. Others would walk along the river bank to High Torr caves or even as far as Matlock Bath, where a cheery café owner would give them egg and chips conjured up somehow from dried egg powder. The Matlock people were very kind and invited us into their homes. I still visit a family there. Some patients though would hide away in their rooms and never come out. They had completely lost their confidence in themselves.

'I used to read the papers a lot in the Matlock library, and I remember just after the Cologne raid reading that a Jehovah's Witness was fined £2 for not presenting himself for medical examination when his call-up papers arrived.[24] And at the same time I saw the Yorkshire miners at Cortonwood were on strike for more pay, and I couldn't help thinking that some people could please themselves whether they got killed or not but for us there was no alternative. Sooner or later someone would decide that we were fit to go back flying. And how long would that last? If the flak did not get us, our nerves would. It would then be court martial, demotion and disgrace.'

Perhaps it was the thought of this shame, which not only he but also his family would have to bear, which caused another patient at Rockside to put a quick end to all the worrying about the future. It happened one night as Catherine Price was going on duty. As she approached the front door, her eye was caught by the movement of something white right at the top, immediately below the roof of the twin-towered building. To her horror, the next moment a pyjama-clad figure came crashing down onto the hard concrete drive.[25]

No one knew why for certain. Some thought that the man might have been disorientated with drugs and did not know what he was doing. Perhaps he could not stand the thought of having that awful label on his documents – 'Lack of Moral Fibre'. Whatever the reason, no one heard much about it. Everything was hushed up, as

---

* The officers went to Torquay. Matlock was for NCOs only.

was this whole chapter in the history of the Royal Air Force in the Second World War.

But in Rockside they still remember the tragedy. It is said that girl students sleeping on the top floor are sometimes troubled at night by a feeling of someone or something being there, and by footsteps that go one way – and do not come back![26]

A third of those patients at Matlock did in fact go back (as did the Torquay officers). They went back to the nightly operations, to the unremitting bomber offensive, battling on for a further three long and bitter years after that momentous thousand-bomber raid on Cologne, steeling themselves against fear and memories.

Sadly, in those lonely battles in the night sky above Germany, 56,000 young aircrew of Bomber Command met with violent death.

On 8 May 1945 it was all over in Europe for the British and Commonwealth and American bomber crews. And the pilots, navigators, bomb-aimers, wireless-operators and gunners suddenly realized what that meant. Peace. They had now reached the beginning of a new road down which they were going to walk like ordinary people, to end their days in a natural and less violent way than the friends they had lost.

Today, some forty years on, as they look back on those hectic times, those five long years of fear, of danger, of excitement and comradeship, of being 'brassed off', when operation were scrubbed, and being 'brassed off' when operations were on, what do they say? Surprisingly, for the listener, perhaps even for themselves, the words that round off their reminiscing almost invariably are: 'I wouldn't have missed it for worlds!'

9. The Summing Up

'I am sick and tired of war. Its glory is
all moonshine ... War is Hell.'
US General Sherman, to Michigan
Military Academy, 19 June 1869

Shortly after mid-day on 28 January 1945, when the 'All Clear' sounded over the bitterly cold city of Cologne, few people realized that the last real air raid was over. There was nothing to mark the end of the terror that had begun with that thousand-bomber raid in May 1942. Nothing to celebrate. But as one peaceful night gave way to another there came a dawning of hope. Those terrifying whistles of falling bombs, the nerve-shattering thuds which for so long had broken the peace of the night and day, causing haggard faces to blench even whiter, had disappeared. Clearly the air raids at least were over.

And what had those raids proved? Had they shown that Prime Minister Churchill, Chief of the Air Staff Portal and 'Bomber' Harris were right in thinking that air bombardment would destroy German morale and that terrorization of civilians would win the war?

The citizens of Cologne had faced the reality of death and destruction, they had not panicked and they had learnt to live with the ever-present threat of a violent and terrible end to life. Morale did not crack; somehow people adjusted to the situation; they bent under the whirlwind that had been delivered and they adapted their lives to the needs of the moment, displaying remarkable ingenuity in carrying on. They were not defeated in spirit; it was almost a victory, but a tragic victory.

The death of fit young men in battle is something that nations have, over the centuries, been conditioned to expect – the general public does not see it happen – but the tearing apart of young children, the mutilation of civilians of all ages is a different matter. Having seen all that, everyone knew what war was like. War was bloody and brutal.

It was bloody and brutal also for the aircrews. Bomber Command lost more men in the Second World War than did the whole of the British Army in officers in the First World War.

What then is the verdict of history?

Those who are critical of the Strategic Bomber Offensive can argue that many of these lives were lost in vain; they can produce evidence to show that German war production was not severely cut back by the bombing of industrial areas. Timely decentralization of factories enabled German war production to reach its highest output in 1944 – at the peak of the bomb offensive. They can say that it was morally wrong to bomb residential areas of cities and that this policy did not bring Germany near to defeat by breaking morale.

But this is only one side of the story. There is that of the Churchill-Harris side to consider. Supporters of their bombing policy can argue, and with good grounds, that it was this method of bombing that ultimately triumphed. Maybe not exactly in the way Harris planned, but the first signs came immediately after that thousand-bomber raid on Cologne for it was then that the German Air Force began to strip Army units of air cover on the Eastern Front to concentrate more on the defence of the Fatherland itself. After the devastating raids on Hamburg in July 1943 the Luftwaffe gave absolute priority to the defence of the Home Front.

The final decisive victory came not through the destruction of factories and cities but through the destruction of the German fighter force. As their tired pilots rose, day after day, to combat the attacks, they received the final *coup-de-grâce* from a new long-range American escort fighter – the P51 Mustang, far swifter and more manoeuvrable than any of its opponents.

Air supremacy was won. The invasion could now be launched, and the combined air fleets were free to attack oil installations and transportation until the German war machine shuddered to a halt. However, the fact that the invasion could wait until the Allies were ready was due partly to the efforts of those gallant Bomber Command crews who took the war into Germany until 1944, took some pressure off the Russians, convinced the Americans that the bomber offensive was a meaningful menace and, in short, bought time to ensure that land battles in Normandy were waged on the most favourable terms possible for the Allies.

No doubt the controversy will continue as long as there are air marshals still writing to *The Times* and the *Telegraph*, and military historians delving into the archives. But the evaluation of all the evidence, with the benefit of hindsight, should be set against the background of crisis and uncertainty that existed in Britain when the thousand bombers were launched; those war-time days, with all their frictions, frustrations and resolutions, are a far cry from the academic desks of peacetime.

We would do well to remember also the words of President Harry Truman, in September 1945, when he paid tribute to the contribution of Air Marshal Harris and the 'indomitable' men of Bomber Command to the winning of the war. He said of Harris, 'He forged in the Royal Air Force Bomber Command one of the most potent weapons of war which brought about the total destruction of the enemy.'

And finally, in this summing up, we should always bear in mind the warning given by General Eisenhower as he contemplated the ruins of the bomb-torn Cologne Cathedral which still stood defiantly above the rubble of the city: 'No edifice, however sacred, will survive atomic war. The bombed ruins of Germany provide but faint warning of what future war could mean to the people of the earth.'

Epilogue

'The youthfulness of our dead warriors
is something which those of us who
make it back from wars – the survivors
and spectators – all too easily forget as
the years go by. We grow older and
greyer, sometimes in the head as well as
on it, and when we think of our dead
we still consider them contemporaries
– as being like ourselves, the elder solid
citizens which most of us have since
become.

'But the fact is: these dead warriors
never did grow old.'

From Memorial Address by former
bomber pilot Arthur Hailey

In the early spring of 1984, in a quiet hillside cemetery at
Goring-on-Thames, 'Bomber' Harris was buried. At the precise
moment when earth rumbled onto his coffin, there came another
rumble, slowly increasing into a roar, as the last surviving bomber
of the Second World War – a four-engined Lancaster – flew by at
100 feet to give a final salute to the wartime Commander-in-Chief
of Bomber Command, a man much loved and respected by those
who served under him. Mourners at his graveside could be excused
for thinking that this final tribute was also being paid to the 50,000
young British and Commonwealth aircrew who died in the bomber
offensive against Germany and for all the dwindling number of
surviving comrades, men who had the courage and tenacity to carry
the war into Hitler's fortress of Europe, with strength far exceeding
anything previously known, and for a longer period than any other
formation of the Armed Services – men, it seemed, that many
politicians wanted to forget.

Why was this?

During the early years of the war, when Britain was at bay, driven out of Europe, threatened with invasion and being blitzed by day and by night, the Bomber Command leaders and their men were hailed as heroes. They were the only ones hitting back. And whilst the battles of north-west Europe were being fought and London was being attacked by the V2 rockets, the bomber crews again were given all credit due to them.

But with the coming of peace, and with it a Labour Government, there came also a change of attitude. The morality of the bomber offensive came to be questioned, and 'Bomber' Harris and his men were denied the accolades of victory. The man who had revitalized Bomber Command – and relentlessly pursued a policy which he believed would spare the youth of Britain from the carnage of prolonged land battles across Europe – was not named in any of the post-war lists of honours. And when he asked for a special campaign medal for his men, he was refused. They could wear the Defence Medal – for which the Home Guard and fire-watchers could qualify.

The laurels and adulation were reserved for the defenders: Fighter Command. The Battle of Britain pilots got a campaign medal for their efforts in the summer of 1940; Bomber Command had fought with equal dedication and self-sacrifice for five years. In the Battle of Britain 507 fighter pilots were killed; Bomber Command could lose as many as that in one raid – as with that on Nuremberg in March 1944 when 545 were killed. More than twice as many men flew in the thousand-bomber raid on Cologne as took part in the whole of the Battle of Britain.

Why was it that Bomber Command was treated so shabbily? How could Britain let one of its greatest wartime commanders retire unhonoured into obscurity in South Africa? And why were the deeds of his men brushed aside without due recognition?

The responsibility for this rests squarely upon the shoulders of the new men who came into power with the elections of 1945. Then, with the benefit of hindsight and with the security of peacetime, it became increasingly acceptable for politicians of all parties to criticize the way the bomber offensive had been handled and to throw grave doubts upon the morality of it all.

It was this same Socialist Government that held sole power in August 1945 when the decision was made for the most horrific air raid of all time. On 6 August the Government agreed to the dropping of the first atomic bomb, ironically code-named 'Little Boy', on the crowded Japanese city of Hiroshima. And then, three days later, in full knowledge of the appalling consequences of the first bomb, the Government acquiesced in the dropping of the second one, of a different design and presumably bigger from its code-name, 'Fat Man', on another densely populated city, Nagasaki. The Japanese were ready to surrender after 'Little Boy', and 'Fat Man' need not have been dropped. The politicians who claimed to have been so horrified at what Harris had done did nothing themselves to stop 'Fat Man' killing a further 80,000 and mutilating goodness know how many more.

Why were these bombs dropped? The pat answer was: 'To end the war more swiftly, thereby saving a million or more soldiers' lives.'

Japan surrendered five days later. Bombing, as Harris had always said, could, and did, end a war. But the enemies of Harris continued to denigrate the achievements of Bomber Command and its commander. (There could also be another reason for the 'shameful treatment of Bomber Command' associated with the fact that Harris once raised doubts on grounds of security, of having a former member of Sir Oswald Mosley's Fascist party employed in the Directorate of Bomber Operations, at Air Ministry. This man, Squadron Leader John Strachey, had such an 'unstable political background', having been both a Fascist and a Marxist, that Harris thought he should be removed from the Directorate. But Strachey had supporters and not only did he keep his job but he was promoted to Under Secretary of State of Air in 1945 by the new Secretary of State for Air, William Wedgwood Benn. It has been argued that personal animosity was partly responsible for Harris's being left out of the honours list. The whole unsavoury saga is recorded by Harris's official biographer, Group Captain Dudley Saward in *Bomber Harris*.)

No doubt people were shocked when pictures of the appalling devastation of German cities came back to Britain. And Ministers hastened to dissociate themselves from the bombing faction. To award honours and medals to Bomber Command leaders and men could smack of condoning all that had been done. So it was that the efforts of men who had fought with great devotion to duty against the forces of a ruthless Nazi Germany were declared unworthy; and the memory of those who had died was tarnished.

True enough, there were times when aircrew were sickened by

what they were doing. 'We knew we were setting fire to ordinary men, women and children in their homes. And we didn't like the idea. It left us confused and we didn't feel proud of ourselves,' said one bomber air gunner, David Craven. 'But it wasn't our choice. We felt much better bombing marshalling yards.' Many aircrew were indeed horrified, but in the whirl of combat there was no time for doubts on the morality of it all. Their tasks were complicated enough and they had to be absolutely single-minded of purpose. But in the quieter moments, back on the station, these doubts were most disturbing.

What made it worse was the fact that they could not talk about their feelings of guilt, their doubts or their remorse. Even in freedom-of-speech-loving Britain, 'defeatist' talk was a punishable offence, as one of the best-known bomber pilot of them all, Group Captain Cheshire VC, DSO and bar, was to find in his earlier days when he was placed under open arrest by intelligence officers who had objected to his outspoken comments about area bombing and his remark that the British traitor 'Lord Haw Haw' broadcasting from Berlin was often nearer the truth than British propaganda.

And so, as the area bombing increased after the thousand-bomber raid, those who had doubts often bottled them up. But when these pent-up feelings were released later, the effect was sometimes traumatic.

Immediately after the war, for example, David Walker, with a DFC and over sixty operations to his credit, found there were times when the horror of it all came back to him so vividly that he broke into a cold sweat, and he would sit shivering for half an hour before the attack passed. Ultimately, so bad did it all become, he had to give up his well-paid job with a chemical firm and offer some form of restitution. Backed by his wife, Barbara, the girl he had known in Lincoln, he sold their comfortable home and flew out to the barren altiplano of Bolivia to become a missionary. He worked for twelve years in the high-altitude villages.

'In my Royal Air Force days,' he recalled, 'I had been taught always to use oxygen when flying at over 10,000 feet. There we were living and working at nearly 12,000 feet with no oxygen masks. What a struggle it was, climbing up the steep hills of Lapuz, gasping for oxygen in the rarified atmosphere, during our visiting from house to house. When I think back to that terrible night when we bombed Cologne, it makes me feel sick to think of the destruction and suffering I caused.'

He was not alone. Many former aircrew had similar feelings – and not surprisingly, for here were young men in the most impressionable period of their lives receiving the direct impact of all the horrors and heroism of war. Few came through unscathed. Lives were completely changed. The best-known example again is of Group Captain Cheshire who eventually witnessed the dropping of the first atomic bomb and after the war decided to devote the rest of his life to caring for those who were unable to care for themselves. Thus the man who had originally studied for a lifetime in law set up and ran homes of refuge of the incurably ill.

His judgement on the moral implications of the bomber offensive was made when he visited Cologne immediately after the war. He was shocked at what he saw. 'I think Cologne depressed me even more than Berlin. The devastation, the cold and the despair on people's faces helped me to grasp for the first time what saturation bombing meant to the victims. Piloting a bomber was a cold, impersonal game. We were concerned with switches and markers and flak, not with life and death. Now I understand the other side of the problem.'

Group Captain Cheshire's reaction was to be echoed many times immediately after hostilities ceased when the official 'conducted tours' for bomber crews took in the main cities that had been bombed. Many of the Canadian aircrew who returned to their base at Tholthorpe, Yorkshire, for a reunion in 1986 still recalled their feelings of horror as they gazed down upon the ruins on those low-level 'sightseeing' trips before being repatriated to Canada for demobilization.

It was no wonder that survivors found that coping with peace was going to be a more complex problem than they had ever imagined. Many are still tormented by nightmares, many still live with ghosts of the past, and they wonder what it was all about – all that courage and self-sacrifice on the bomber stations so long ago.

Those airfields are still there. Abandoned, disowned, neglected, overgrown, forgotten, as if no one wants to accept responsibility for them. Symbolic, surely, of the disgraceful way Bomber Command was treated after the war. Upon these ruins there are no official memorials beyond those built by Squadron Associations but something lingers still. There is a message.

Listen for it as you walk onto one of these ghostly airfields in the fading light of late afternoon when the mist rolls up from the coast; wander through the dispersal points overgrown with weed;

approach the crumbling Nissen huts where rusty windows hang ajar, and once again you can, with a little help from the imagination, get the sounds and smells from the past. From far off comes the roar of an aircraft engine being tested, the happy cries of 'Naafi up', greeting the arrival of the tea wagon (and you can taste again the saccharine in it). Carried to you on the faint cool evening breeze will come the staccato cough of the Fordson tractor hauling a clattering train of bomb trolleys. Enter what remains of the old dining-hall and feel once more the warm air smelling of damp overcoats and fried kidneys, bacon and 'bubble and squeak'. Hear again the hissing of steam from the plate-washer and the backchat from the WAAFS behind the stainless steel hotplate, whilst from somewhere in the back of the kitchen someone impersonating the voice of a Negro sings: 'Pardon me, boy, is that the Chattanooga Choo Choo? Track twenty-nine. Then you can give me a shine.'

From a nearby Nissen hut it is easy to get the illusion of an old wireless from which the solemn voice of a newsreader says: 'Last night aircraft from Bomber Command attacked the railway marshalling yards at Hamm, causing extensive damage to rolling stock and buildings. Nine of our aircraft our missing ...'

Everything comes back to those who are tuned in to the memories held by those forgotten fields from which young men fought and died. Once, long ago. Men who are white-haired now, or dead these forty years ...

To them, on these abandoned airfields, there may be nothing to commemorate their stay but something definitely lives on. Somewhere over the whole scene there hangs Harris's own epitaph to his 'boys': 'There are no words that can do justice to the aircrew who fought under my command. There is no parallel in warfare to such courage and determination which at times was so great scarcely one man in three could expect to survive his tour of thirty operations. It was moreover a clear and conscious courage, by which the risk was taken with calm forethought; it was, furthermore, the courage of the small hours with long drawn out apprehensions of going over the top. Such devotion must not be forgotten. It is unforgettable by anyone whose contacts gave them knowledge and understanding of what these young men experienced and faced.'

There are not so many of them left now, but they remember it all so well. One former Canadian pilot, now living alone in Yorkshire, told how it is with him every Remembrance Day when he sits and watches television showing the service at the Royal Albert Hall. 'I'm not an emotional man but once the RAF March Past is played and the standards are brought into the arena, all the memories come flooding back. And I stand up to attention and my eyes brim over with tears. Nobody can see me. And I wonder how many there are now who can even begin to understand ...'

From those abandoned airfields, from all those memories, there comes a message, loud and clear: whatever view is taken of Bomber Command's offensive, no one can deny the bravery of the young men whose destiny it was to fly from those airfields. No one can deny that the picture of those devastated cities is firmly implanted in everyone's mind. The horror of it lives on in the common imagination. So powerful is its hold that the idea of any repetition is repellent. Never again do we want to risk another war, especially with the new generation of aerial explosives.

As General Sherman said, over a hundred years ago: 'War is Hell.' It is Hell – Hell for the warrior and civilian alike, and from this knowledge has come more than forty years of peace. Perhaps this, after all, is the greatest legacy left to us long ago by those young men of Bomber Command.

Appendix A.
What Happened to Them All?

'When we look back on all the perils
through which we have passed ... why
should we fear for our future? We have
come safely through the worst.'
Winston Churchill, 16 August 1945

Some came safely through. Others did not. Few came through
unscathed. But at last it was all over, the days of war had run their
course and, for those who had survived, there was a future. And, for
the first time for many years, they could seriously think of it and
plan ahead.

But it was not easy for everyone to adjust to the routine of
having one day so much like another. For Bomber Command crews
in particular, it took a long time for the feeling to fade that at any
moment the tannoy would crackle again. Gradually, though,
occupied with personal problems, with the resumption of old civvy
jobs and the taking-up of new ones, most of the returning aircrew
slipped into the routine of peacetime; some more smoothly than
others.

The reader might like to learn a little more of the chequered fates
of those mentioned in this book through whose experiences the
story of that first thousand-bomber raid has been told. Briefly they
are listed in alphabetical order for ease of reference.

Baldwin, Jacky, Air Marshal Sir John Eustace Arthur, KBE, CB,
DSO, had been commissioned in the RAF in 1918 and first bombed
Cologne a few months earlier. He had, in fact, retired from the RAF
in August 1939, but only for twelve days. He was recalled to
command No. 3 Group Bomber Command. In 1942 he became
Deputy Air Officer Commanding India and then, from 1943 to

1944, he commanded No. 3 Tactical Air Force. He retired from the RAF for the second time in December 1944, aged fifty-two, and became a director of the York chocolate firm Jos. Terry & Son and of Atlantic Shipping and Trading.

Clarke, Eric survived the number 13 jinx, came back safely from the Cologne raid and, despite his affliction of air sickness, completed twenty-nine operations. The last one was an eventful trip in a Lancaster by daylight to Milan. The pilot was J.K.M. Cooke DSO, DFC, whom he would very much like to contact again. After the war Eric Clarke began a career as a local Government officer and studied hard to qualify eventually for a post of Deputy Chief Finance and Rating Officer.

Craven, David, flew in a Hampden from Cottesmore, completed sixty more operations after that thousand-bomber raid and earned a DFM. He was told of the award whilst on the dance floor, by Air Commodore 'Gus' Walker (now Air Marshal). He still finds, after all these years, that there are times when the horror of all those burning cities comes back to him vividly and disturbingly.

Davidson, Jim, the gunnery leader from Croft, survived the Cologne raid and completed two tours of operations. He returned to view Cologne Cathedral thirty-seven years later and met, with the writer, Adolf Galland, General of German Fighters, and the Mayor of Cologne. (See photograph.) His RAF service had taken its toll on his health, though, and he died before publication of this book.

Ennis, Tony, squadron leader, skipper of the Halifax from Leeming in which Fred Simpson and Bertram Groves flew, was killed in 1943.

Bertram, Groves, sergeant rear gunner, in Ennis's Halifax, recovered from wounds sustained on the Cologne raid and received the DFM.

Harris, Sir Arthur Travers, Bart., GCB, AFC, Marshal of the Royal Air Force. Shortly before the Second World War ended and when the arguments over the bomber offensive against Germany were being voiced more loudly, Air Marshal Harris was offered another post – a way out of all the controversy: the Governorship of Southern Rhodesia. He declined. He wished to stay to the war's end with his men of Bomber Command. Next he was offered the post of Commissioner of the Metropolitan Police. He declined again. Then, shortly before the General Election of 1945, Churchill offered him the Governorship of Bermuda. This Harris was prepared to accept, but surprisingly Attlee, after becoming Prime Minister, cancelled the pending appointment.

In January 1946 the former bugle-boy of the Rhodesian Infantry Regiment was promoted to the highest rank in the service – Marshal of the Royal Air Force. But he was left out of the Victory Honours List, and his handling of the bomber offensive was attacked with increasing fervour by the politicians by then in power. However, whilst many in Britain adopted a 'holier than thou' attitude to Harris's efforts, the Allied Governments recognized fully his contribution to victory, and they continued to do so long after Harris had retired to a civil job as managing director of the South African Marine Corporation, a new shipping line sailing the USA-South Africa route.

During all the years the controversy raged over the bomber offensive Sir Arthur Harris kept quietly out of it all, harbouring no bitterness about his own treatment but saddened that his men should have been dealt with so despicably.

However, let us leave him now with that fine tribute paid to him by US President Dwight D. Eisenhower, who sent a special message on the twentieth anniversary of the D-Day invasion of Europe, in which he said: 'Never during the two decades that have passed, have I ceased to render daily and devout thanks to a kindly providence for permitting us to achieve in eleven months the complete victory that so many believed would require years ... To you, one of my close associates in 'Overlord', I am impelled to send, once more, a special word of thanks. Your professional skill and selfless dedication to the cause in which we all served will be noted in the histories of those dramatic months, but no historian could possibly be aware of my obligation to you.' Let us hope that historians will eventually set the record right.

Marshal of the Royal Air Force Sir Arthur Harris died at the age of ninety-two in the spring of 1984 and was buried at Goring-on-Thames. In the minds of the few survivors of his gallant force now, the memory of 'Bomber' Harris lives on; for them he was a great commander.

'For thou has been
As one in suffering all, that suffers nothing,
A man, that fortune's buffets and rewards
Has ta'en with equal thanks:'

William Shakespeare, *Hamlet*

Henderson, Doug, the Scot who liked a 'wee drink', earned a DFC with two tours and adjusted to civil life, again with the help of a 'wee drink' which did not appear to interfere too much with the way he did his job, but he died before drawing his pension. There are those who think he was yet another casualty of war-time stress.

Hudson, 'Rusty', pilot, put in a request to be taken off operations immediately after the Cologne raid. His request was granted on medical grounds and in view of the number and severity of the operations he had completed. He married Jackie and spent most of the remaining war-time years on flying control duties. He did not, however, manage to face a resumption of his dental course at the university but instead made a successful career with an international seed and fertilizer firm. Now retired.

Lawson, Ron, survived the Cologne raid with Micky Martin and went on – wearing his old lucky trousers – to complete two tours of operations including seven trips to 'the Big City', Berlin. When peace did come, his trousers were threadbare but he had at least survived to return to his old job as a civil servant. Now retired.

Macfarlane, John, who had a relatively quiet trip to Cologne and back, was posted to the Middle East and was eventually shot down over Crete. He evaded capture and fought with the partisans for some months before escaping by submarine. He was awarded the Military Medal. After the war he trained for teaching and now enjoys a well-earned retirement in the North-East.

Martin, 'Micky', skipper of Ron Lawson's bomber, returned safely from Cologne and then later left 50 Squadron for the famous 617, the Dambusters, and surprisingly, considering the nature of the raids he undertook, survived. He is regarded along with Gibson and Cheshire as one of the great bomber pilots of the war. In peacetime he stayed in the RAF to become Air Marshal Sir Harold Martin KCB, DSO, DFC, AFC.

Maudslay, Henry, who had flown the 'cannibalized' Manchester bomber from Waddington to Cologne that May night also joined the Dambusters Squadron. On the night the Möhne Dam was breached he went on to attack the Eder Dam. Mist and the surrounding hills made the approach very difficult. He made two attempts to get down for a level bomb-run but each time failed. On the third attempt he pushed the nose of the bomber hard down and flung it into the valley until he was running straight and true for the wall. His height and approach seemed perfect. The massive ball of a bomb, specially made for the job, dropped. Then those who were watching saw a huge tongue of flame reach up to the frail bomber and lift it upwards. The bomb had hit the top of the dam directly below the bomber. A vivid flame lit up the whole valley and the bomber just disappeared. Completely. There was no burning wreckage, no aircraft afire in the sky. There was nothing. The explosion had consumed everything.

Milne, Sandy, got back safely from Cologne in the old Whitley he had been advised not to take over the Pennines, and completed a full tour of operations before beginning a strange assignment. He was posted to Cambridge university and flying a Link Trainer pushed himself all the time to the limits of fatigue. During these sessions he would be given pills specially prepared to keep him alert and one hundred per cent operationally capable. At that time Bomber Command was losing an alarming number of aircraft on return to base through pilot error directly attributable to excessive fatigue. The drugs Sandy Milne was testing were to prevent the drowsiness causing pilot error. When this attachment finished, Sandy Milne was sent back to his unit in a state which put him straight into sick quarters, suffering from violent stomach pains. After the war he resumed his studies at medical school, still hoping to become a doctor, but his health was not up to this strain. His body erupted in boils. He was also suffering now from deafness. Eventually he received a war pension and through sheer determination completed a course for a Master of Arts degree and worked in various Scottish academies. Now retired and living in Scotland.

Mitchell, Vic, was at Finningley when the 'Awkward Squad' failed to return. They later telephoned from Skegness, much to the amusement of the sergeants' mess, to say they had made a forced

landing there. But the laughter was short-lived, for they had been
to Cologne in the hastily patched up Wimpy which everyone had
said would get no further than Bawtry, and they had bombed the
target. Vic Mitchell was later shot down over Belgium and forty
years later received a letter from the Mayor of Lomel in Belgium,
inviting him to a ceremony at the lifting of his wrecked Lancaster
from the marshland of the forest there.

Price, John, who had flown to Cologne with a scratch crew from
Harwell in an old Whitley drogue tower, survived a dozen more
operations over Germany and a crash into electric grid cables
before being posted to the Middle East in time for the battle of El
Alamein. He completed thirty-seven operations. Eventually he
resumed his civilian life but not without some legacy of ill health
attributable to the stress and tensions of combat. Nevertheless, he
feels it was a job which had to be done and has a sense of
satisfaction that he played his part in the overall effort.

Prince, Eric, was halfway through his gunnery course when taken
for the raid from Harwell. The following night his aircraft was
badly shot up over the Dutch coast and he baled out over the
balloon barrages around Harwich. He landed on the railway track
and escaped with a badly twisted ankle. The Australian navigator,
who jumped a second or two before Prince, landed in an open
railway truck and regained consciousness in London. He was
missing for four days and on return was posted to the Middle East.
Four days later he was dead. Eric Prince completed his course and
was posted to the Middle East in time for the battle of El Alamein
and completed a full tour of operations. He too was troubled with
nervous reactions on his return to civil life. These would come over
him unexpectedly, as when travelling in a train entering a tunnel he
would break out into a cold sweat and emerge trembling –
symptoms which many aircrew of Bomber Command have spoken
about.

Simpson, Fred, flight engineer on a Halifax from Leeming, has
never stopped flying. He completed forty operations before going
on to instructor duties and then after the war worked with a wide
variety of civil airlines, some with strange names flying from
strange parts of the world. At one time he was on the 'Ghurka
Shuttle', ferrying those gallant warriors between their mountain

home in Nepal and operational theatres. Even today Fred finds difficulty in keeping away from Gatwick and Heathrow but I hope one day soon he will settle down long enough to write his memoirs. They will be worth reading.

Walker, David, of 44 Squadron returned safely from the Cologne raid on his twenty-first birthday and went on to complete sixty operations, earning a DFC. He tells an amusing story about this. Whilst he was waiting in line to receive the medal from King George VI at Buckingham Palace, he stood just behind a burly, six-foot-three Royal Marine commando. Ahead were a dozen women of the ATS who had been well drilled in the procedure, three paces forward, curtsey, shake hands and receive the medal. One, two, three, bob down and shake. So mesmerized was the big commando with this drill that when his turn came he went into the same routine: one, two, three, bob and shake hands. His face was aflame as he walked away.

After the war David Walker went back to his old job – a good one with a chemical firm – but he was so full of guilt and remorse for his part in the bomber offensive that he gave up the job, sold his house and with his wife Barbara went out to South America as a missionary, staying for twelve years, working at altitudes of 10-12,000 feet. A Jehovah's Witness, David is back in the North-East, leading a somewhat quieter life.

Williams, Ken, the wireless-operator/air gunner, returned unscathed from the Cologne raid and completed fifty operations before going to the American 8th Air Force instructing on Liberators, the Fortress and the B26. After the war he returned to Bradford and became shipping manager for Jowett Cars. He recalls his grief when he found that twenty out of his school class of thirty had 'got the chop'. One of these was his best pal, **Bill Whitehead**, whom we have already met telling Air Marshal Baldwin to get out of his way in no uncertain terms. Flying for so long at high altitude has left Ken Williams with both ear and eye trouble for which he still has hospital treatment.

Wilson, Jack, the keen former civil flying instructor, returned safely from the Cologne raid and then went on to a Pathfinder squadron. In his typical deliberate and painstaking fashion he was pressing home his run-in for marking the target in Hamburg when he was shot down and killed in 1943. His wife remembers that day well for he was unusually quiet and thoughtful beforehand. They lived within walking distance of the airfield, and often he would be at home in the afternoon before going off on the night raid. On that August day it was almost as if he knew it would be his last on earth; he lay in a garden hammock taking in the beauty of the summer's afternoon. The following morning he was not back for breakfast in the usual way. The padre came to break the news — but his wife already knew. She had seen a jeep-load of aircrew go by, and one of them raised his arm as if pointing to the house. That was enough.

Winfield, Roland, who simultaneously pursued two careers which complemented each other — pilot and aviation medicine specialist — eventually completed ninety-eight missions against Germany and gained both the Air Force Cross and the Distinguished Flying Cross. His notes on these operations formed the basis of a book (*The Sky Belongs to Them*) which gave a profound insight into the stressful lives of Bomber Command aircrew. By writing about the war he hoped to show young people what the reality of it all was, so that it could be seen in its true colours and not the glamorized ones of fiction and film. A true presentation, he thought, might help prevent the young ever becoming involved in another war. He died before his book was published.

Appendix B. Airfields Revisited

'There are more things in heaven and earth, Horatio,
'Than are dreamed of in your philosophy.'

Shakespeare, *Hamlet*

What is the secret of the ghostly airman who still haunts a rural airfield forty years after World War II ended?

A mysterious figure, wearing a flying-suit and carrying a bundled-up parachute has been seen wandering the wartime airfield of East Kirkby, Lincolnshire. The writer went to investigate this phenomenon for himself. All over England's eastern counties are scores of neglected, overgrown wartime bomber airfields where RAF and USAAF crews were stationed and where such stories abound. Clearly something lingers on as a reminder of the young men whose lives were cut short these forty years ago.

Sometimes it is difficult to sort out the fact from the fiction in these reports because it is often not possible to speak to the eye-witnesses of such paranormal phenomena. But at Lincolnshire's East Kirkby airfield there are no such difficulties: the reports are recent and given in simple, straightforward language without any elaboration or intention to impress the listener.

'The first time I saw anything strange,' said Fred Panton who farms the old airfield, 'was one morning at about six o'clock when I was driving down the perimeter track and something impelled me to stop the car, get out and just walk down the runway. It was then that I got the unmistakable eerie sensation of returning bombers and quite a noise of engines. That's happened several times since.'

Fred and other people have seen the figure of a suited airman carrying his parachute to the watchtower. His unemotional account is certainly intriguing.

'I had been working late one night and I remembered that our local fish-and-chip shop was frying, so I jumped into my car and began to drive slowly along the airfield road when something or other caught my eye and made me glance towards the nearby hangar. And there, with a shock of surprise, I saw a tall man carrying what I, at first, took to be a big bundle of white plastic bags, and I stopped because I hadn't seen anyone around all day and I said to myself: "What the Hanno is that?" But then I thought, well, he's doing no harm, and continued on my way to the chippy. It was only when I got onto the main road that I realized that what I had seen was the same as other folk had – an airman carrying a bundled-up parachute. I am convinced now that is what I saw.'

Several people can give accounts of apparitions and agonizing screams there. 'We were working in an old hangar when suddenly from out of nowhere there was a horrifying scream. It was shattering to hear. We had no idea what caused it, and though we looked around all the other buildings we found nothing there,' said another local resident.

'I was standing under the balcony of the watchtower one evening,' said another woman, 'when I saw two people walking diagonally across the ploughed part of the field in front of me. But they seemed as though they were walking along a path. And then they went behind a tree and never came out the other side.'

Irish May Handson, who used to serve these young men with their pints of bitter at the Red Lion, East Kirkby, remembers going into one of the old buildings one summer afternoon and suddenly feeling very cold. She was gripped by a feeling which made her stand still for a moment in wonder as if in the presence of something she could not comprehend. She could not stay in the building.

Dennis Brown was working one Sunday afternoon in what used to be the signals' room of the watchtower when he heard the outer door creak open noisily below, and then footsteps came purposefully up the stone steps. It sounded like Ron, his friend, so Dennis carried on working until he heard the door of the neighbouring room being flung open, scraping over the concrete floor. Dennis, walked towards the other room, calling out, 'Is that you, Ron?' There was no answer. There was no one in the other room. There was no other way out of the building. The door was still quivering as it had caught on the concrete. Dennis Brown dashed downstairs, across the tarmac to his own bungalow, where he sat shivering in a chair. Since then they have tried to make the watchtower door quiver on the concrete, but they have never succeeded.

'I cannot explain what it was. I don't know. I don't believe in ghosts and yet I do believe that it was something. And I have the feeling that it was something nice. Not threatening.'

Fred Panton's elder brother Christopher was killed in action in the Nuremberg raid in 1944, and Fred has now restored the watchtower in his brother's memory.

Scoffers could perhaps offer 'rational explanations' for all these mysterious happenings. But who can be one hundred per cent sure of anything like this? As the erudite Dr Samuel Johnson once wrote: 'The whole of the argument is against the existence of ghosts but the whole of the feeling is for it.'

When you visit these abandoned airfields today, it is easy enough to ponder on the thought that this was the last place on earth to be seen by aircrew who never returned, and to contemplate, perhaps, the motto of 57 squadron who flew from East Kirkby: 'My body may change, but not my spirit.'

Appendix C. Extract from AIR/49/357: A Pilot's Own Story P/O M.K. (aged 27)

It is rare to find a report of a crash written with such attention to detail, especially in the recording of very personal feelings. The usual 'combat reports' written for the squadron records are very short and deliberately dispassionate. The report of this pilot, who became a navigator, was not written for perusal by his own squadron officers but for an attentive and sympathetic medical officer in whose professional integrity and confidentiality he trusted.

Such confidentiality has been honoured until very recently when files were released in the Public Record Office. From such a report we can now see more clearly the stresses involved in air warfare and the problems facing the commanders.

This is the second instance, in the Air Force, that I have been asked to write a detailed account of a crash, in which I was an active participant.

The first one being a little over a year ago, when a 'plane in which I was flying solo went out of control and necessitated a crash landing, wiping out the aircraft but resulting in no serious injury to myself, except to make me feel completely incapable of performing a successful landing again, with the effect that it was found feasible to give up piloting and undertake the role of a navigator. It was in this capacity I was serving on the operational trip of 6th July 1941 – in a Wellington – D for Donald – on a bombing trip to Dortmund – just east-north-east of the Rurh Valley – the hottest spot that has ever been entered in a flying crew's log.

This account is a little difficult to relate – as there have been many times since that the flight has been re-lived, and each time new thoughts intruded themselves – should we have done this – or that; why didn't I *insist* on being taken to the Intelligence Officer, in order that he could have given a completed report to the Air Ministry on the Squadron's results; and other similar events. That is the reason for the general start to this note – it might result in a clearer picture. Perhaps it was fortunate that I was the only conscious person when we were rescued – it gives rise to some confusion.

The flight to the target was, in the main, uneventful – as far as these things go. Naturally, we flew quite close to Rotterdam, which put up its usual welcome in a slight barrage of lights and anti-aircraft shells – but we de-synchronized and took evasive action – and that incident was soon behind us – forgotten.

'What time are we due over the target?' The Captain speaks for the first time.

'At 12.30,' I answered.

This is always arranged by the Wing Commander – so that all the Squadron – in conjunction with any others taking part – arrive over the target at the same instant, in order to divide the ground defences among many – rather than any one kite receiving the full blessing from the earth.

The time now escapes me – but after checking our position by the stars – and re-checking by radio loop bearings, I was satisfied that we were well on track – the prevailing wind would hold good – by the appearance of atmospheric conditions – and a consultation with the met. forecast form – so I settled down to munch on an orange.

Of course, we were de-synchronizing and flying in an evasive manner all this time – in order to confuse the detectors – but the average course, air speed and height were all to a navigator's satisfaction.

It must be understood that all this time countless ribbons of light were cutting the darkness all around us – and now and then a burst would rock us ever so slightly – that was fine – it meant that locating our kite was proving to be a bit of a task to them – and they only fire when sure that your position is accurately plotted – so, as long as the bursts just rocked us – well, the detectors were picking up the wrong note.

Again, it must be understood that this takes longer to tell than it takes in the actual flight – and the navigator manages to get about two successive bites out of the orange – the rest of the time checking and re-checking position, air speed, course, height, track and ground speed; plotting star sights and fixes, radio loop bearings, fusing the bombs; setting the distributor arm in order to drop the stick in the most effective way.

'Our height is 12,500 feet,' I said to the Captain, 'and we should bomb from 10,000.'

'Got it,' said the Captain, Ronnie Fraas, 'I will glide down now.'

'Hold back the speed as we are ahead of time, now,' I warned.

'Fine – but it is rather quiet tonight, isn't it – probably night fighters. Hello, front and rear gunners – keep a sharp eye. Take over Bill [the second pilot], I want some coffee.'

So back he piled – clapped me on the back and we toasted the blitz of Dortmund in our thermos tops. And back he went.

Up to the astro-hatch I went to have a look round – only to be completely dazzled by a perfect wall of light – which seemed to envelop us – and hold like the very devil – and then came that unmistakable sound of bursting ack-ack shells – a sound that is almost impossible to describe – I think if you magnified the cracking of a nut under water you'd have it.

There was the one that was close – we pitched from it – and yet another after another – yes, they had us buttoned – those ground boys were sure on their toes tonight and each one came closer and closer – no doubt we were for it, unless, yes – to drop a parachute flare – that usually blinds them and gives us an escape.

'Going to drop a flare,' I fairly blasted the intercom.

'Good show,' the Captain had tense tone.

So, seizing the bulky flare I staggered – yes, with the furious tossing and pitching about the sky of our kite – a crawl would describe my journey better.

Opening the flare chute, I was startled to see a searchlight streaming right up into my face, nothing is more surprising than that – and unnerving – it makes one positive that it was meant for you alone – and although the impossibility of it is obvious, you are sure that the ground can see you clearly. However, to drop the flare and ease the situation – with a ring and a rasp it was gone and without waiting for any effect I tumbled back to my table – as I was a bit faint from lack of oxygen and a horrible suspicion came over me. Yes – Good God – we were smack over the *Ruhr Valley* and the time – 12.30 – *ten minutes to fifteen ahead of schedule* – which meant that we were alone – terribly alone – just the right meat for that terrible barrage – no wonder it seemed worse than anything previous – we were getting all of it!

Here I become slightly confused – as there have been many times the next few moments have come back to me – but I shall make an honest effort to confine my recording to the actual facts as they presented themselves.

This I am sure of – there isn't time to worry over the ground now – the flare had its effect, but we all felt that 'Jerry' was too good tonight and we would soon be twisting and twitching about the sky very soon again. We are dead on track and will be over our particular target in eight minutes – all things allowed. Up to the bomb compartment I went and lay on the floor over the glass panel – to guide the kite to our point – only to be almost blinded by a battery of lights from the ground. Quickly I closed my eyes – for too much of that light could blind me to the target – Jerry's plan, of course.

'Let the bombs go,' the Captain really shouted – if I had only listened.

'But we aren't over the target yet.' I took a quick look at my watch.

'Let the bombs go,' he repeated.

And knowing full well he was remaining cool – I took no notice – as I could see the Dortmund-Ems Canal docks ahead – and the chance to get our target had too strong a hold on me – I honestly didn't know that the frightful barrage of lights and shells existed – two minutes would see our job done – and by the look of things – done well!

'For God's sake drop those damn bombs, boy.'

'Yes, Captain.' For now the target was coming down the drift wires of the bomb sight.

How well I remember that the next few seconds were like hours – could I hold off long enough? It never occurred to me that I was in no position to judge. The Captain should be obeyed on the spot and the argument dealt with in the safety of the Mess. But I do want to make it clear that the chance of 'doing the thing' was too overpowering – and who can criticize?

I seemed to push that switch with my whole body and it seemed a great relief that I sang out, 'Bombs going, going, going – GONE!' Only to find – on peering out to see their work – myself thrown clear back under the pilot's feet, after what seemed an ear-splitting crack.

And not a word was said by anybody. After all, even if it was the heaviest blast, we had been throwing about a great deal, but 'The starboard engine has packed up,' and the Captain sounded quite cool.

The last burst had done its work – and we now had one engine to travel six hundred miles.

After giving the course home I sat down – or tried to – what with our twisting and turning – then jumped up and gave another course in order to fly us north of the Ruhr. Coming in had been too hot.

Then a multitude of thoughts roared on me – the same thoughts that actually roar in on me now; we had arrived too early; why; whew! It was hell; had my navigation gone wrong; must check it; can't find anything wrong; had our speed been too much, on the glide; the log said no; should I have led the Captain on; why were we ahead of schedule; should have dropped them when ordered; but I am the bomber and I give the orders on that; was my last fix incorrect – and on and on in the same channel.

We were losing height steadily, but not quickly and we had plenty to spare. But it meant working like the devil on the navigation.

We had to get home as quickly as possible – and our early arrival on the target had shaken my faith.

After an age I could see the Zuyder Zee coming up and a perfect hell of flak beyond it – that would be Rotterdam – and it was right on track. We must go round – our altitude was too risky and easy for the light flak.

So I gave the Captain a large alteration to starboard – as the Jerry fighters were too thick south of the city.

Over the Zee now – and then bright flashes of light came through the starboard windows and then 'The engine's on fire!' The second pilot speaking.

Not badly – just a low, slow flame, more inside the cowling than out – but the wing petrol tanks.

And now we were visible for miles – any fighter would be able to see us – I can almost see the gunner straining through the darkness for a dark, fast-moving shape.

Now we were over the North Sea – and this was the time really to work.

Asking the wireless to get me a loop from X – I went back to take a star sight – but the flames from the engine were now bright enough to interfere with the proper use of the sextant.

How the devil was I to get a sure fix now – the wireless handed back the loop reading and it was duly plotted on the chart – but in too much of a fore and aft line to check ground speed – but wait – that loop station was not useless after all – it was only about ten miles north of our aerodrome – why not fly that bearing until the coast came up?

No time was lost in giving the new course, and my work was eased slightly – it had been impossible to work out an estimated time for the coast.

Muffled explosions were coming from the engine – and with each one the flames went higher and higher. Honestly, each explosion seemed to ask each one of those questions over and over again. I tried working faster and harder – making the wireless sweat giving me the same loop over and over again. At least we are making good the required track.

'Hello, boys,' the Captain in that same cool tone, 'we are losing height and may have a spot of rowing to do – I am doing my best.'

God knows, he was flying like a genius.

'Better jettison everything,' the Captain was a little worried now – the engine was a mess, 'flares, floats, ammunition, guns.'

So the three of us went to work – we opened that chute and every loose thing we could put hands on went down to the sea. The fire had us badly worried – we had heard too much about charred remains being washed up – yes, we were three nervous lads. Two of us will never fly again.

Nothing to do now, but sit and wait. We tried eating our chocolate and currants, but they were tasteless. I'll never forget those moments.

The fire was bigger and much worse – the sea was close and relentlessly beneath us. Our track through the sky was like a comet – surely a fighter would see us and attack, let's hope they aren't patrolling the coast.

Quickly checking the track again – I looked out and could see a long dark shadow. That must be the coast – and I really prayed. But we were losing height near those cliffs north of Flamborough.

'Alter course twenty feet port,' I shot at the Captain. Quickly mentioning the cliffs, I added, 'there's a good chance of pin-pointing south of Flamborough.'

'Good lad.' And his words cheered me amazingly well.

How we were losing height; how that fire was blazing; how did it all happen? Yes, it was, *it was* all my fault – I must clear by getting us home – right down on our own aerodrome.

'Coast ahead, and a beacon flashing – where is that beacon, navigator?'

Checking with the list and the map – we were south of Flamborough all right and heading further south – into Hull – and a balloon barrage.

My God – what is the matter with me – my navigation has gone right to hell.

Working like the devil – everything seemed twice as heavy and difficult – I gave a course that would bring us over D – aerodrome, the nearest one to the coast just east of our station – then I started to laugh.

Here I was – graduated from OTU in top place with a rating of 'About the Average' – here I was going absolutely haywire. *Of course*, all this was my fault, right from the start – 'Will be of immeasurable value to his squadron and crew' – Ye gods!

'What's that beacon?'

Running up and looking I saw – with extreme relief that it was D – but our height – dangerously low – and the engine fire was an inferno – spreading well out on the wing. How in the name of God were the flames avoiding that petrol? We had expected to blow up a long time ago – and what a suspense that had been.

'Land at D.' Now the second pilot was excited, 'We'll never make back. Land at D!'

The skipper didn't answer and I automatically gave the course for base.

My work was finished and try as hard as I could my head wouldn't settle. Our height was negligible – and the second pilot was pouring instructions out to the skipper – one right after the other.

'Should have landed at D – we'll never make it.'

'There's the green light. You missed it.'

'Land down wind – off the runway – but land quickly.'

The fire was now roaring and drowning the sound of our one engine. The wireless op. was pulling my arm.

'Lie down on the floor,' he actually shrieked in my ear – and he proceeded to do so.

'Shall I come up front?' asked the rear gunner.

As I started to crouch – the kite seemed to turn right over – and there was a terrific tearing sound.

Here I have to stop and wait – I know what happened in the

next few moments, much thought has made it clear to me. But I want to record truly my mind as it worked in these moments – and what I physically felt.

Hot, burning flames were all around. I screamed – the wireless op. just disappeared – now there screams all around me – dreadful screams – searing, blasting, searing flames – and a dirty, filthy odour – strong of burning fabric, oil and wood, with a strong impression of burning hair. Still those screams – vaguely I knew my own voice was nowhere in that sound. My face seemed to be passing right through solid walls of fire – it couldn't have been – but the flames, that were everywhere, were deluding me – and still that vile smell. Even now its impression is quite strong.

The crashing tumble was over – and I just sat there – why, I don't know – but just sat there and knew that my left arm was hurting like the devil somewhere under and behind me. The stillness – such a stillness – was broken only by the sound of the fire. I must get away and tried to – but something – cables, wires, I don't know what – was wound around my chest and legs preventing my moving – I tore at them with my right hand – tore like fury, over my head, stood up and tried to kick my legs free. Then an arm of fire shot at me – it seems right through me – and again I screamed – then as if my voice had been a signal, there came the most horrible screams I think I will ever hear again.

At last I was free, and I stumbled to my right – the way was blocked – I turned again and threw myself clear and lay on the ground – no fire – just cool air and ground.

How long I was there I don't know, but I got up and looked at the wreckage – it seemed to be spread over yards and the flames were white and high – then I saw Tom, the wireless op. slowing moving up and down in what seemed to be the spot from where I had come – his face and hands were black and he seemed to be looking at me – and I *swear* those two white eyes seemed to be accusing me – 'You did this!' – and I felt guilty, dreadfully guilty – and coming in a little closer I wave my hand and yelled at him – 'This way, Tom' – my face and hands were now stinging intolerably and I turned away, went a few steps and turned back – Tom was just standing there – again I waved and yelled – surely he could see me – other screams prevented his hearing me.

Then I heard voices and shrubs crashing – turning I saw the boys coming from the aerodrome – I ran to them calling for help and two of them took hold of me – one of them hurting my arm very much.

'Come along now.'

But I won't – I just stood there and looked at that inferno. 'Get the boys out, they're still in there.'

'All right, old man, somebody is taking care of them.'

Looking, I could see figures running around and, in that fire – when suddenly there was a series of smashing explosions and thousands of tiny flaming particles seemed to roar up into the sky – the spare petrol – now myriads of colours – the Verey cartridges.

'Oh, you'll never get them out now – all of them are done.' My voice sounded miles away.

During this time the two lads had been trying to get me on to the stretcher – and now, it was all done, so down I went.

The arm and hand were hurting me fearfully.

Next I remember we were in the sickbay and voices and people all around – who was moaning like that – turning my head I saw other stretchers around with somebody in each one – the boys *had* pulled them out – it was marvellous.

I knew that black face next to me.

'Hello, you.'

'Hello, Mac – hear the skipper?'

So it was the skipper moaning like that. Who had been screaming?

'Skipper – hello – I'm sorry.'

And that's all I knew.

Medical Note

As stated, this officer has lost his confidence in flying as a result of his experience and will not be fit to fly from a psychological point of view for some months. He has quite considerable nervous predispositions. His background at home is not stable and his parents do not get on together. He is imaginative and intelligent, but before joining the RAF showed a tendency to over-conscientiousness and was inclined to overwork. He had considerable responsibility for one so young. He joined the RAF for various motives, partially to escape from his work, and never really achieved complete confidence in himself as a navigator. He is inclined to blame himself for his aircraft being damaged as a result of this fact. This self-blame and lack of confidence persist. I am not at all sure whether one will ever get this man to fly again operationally although he may well fly in another capacity. He is improving and dreams less about the accident. I would agree to his being sent to Canada and suggest A4B category for three months.

In his description of the accident he showed his nervous temperament and tendency to dramatisation to an abnormal degree.

His physical injuries were moderately severe burns of both hands and arms, responding well to treatment with considerable use of both hands. Very mild burns of the face have produced no disfigurement.

DISPOSAL: Sent to Canada.

Appendix D. Extract from the Files of 'Köln im Luftkrieg' (Cologne City Archives)

Summary of Effects of Raid, 30/31 May 1942
Damage to buildings:
Damaged: 12,840 of which:
3,300 were completely destroyed beyond further habitation
2,090 extensively damaged and needing rebuilding
7420 damaged but habitable after repairs

Residential units damaged:
13,010 totally destroyed
630 severely damaged
22,270 needed repairs

Commercial enterprises and buildings
1,505 totally destroyed
630 severely damaged
425 in need of repairs

Factories
36 totally destroyed
70 severely damaged
222 damaged sufficiently to reduce production by 50%

Essential services affected
Water mains broken in 17 places
Main electricity cables broken in 32 places
Telephone cables broken in 12 places
Gas mains broken in 5 places.

City transport: Tram services not operative for one week and rail traffic suspended for several days.

Casualties:
Killed: 469
Injured: 5,027

Numbers rendered homeless
45,132.

References

Prologue

1. The German Army's achievement on this Western Front has often been under-rated. They inflicted casualties of over one hundred per cent on many of the Allied infantry units. British and American commanders soon had to rely on massive bombardment from the air and by artillery to overcome the extraordinary skill and determination of German soldiers defending their Fatherland. This factor must be borne in mind when considering the contribution made to victory by the new bomber offensive which began with the first thousand-bomber raid on Cologne. General J. Collins saved the twin towers of the cathedral from artillery fire by forbidding the gunners to register on it. But who saved it from the RAF night bombers? Was it superb bomb-aiming? Was it amazing good luck? Or was there some other, superior power?
2. Alan Moorehead, *Eclipse*, p.200.
3. Frau Löhr witnessed the scene and related it to the writer in Cologne 1978 when he was researching *Frontstadt Köln*.
4. Frau Löhr report to writer, 1978.
5. A. Moorehead, op.cit., p. 201.
6. R. Martin, *The GI War*.
7. Former Sergeant James Osborne to the writer, Frankfurt, 1979.
8. *Stars and Stripes Edited*.
9. Frau Löhr to writer, Cologne, 1978.
10. J. Toland, *The Last Hundred Days*.

1. The Gathering of Eagles

1. Group Captain Tom Sawyer, DFC, *Only Owls and Bloody Fools Fly by Night*.
2. Related personally to the writer by David Walker, Ferryhill, Co Durham, 1986.

3. Mr Cyril Manser, brother of Leslie Manser VC to the writer personally, June 1986.
4. Guy Gibson, VC, *Enemy Coast Ahead*.
5. Eric Clarke to the writer personally, January 1986.
6. To the writer personally, shortly before his death, 1985.
7. To the writer personally by Mrs Christina Galbraith.
8. Told to the writer by Mr Max Pexman, brother of Ken, 1978.
9. Told to the writer in letters and personal interview, January 1986.
10. Told to the writer in personal interview, December 1985.
11. Interviews with the writer at Guisborough and York, December 1985.
12. Interview, Cleveland, January 1986.
13. Roland Winfield, a medical officer engaged in research into aviation medicine, was also a qualified pilot who flew as second pilot and air gunner on 98 operations over Germany. He took part in the first thousand bomber raid. He explained his philosophy in his book *The Sky Belongs to Them*.

2. The Great Dilemma

1. Air Vice-Marshal D.C.T. Bennett CB, CBE, DSO, *Pathfinder*.
2. Group Captain Dudley Saward, *The Bomber's Eye*.
3. Group Captain Dudley Saward, *Bomber Harris*.
4. Ibid.
5. Ibid.
6. Ibid.
7. BBC interview, 1979
8. Ibid.
9. Sir Arthur Harris, *Bomber Offensive*
10. Ibid.
11. Ibid.
12. Ibid.
13. Ibid.
14. Speer told the writer in a personal interview, 1972.
15. Norman Longmate, *The Bombers*, p.221.

3. A Fine May Evening in Cologne

1. Interviewed by the writer in Gütersloh, 1979.
2. Interviewed by the writer in Cologne, several times 1978-9, 1982.

3. Klara Zarges told her story to the writer personally and through letters.

4. Hildegard Steinborn, being the wife of a photo-journalist, told her story to the writer from notes and an account written a few days after the raid.

5. Willy Niessen opened his files and collections of material to the writer and greatly assisted in the interviewing of eye-witnesses.

6. Correspondence and personal interviews with the writer.

7. Toni Stellmaszyk told his story through letters and personal interview, 1978-9.

8. Account given to the writer by Hans Heines through letters, military documents and personal interview.

9. Adolf Galland – personal interview Cologne 1979, and see *The First and the Last'*.

10. Erika Wagner's letters to the writer and personal interview, 1978.

4. Count-Down

1. In the introduction to Guy Gibson's *Enemy Coast Ahead*.

2. Interview with the writer, January 1986.

3. Correspondence and interview with the writer, February 1986.

4. Interview with the writer, January 1986.

5. Interview with the writer, January 1986.

6. Interview with the writer, January 1986.

7. Correspondence and interview, February 1986.

8. Correspondence and interview with the writer, February 1986.

9. Interview with the writer, February 1986.

10. Former wireless operator interviewed by the writer, December 1985.

11. G. Gibson, op. cit.

12. Correspondence and interview, January 1986.

13. Squadron Leader Jack Currie, *Lancaster Target*.

14. As we have already seen, there had already been more than one 'slip-up'. Mrs Elizabeth Stebbing leaving Command Headquarters at High Wycombe was told by an unknown woman at the bus-stop that it was a nice evening to be sending a thousand bombers to Cologne (page 57); WAAF Corporal Irene Shaw receiving a top-secret message in plain language at RAF Finningley (page 81); opera singer Erika Wagner in

Cologne being told by the colonel of the barracks not to go there to sing that evening as they were expecting a big raid (page 73). Cyril Ainley of RAF Lichfield was told by civilians standing on the hump-backed bridge by the station that the aircraft taking off were going to Cologne (page 96).

That week the *Northern Echo* newspaper reported the case of a Mrs Margaret May Alderson who was charged at a north-east court with 'having communicated to other persons information appertaining to aircraft operations, personnel, crashes and casualties which might, directly or indirectly, be of value to the enemy'. This sort of 'careless talk' was happening far too often. German agents in Britain at that time gained eighty per cent of their information from careless talk, just as British agents in Germany were getting theirs from idle chatter and 'pillowtalk' reported back through intelligence officers.

5. Every Six Seconds!

1. Peter Greenham in interview with the writer, February 1986, at Brandon.
2. I am indebted to Max Pexman of Scunthorpe for details of the raid as far as it concerned his brother and also to the account in Ralph Barker's fine book *The Thousand Plan*. Mr Pexman received details from crew members later.
3. Air Vice Marshal Baldwin's account was published shortly after the raid in *Bomber Command* publication.
4. Account given to the writer by Bill Whitehead's school friend, Ken Williams. Bill Whitehead was killed shortly after the raid.
5. Accounts by Cyril Ainley by letter to the writer and subsequent conversations, 1986.
6. John Prince gave details to the writer from his home in Devizes, 1986.
7. Account by Vic Mitchell of York to the writer, 1985.
8. Fuller details given in R.V. Jones, *Most Secret War* Cajus Bekker, *The Luftwaffe War Diaries*.
9. Briefing at Croft reported to the writer by Jim Davidson.
10. Account given to the writer by Klaus Kuhnberger of Bielefeld.
11. Details given in an interview with the writer, Durham, 1986.
12. See Noel Monks, *Squadrons Up*, and also a full account by 'Johnnie' Johnson in *Wing Leader* and in Laddie Lucas, *Out of the Blue*.

13. Details given in interviews with the writer, December 1985 and February 1986.
14. Town Archives, Cologne.

6. *Lake of Fire*
1. In *Bomber Command*, Air Ministry publication, 1942.
2. Max Hastings, *Bomber Command* (see Bibliography)
3. Interview with writer, 1985.
4. *The Times*, 4 June 1942.
5. *The Times*, 9 June 1942.
6. D. Saward, *Bomber Harris*.
7. Interviews with writer, 1979.

7. *The Way Out*
1. As told to the writer by Toni Stellmaszyk.
2. Letters and personal interview with the writer.
3. Story related to the writer in a personal interview, 1977.
4. The film was placed in the archives at Düsseldorf and then removed by the Allied Military Government. The writer has not yet traced the film.
5. I am indebted for this account to Mr Cyril Manser, brother of Leslie Manser VC, who had spoken to the farmer and the crew.
6. Letter from Norman Worthington and subsequent talks with him.

8. *Aftermath*
1. Cajus Bekker, op.cit.
2. *The Goebbels Diaries*, ed. Lochner.
3. Personal interview with the writer in 1972.
4. Harris, op.cit.
5. *The Times*, 3 June 1942.
6. *British Intelligence in the Second World War*, Volume II, Chapter 20.
7. *Daily Telegraph*, 29 Nov 1978, reporting speech made by Averell Harriman on 28 Nov 1978.
8. *New York Times*, 20 May 1942.
9. *British Intelligence in the Second World War*, Volume II, Chapter 25.
10. Max Hastings, op.cit.
11. Winston Churchill, *The Second World War*, Volume IV.
12. Dr Roland Winfield, DFC, AFC, *The Sky Belongs to Them*.

13. Ibid.
14. Public Record Office File, Air 49/357.
15. Ibid.
16. Interview with the writer, March 1986.
17. Currie, op.cit.
18. R. Winfield, op.cit.
19. Interview with the writer, March 1986.
20. Interview with the writer, March 1986.
21. Personal interview with the writer, March 1986.
22. Interview with the writer, March 1986.
23. Letter to the writer from Matlock, March 1986.
24. *Derbyshire Gazette*, 2 June 1942.
25. Account by Catherine Price to the writer at Matlock, March 1986.
26. Administration staff to the writer, March 1986.

Bibliography

In addition to the files in the Public Record Office and in the German Archives in Cologne and Koblenz, I have found the following books useful in providing information to add to the accounts of the eye-witnesses.

Barker, Ralph, *The Thousand Plan*, Chatto and Windus, 1965
Bekker, Cajus, *The Luftwaffe War Diaries*, Macdonald, 1964
Bennett, D.C.T., *Pathfinder*, Muller, 1958
Hinsley, Thomas, Ranson Knight, *British Intelligence in the Second World War* Volumes 1 – 3, HMSO, 1979-82
Charlwood, Don, *No Moon Tonight*, Angus and Robertson, 1956
Cheshire, Leonard, *Bomber Pilot*, Hutchinson, 1943
Churchill, Winston, *The Second World War*, Cassell, 1948-54
Currie, Jack, *Lancaster Pilot*, New English Library, 1977
Eisenhower, Dwight, *Crusade in Europe*, Heinemann 1948
Frankland, Dr Noble, *The Bombing Offensive Against Germany* Faber, 1965
Galland, Adolf, *The First and the Last*, Methuen, 1955
Garbett, Mike, and Goulding, Brian, *Lancaster at War*, Ian Allan, 1961
Gibson, Guy, *Enemy Coast Ahead*, Michael Joseph, 1946
Goebbels, Joseph, *The Goebbels Diaries*, Hamish Hamilton, 1948
Harris, Sir Arthur, Marshal of the RAF, *Bomber Offensive*, Collins, 1947
Jones, R.V., *Most Secret War*, Hamish Hamilton, 1948
Lee, General Raymond, *The London Observer*, Hutchinson, 1972
Longmate, Norman, *The Bombers*, Hutchinson, 1982
Martin, R. *The G.I. War*, Little Brown, 1967
Moorehead, Alan, *Eclipse*, Hamish Hamilton 1945
Roskill, Captain S.W., *Churchill and his Admirals*, Collins 1977
Rumpf, Hans, *The Bombing of Germany*

Saundby, Sir Robert, Air Marshal, *Air Bombardment*, Chatto and Windus, 1961

Saward, Group Captain, Dudley, *The Bomber's Eye*, Cassell, 1959

Saward, Group Captain, Dudley, *Bomber Harris*, Cassell, 1984

Sawyer, Group Captain, Tom, *Only Owls and Bloody Fools Fly at Night*, William Kimber 1982

Speer, Albert, *Inside the Third Reich*, Weidenfeld 1970

Spender, Stephen, *European Witness*, The Right Book Club, 1946

David McKay, Edited, *Stars and Stripes*, 1954

Shirer, William, *The Rise and Fall of the Third Reich*, Simon and Schuster, 1960

Taylor, Eric, *Frontstadt Koeln*, Droste Verlag, 1980

Toland, John, *The Last Hundred Days*, Random House, 1966

Webster, Sir Charles and Frankland, Noble, *The Strategic Air Offensive Against Germany*, HMSO, 1961

Winfield, Roland, *The Sky Belongs to Them*, Kimber, 1976

Winkelnkemper, Dr T, *Der Grosseangriff auf Koeln*, Zentralverlag der NSDAP, 1942

Index

Index